T0339178

SUNSET CLUSTER

H. ROGER GRANT

SUNSET CLUSTER

A SHORTLINE RAILROAD SAGA

INDIANA UNIVERSITY PRESS

This book is a publication of

INDIANA UNIVERSITY PRESS
Office of Scholarly Publishing
Herman B Wells Library 350
1320 East 10th Street
Bloomington, Indiana 47405 USA

iupress.org

*Manufactured in the United
States of America*

First Printing 2023

Cataloging information is available
from the Library of Congress.

ISBN 978-0-253-06671-8 (hdbk.)
ISBN 978-0-253-06673-2 (web PDF)

In memory of

(1872–1932)

Champion of a sunset cluster railroad

CONTENTS

PREFACE

RAILROADS HAVE LONG FASCINATED ME. FROM A TENDER AGE, I delighted in watching freight and passenger trains of the Chicago, Burlington & Quincy, Minneapolis & St. Louis, and Wabash Railroads in my hometown of Albia, Iowa. Abandoned rights-of-way likewise intrigued me. I vividly recall the Lee's Hill cut northwest of town. A farm pasture contained this remnant of the Interurban Age, where the Albia Light & Railway Company (née Albia Interurban Railway) once ran between Albia and the coal-mining town of Hiteman. Grandmother Dinsmore, who had regularly ridden the line, inevitably pointed it out when we drove along a nearby county road. Seeing that earthen scar brought back memories for her and my mother. Another interurban once served Albia. In 1948, the freight-only Southern Iowa Railway (née Iowa Southern Utilities) retired its ten-mile northern segment between Albia and Moravia. I vaguely recall the removal of the rails and ties, and for years I watched the former right-of-way become less visible. In the spring of 1962, as a senior in high school, I embarked on a one-day adventure with a friend. For some reason, I wanted to see what remained of the Creston, Winterset & Des Moines Railroad. We drove to Macksburg, northern terminus of this long-abandoned shortline. West of town we located the right-of-way and began our walk. It had rained heavily the previous day, and we endured the discomfort of Iowa mud. We negotiated fences, grazing cattle, and cow pies, but the rapidly flowing Grand River stymied our advance toward Creston. In addition to portions of the right-of-way, we found the rotting remains of a wooden deck bridge. That was a highlight.

Decades after the Macksburg outing, I turned my attention to producing an academic study of railroads that appeared late in the Railway Age. My efforts resulted in *Twilight Rails: The Final Era of Railroad Building in the Midwest* (University of Minnesota Press, 2010), featuring case studies from eight states, including the "Crazy Willie & Dandy Molly." In some ways, *The Sunset Cluster* is a companion work. This time I remain in Iowa and examine five shortline railroads that appeared after 1907 in the western section of the state. Four opened, and one was only partially graded.

These case histories have value. They provide a window into the intent of latter-day shortline builders and the challenges they faced. They show, too, an almost desperate desire by communities to benefit from steel rails before the regional railroad map finally jelled. Although the four operating roads had disappeared by 1920 (except for the original part of the Atlantic Northern & Southern, which continued until 1936), each had an immediate and lasting impact on its service areas. Hamlets, villages, and towns prospered, and several new townsites emerged. After the rails were lifted, some communities collapsed or declined rapidly. Most places experienced a slow downturn in population and vitality, hurt by agricultural depressions of the 1920s and 1930s, the drought of the "Dirty Thirties," agricultural mechanization, farm consolidations, and motor vehicles operating over an expanding network of improved roads. Fortunately, the county-seat towns served by the cluster carriers did not waste away; in fact, Atlantic and Creston have become big-box shopping centers. In recent decades, Treynor, the focal point of the Iowa & Omaha Short Line, has developed into a flourishing bedroom community for the greater Council Bluffs area. It presently claims more than a thousand residents, approximately ten times larger than when rails arrived.

It would be a mistake to believe that the five shortline cluster in Iowa is unique. While scholars have not examined sunset era railroads in any systematic fashion, these railroads existed beyond borders of the Hawkeye State. But how many and where are not fully known.

The Wiregrass country of South Georgia saw the shortline cluster phenomena. During the waning years of the nineteenth century and the first decade of the twentieth century, various mostly lumber-carrying shortlines emerged. Between 1906 and 1908, John Skelton Williams, a banker and railroad executive from Richmond, Virginia, took all or part of four closely spaced independent roads and fused them into the southern portion of his newly organized Georgia & Florida Railroad (G&F). By the late 1920s, the company had become a 501-mile carrier operating in South Carolina, Georgia, and Florida. The G&F struggled financially and claimed the dubious distinction of being the longest Class I road in receivership. Was this late-date railroad a good idea? The answer is yes and no. Communities, businesses, and farms developed, but investors lost. The story of the G&F replicates some of what occurred in western Iowa, although the G&F survived until the early 1960s before entering the orbit of the Southern Railway and then being largely abandoned.

Although this study fills a void in the literature of railroad history, there is a limitation to any examination of these sunset cluster carriers. Much inside information and insights have been lost because participants have long since passed. Still, the basic conclusions contained in this work are likely correct. Contemporary newspapers, government reports, and other sources help to tell this story, bringing a vanished slice of railroad history to life and revealing the whats and so whats of these obscure and virtually forgotten shortlines.

ACKNOWLEDGMENTS

AS WITH PREVIOUS PUBLICATIONS, I AM GRATEFUL TO A variety of institutions and individuals. My research would have been more challenging without the extensive help I received from librarians and historical society staffs. The Information Sharing Office of the R. M. Cooper Library at Clemson University made it possible to obtain books and reports. Anne McMahan Grant, the resourceful subject librarian for the Department of History, arranged for my online access to back issues of the *Council Bluffs* (IA) *Nonpareil* and provided additional assistance. Nick Fry at the John W. Barriger III National Railroad Library in St. Louis, Julia Jessen at the Museum of Danish America in Elk Horn, Iowa, and Chris Rockwell at the California State Railroad Museum in Sacramento also have been helpful.

Multiple individuals deserve to be acknowledged. They include the late Elaine Artlip, Mike Bartels, Diane Burdette, Dana Grefe, Sue Hiott, Tom Hogan, Tom Kuehn, Dave McFarland, Larry Polsley, Mary Ward, Warren Watson, and Dick Wilson. Don Hofsommer and Tom Hoback kindly commented on early drafts of the manuscript. Not be overlooked is the support and encouragement given me by my daughter Julia Grant.

Then there is my gifted mapmaker, Dick van der Spek, a retired cartographer for the Dutch Ministry of Defense. Working from Udon, Thailand, he patiently created an overview map of the southwestern quadrant of Iowa, showing the five sunset cluster roads and the immediate network of Burlington, Great Western, Rock Island, and Wabash lines.

Monetary assistance is always appreciated. A research grant from the Department of Cultural Affairs of the State of Iowa aided immensely.

I continue to be thankful for the financial commitment made by the Lemon family to my Kathryn and Calhoun Lemon Professorship. Although the COVID-19 pandemic disrupted my research activities, I benefited from a sabbatical leave during the fall semester of 2021.

With my previous ten books with Indiana University Press, staff members have continued to be professional and supportive through the publication process. This has been a wonderful relationship.

H. Roger Grant
Clemson University
Clemson, South Carolina

SUNSET CLUSTER

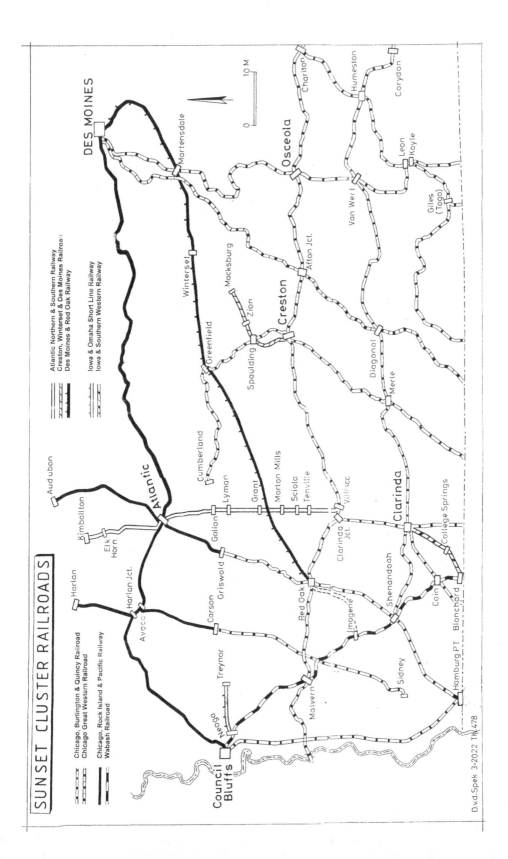

SUNSET CLUSTER RAILROADS

Chicago, Burlington & Quincy Railroad
Chicago Great Western Railroad
Chicago, Rock Island & Pacific Railway
Wabash Railroad

Atlantic Northern & Southern Railway
Creston, Winterset & Des Moines Railroad
Des Moines & Red Oak Railway

Iowa & Omaha Short Line Railway
Iowa & Southern Western Railway

10 M

0

DES MOINES

Audubon

Kimballton

Elk
Horn

Harlan

Atlantic

Harlan Jct.

Avoca

Treynor

Neoga

Council
Bluffs

Carson

Griswold

Galion

Lyman

Cumberland

Grant

Morton Mills

Sciola

Tenville

Villisca

Clarinda
Jct.

Clarinda

Red Oak

Imogene

Shenandoah

Coin

College Springs

Blanchard

Hamburg PT

Sidney

Malvern

Greenfield

Winterset

Martensdale

Macksburg

Zion

Spaulding

Creston

Afton Jct.

Diagonal

Merle

Van Wert

Chariton

Humeston

Corydon

Osceola

Leon

Koyle

Giles
(Togo)

D.v.d.Spek 3-2022 TN 478

ONE

SUNSET YEARS

RAILROAD FEVER

FOR MORE THAN THREE QUARTERS OF A CENTURY, RAILROAD fever gripped the United States. By the mid-nineteenth century, an increasing number of Americans had realized that iron rails would become their pathways for economic prosperity and enhanced mobility—proverbial magic carpets. No longer would they need to endure the shortcomings of existing means of travel and transport, whether stagecoach and wagon, canal packet and freighter, or lake and river steamboat. The consensus grew that both conveyances powered by animals and on water were impractical for long distances, the former being limited in capacity and the latter in scope. This would be the age of steam-propelled land transport. If a community gained access to a railroad, residents would want additional outlets, preferably built by competing carriers. Competition would lead presumably to better service and lower transportation charges.

In 1850 Henry Varnum Poor, manager and editor of the *American Railroad Journal* (the premier industry publication of the pre–Civil War years), captured the growing sentiment of the citizenry: "The construction of railroads is probably the most engrossing subject now occupying the attention of our people. Every portion of our country is aroused to their importance. In the West, the feeling in their favor amounts almost to mania, and every farmer there is contriving how he shall secure one within convenient distance." "Their influence, as instruments of wealth," he added, "are now thoroughly appreciated, and the social advantages which they confer, are scarcely less valued." Poor concluded: "People will have railroads, this is a settled fact, and their construction will go on til every section of the country is penetrated with them."[1]

The American railroad network grew steadily and impressively, increasing from a paltry 23 route miles in 1830 to 30,626 miles on the eve of the Civil War. Although the 1880s marked the greatest surge of railroad construction in American history, with mileage soaring from 92,147 in 1880 to 163,359 in 1890, the national network continued to expand during the formative years of the twentieth century. In 1900 mileage stood at 193,346; in 1905 it climbed to 218,101 miles and reached 240,293 in 1910. Six years later, route mileage peaked at 254,251. In the 1920s additional trackage appeared, but new construction failed to keep pace with abandonments. As the decade opened, the national network stood at 252,845 miles. The following year, *Railway Age* commented on this shrinkage: "The total miles abandoned since the last annual compilation reached 713 miles, some twenty-four miles greater than that for 1919, but what is more to the point, some 400 miles more than was constructed during the same period. In other words, the lines abandoned exceed the new construction in the ratio of over two to one." The high percentage of shortline railroads built during these "sunset" or "twilight" years contributed to that decline. Mileage remained somewhat steady until the post–World War II years, but by the present century, the one-time cobweb of rails had shrunk dramatically to approximately 125,000 route miles before stabilizing. A combination of less regulated, well-managed, and profitable Class I, regional, and shortline carriers explains the shrinking. Even the long-powerful Interstate Commerce Commission (ICC) was laid to rest in 1995, replaced by the less intrusive Surface Transportation Board.[2]

In the span of a lifetime, the nation witnessed the dramatic evolution of the railroad. The puny, slow-moving locomotives that made their debut in the 1830s and 1840s gave way to faster, huskier ones. These "iron horses" initially traveled over iron-capped wooden rails; soon more durable iron T-rails emerged, and in the 1870s steel rails became available. Consists grew longer, heavier, and for passengers more elegant. Starting in the early 1850s on a New-York & Erie Railway train, control by telegraph made operations safer and more efficient. By the immediate

post–Civil War period, railroads functioned much as they would in subsequent decades.

Then a flanged-wheel challenger appeared. The short-lived Interurban Era coincided with the final surge of steam railroad construction.
At the dawn of the twentieth century, this competitive form of intercity
transportation, which debuted in 1889, sported 2,107 route miles. Building progressed at warp speed even when interrupted by the financial
panics of 1903 and 1907. By 1910 mileage had climbed to 12,806. Six years
later, it peaked at 15,580 route miles before the virtual collapse of the industry in the late 1930s. Ohio and Indiana became the interurban heart-
land: Ohio reached 2,798 miles and Indiana 1,825. California, Illinois,
New York, and Pennsylvania, however, rivaled the trackage found in the
Hoosier State. The vast majority of these "juice" roads were relatively
short, averaging twenty-five to fifty miles in length. A few, though, were
more extensive: Pacific Electric Railway, the nation's largest interurban,
boasted about 700 route miles; Ohio Electric Railway claimed more than
600 miles; Union Traction Company of Indiana sported 410 miles; Illinois Traction Company (Illinois Terminal after 1937) had approximately
400 miles; and Piedmont & Northern Railway, the most important electric road in the South, operated 125 miles in its unconnected North and
South Carolina divisions.[3]

Not to be overlooked during the final steam railroad construction
cycle were two projects that received considerable printers' ink: the last
"transcontinentals."[4] In May 1909 the Chicago, Milwaukee & St. Paul
Railway (Milwaukee Road), through its Chicago, Milwaukee & Puget
Sound Railway subsidiary, completed a 1,385-mile Pacific Coast Extension between Mobridge, South Dakota, and Tacoma and Seattle, Washington. Six months later, the Western Pacific Railway opened its 927-mile
line between Salt Lake City and San Francisco. Both managements took
comfort in rising railroad usage. In 1910, for example, passengers carried
nationally reached 933 million, a 126 percent increase over 1888 (the first
full year of ICC records). Freight traffic rose more dramatically, soaring
257 percent during this same period. It is no wonder optimism triggered
additional construction. In 1900 railroad companies made up more than
half of US market capitalization, and their bonds were the gold standard

of securities. The industry claimed about $12.5 billion ($394.1 billion in current dollars) worth of assets; the nation itself had an estimated wealth of approximately $90 billion dollars ($2.83 trillion in current dollars).[5]

The Milwaukee Road and Western Pacific brought "steamcar civilization" to existing communities, and they birthed new ones. Other strategic contemporary construction projects did the same. Take the completion in 1913 of the Chicago, Rock Island & Pacific's (Rock Island) St. Paul–Kansas City route, later known as the Spine Line. Although stretching only sixty-five miles between the Iowa towns of Carlisle and Allerton, this trackage spawned or brought to life several places, notably Beech, Melcher, and Williamson. In the pre–World War I years, there remained hundreds of inland towns, villages, and hamlets scattered throughout the trans-Chicago West. Their residents almost always believed that they *needed* a railroad, steam or electric, to have any hope of economic happiness. Population growth, new businesses, and increasing real-estate values seemed to be universal goals. Railroads and prosperity were deemed inseparable. Yet time was running out; the national railroad map was about to jell, and modal competition was emerging. There also existed a less apparent motivation: nonrailroad places sought to bolster local pride. The presence of rail transportation demonstrated to outsiders that community residents were progressive and up to date. Interurbans were widely viewed as "the latest harbingers of a higher state of civilization." Electric roads epitomized the modern.[6]

LAUNCHING A HOMETOWN RAILROAD

How could an inland or single railroad community attract the iron horse? Options varied. The most obvious, to convince a neighboring trunk railroad to provide the connection, had been done for decades with financial support from residents and local governments. Still, risks existed for the cooperating railroad. What if revenues did not justify the initial expense? An appendage had the potential to yield limited business and hence little or no profitability. Would a completing carrier retaliate? Corporate leaders often felt that their road had a "Divine right" to control what they considered their natural domain. They did not welcome interlopers—due diligence was required.[7]

If a trunk road failed to construct a branch or even show interest, there remained other possibilities for achieving a first or second outlet. Citizens might turn to community leaders, outside individuals, or promotion companies to convert grassroots enthusiasm into shortline reality. This was frequently done through public meetings and the local press, though prominent boosters usually did the actual organizing. They named the railroad (perhaps with a euphonious ring or with exaggerated destinations), elected officers (often themselves), and obtained a charter and other required documents.

Outsider involvement became a common occurrence. The rumor mill and personal contacts often brought paper projects to the attention of small engineering and securities construction firms. Their intent was hardly altruistic; they anticipated attractive monetary returns. Occasionally they sought to fleece the flock, exploiting citizens who were babes in the woods when it came to matters of high finance. One trick involved the aggressive sale of watered stock, the American master of which was Chicago traction magnate Charles Yerkes. There always seemed to be the promise that *their* railroad could be built and would generate multiple benefits. There also existed the belief that railroads would become permanent community fixtures. Probably few shortline proponents, including the most gifted promoters, conducted in-depth research on the actual financial prospects of their projects.

The construction process involved numerous stages and options. Legal papers in hand, a wealthy businessman, large landowner, or small group of well-heeled local individuals might underwrite a considerable portion of the financing. They would do so with purchases of stock and mortgage bonds, especially if the projected line was not particularly long or challenging. This method might be practical for a ten- to fifty-mile railroad traversing relatively level terrain, requiring only light to modest grading, and lacking a major stream or streams to bridge. Public taxation in some form became a popular practice. Voters in a county, township, or municipality (or multiple taxing authorities) would pass a tax levy, a ballot measure that might involve high-interest long-term bonds. Some entities had bad experiences with this approach, as in the case of Yankton County, Dakota Territory. In 1872 voters overwhelmingly endorsed a proposal for twenty-year bonds amounting to $200,000 ($4,385,879 in current dollars) and bearing 8 percent annual interest for construction of the Dakota Southern Railway. Because of legal difficulties, the county was unable to retire what became an oppressive debt until 1913. A popular approach involved placing a five-mill assessment on taxable property for one to five years. When voters approved the levy, each taxpayer would receive a certificate for the amount of the special railroad tax. This document could be exchanged for company stock, and options varied on how to use it. An Iowa newspaper editor elaborated on possible strategies: "When the amount of the 5 per cent. railroad tax is a small sum it can be made useful by combining it with such other railroad tax certificates as will make up the sum of $100, and one share of stock in the railroad will be issued for each $100 paid in the 5 per cent. tax, when the $100 certificates are gotten together." He continued: "The combination of tax certificates can be made by several owners joining together, and the several persons can select one of their number to handle the matter for them. Or, a taxpayer who does not care to bother with his certificate can seek a purchaser for it; or, it may be sought for by one who wishes to purchase certificates for the purpose of getting stock in the company." A township or county would occasionally grant an outright subsidy or bonus, but there would always be requirements. Public funds were commonly payable only once the road opened. A customary feature of a ballot victory or grant was the requirement that the railroad be placed in service by a specified date, usually December 31. Contractors often struggled to meet this looming deadline, which could be both exciting and nerve-racking. The race to finish became the storyline for the action-packed 1950 movie *A Ticket to Tomahawk*, produced by Twentieth Century Fox Studios and staring Anne Baxter, Walter Brennan, and Dan Dailey. The climax includes Tomahawk extending its town limits to meet the impending deadline, an action that two Iowa sunset cluster railroads employed.[8]

Before construction could commence, a survey (or perhaps multiple) needed to be run by a locating engineer. The final determination might not be as the crow flies—topography had to be considered, affecting cost and speed of construction. Promoters sought friendly, existing communities and locations suitable for prospective townsites. The property of a large backer or backers might play a role in determining the ultimate route. Usually, the survey process was not too time consuming, but it might involve debate or controversy.

The next step in the process involved obtaining the right-of-way. A portion of the land needed along the projected route, the standard hundred-foot wide strip,[9] might come from donations made by adjoining landowners. During the sunset era, it was more common for the gestating railroad to exchange stock for the needed parcels. In a typical arrangement of this kind, J. A. and Lydia Harris, who farmed near Atlantic, Iowa, accepted "in consideration of the Sum of Five Hundred Dollars in 5 shares of the capital stock of the Atlantic Northern and Southern Railway Company in $100 shares in hand paid by Atlantic Northern and Southern Railway Company." This transaction conveyed "3 and 11/100 acres more or less" for the right-of-way. Farmers wanted access to a railroad, and they anticipated increased property values. Town residents and local governments might gift lots or receive stock for rights-of-way and station facilities. In some cases, the infant company paid for the requisite land. Farmers, though, often sold their property at a nominal price. When a dollar amount could not be arranged, it became necessary to obtain land through the right of eminent domain, a legal process that determined a fair market value for the parcel to be taken.[10]

Although private capital was the popular way to create a railroad, occasionally a local municipality or institution would build one. This probably involved a community that lacked a rail outlet, as exemplified by the actions of the central Oregon town of Prineville. The Oregon Trunk Railroad had bypassed the community, and local development lagged. Prior to World War I, there had been two failed attempts to forge a railroad connection, so local leaders took matters into their own hands by chartering a publicly owned railroad. Success followed. In 1918 the eighteen-mile City of Prineville Railway opened for service, connecting with the Great Northern and Oregon Trunk Railroads at Prineville Junction. It remains a functioning common carrier.[11]

While Prineville created a municipally owned and operated railroad, private institutions occasionally did the same, as in the case of a college in Tabor, Iowa. This southwestern Hawkeye State community, established in the 1850s by Ohio abolitionists "who were unusually radical for the time," was situated on high land to avoid floods and disease. Following the Civil War, villagers launched a Christian college affiliated with the Congregational Church. When the Chicago, Burlington & Quincy Railroad (Burlington) and Wabash Railroads built through the immediate area, they avoided Tabor because of its unattractive physical location, adversely affecting residents and students alike. In the 1880s college officials received an invitation from Red Oak, Iowa, to relocate their school to this county-seat town where the Burlington provided main-line service. Instead of accepting this offer, residents decided to build their own railroad, which they incorporated in 1887. Residents unanimously voted a special 5 percent tax for the proposed Tabor & Northern Railroad, and the college purchased $43,000 ($1,256,067 in current dollars) of first-mortgage bonds to guarantee construction. The newly launched company gave the college enough stock in payment for the bonds for the college to have control. On December 20, 1889, the eleven-mile road opened to a connection in Malvern with the Burlington and Wabash, and the college dean became the president. A decade later, school trustees decided that operating an institution of higher education should not include running a railroad, and the college subsequently sold its holdings to a well-heeled trustee.[12]

The farmers' railroad became another creative way to forge access to the national rail network. If existing service was nonexistent, poor, or expensive, affected individuals, mainly farmers, could build their own railroad. This self-help concept lacked great complexity. A railroad would be organized, incorporated, and surveyed. Everyone who lived along the proposed line would donate right-of-way land, and there would be gifts of building materials and volunteer labor for the construction process. Hometown carpenters would erect bridges, depots, and support structures. Available animal teams would shape the roadbed with field plows and wheeled scrapers; crossties would be harvested from available stands of timber. Organizers would customarily reward contributors with stock, and securities might be sold. With grading complete and ties furnished, the company would bond its gestating road. That financial institution would probably be an area bank. When the company had money in hand, the purchase of rails and rolling stock began.

This inevitably meant used or "relay" rails together with a secondhand locomotive, freight and work cars, and an old passenger coach or two. The fate of the finished railroad would be left flexible. It could be sold or leased to a connecting trunk road with the agreement that customers would receive preferential treatment, or it could operate indefinitely as a home-owned venture.[13]

Even though the farmers' railroad concept possessed utopian qualities, few such roads appeared. The Farmers' Grain & Shipping Company (FG&SCo) was the largest and probably best known. Completed in 1905, its fifty-three-mile line ran between Devils Lake and Rock Lake, North Dakota. The FG&SCo added another thirteen miles when it leased the Brandon, Devils Lake & Southern Railroad, a Great Northern Railway (GN) property. The combined trackage extended operations from Rock Lake to Hansboro, North Dakota, yet it did not take long before the FG&SCo entered the GN orbit.[14]

IOWA COMES OF AGE

Within a generation or two, Iowa had evolved from prairie to corn belt. "The State of Iowa has grown from a wilderness to a great agricultural and industrial commonwealth in the allotted time of man," remarked an early twentieth-century observer. Few places could rival the Hawkeye State's soil fertility; it contained about a quarter of all grade-A land in the nation. Iowa had few marshes, wastelands, and barren knobs unsuitable for cultivation. Its image as a premier agricultural producer grew rapidly, and the corn-hog culture came to dominate. By 1900 the state led the country in corn and hog production. Cattle especially, together with horses and sheep, were also important sources of rural income. Agricultural historian James Whitaker argues that Iowa was not only a corn-hog state but also a corn-cattle one: "Rather than being a passing phase of frontier agricultural development as earlier in areas to the east, cattle feeding in the Corn Belt was a commercial venture very early and remained a major element in the economy of Illinois and Iowa in the middle of the twentieth century." Earle Ross, another agricultural scholar, concludes that the state's farmers from 1897 to the eve of World

War I experienced "unexampled progress and security." This was the golden age of agriculture, being a striking change from the poor harvest years of the late 1880s and the hard times of the mid-1890s. When William Brown, president of the New York Central Railroad, addressed the Iowa Society of New York City in 1910, he made glowing observations about Hawkeye State agriculture: "The farmer, after long years of discouraging struggle, has come into his own, and his prosperity will increase with the years. They are selling their corn for ninety-seven per cent., oats sixty-three per cent. and hay for forty per cent. more than they received ten years ago." He made this point: "With an average increase of eighty-seven per cent. in the price of all kinds of farm produce, they are paying only five per cent. more for their binders and mowers, four per cent. more for corn binders, three per cent. more for hay tedders, and one per cent. more for side delivery rakes and loaders." Later the federal government used these prosperous times as its parity years for agriculture. Statistics generated between August 1909 and July 1914 became the baseline for comparing farmers' purchasing power.[15]

Another way in which Iowa agriculture flourished involved rising land values. "How high will the price of Iowa land go?" asked the *Cedar Rapids Gazette* in 1909. "The question is induced by the recent phenomenal increase in the prices of good Iowa farms and the apparent tendency to still further increases. There seems to be no limit to the possibilities." Remarked newspaperman Edwin Percy Chase from Atlantic, Iowa, in 1936, "The year 1900 brought a new deal to Iowa. At the turn of the century land values, which had remained around $40 to $50 [$1,260 to $1,575 in current dollars] per acre for many years, commenced to surge upward. Within the next two or three years in our section of the State land was selling at from $75 to $100 [$2,365 to $3,155 in current dollars] per acre." His conclusion: "The farmer was coming into his own." Land prices continued that upswing through World War I. Some farms in western Iowa sold for as much as $200 to $250 ($4,110 to $5,135 in current dollars) an acre.[16]

Hawkeye State farmers were not the only residents who prospered in the new century. Main Street merchants realized that most farmers had money and were willing to spend it—profit margins were not razor-thin. This meant strong sales of machinery, lumber, hardware, dry goods, and other consumer items. Others, too, benefitted. Bankers faced less risk with agricultural loans, and professionals—lawyers, physicians, and dentists—earned a good living. Preachers and teachers likewise made gains. Moreover, thousands of Iowans found steady employment in agribusinesses. The state's industrial base became geared to the farming economy, revealing a strong rural-urban symbiosis. Meat packing emerged as a leading industry, with important plants in Cedar Rapids, Des Moines, Dubuque, Mason City, Ottumwa, Sioux City, and Waterloo. Mining operations also flourished, with Boone and Monroe Counties becoming epicenters of bituminous coal production and the greater Fort Dodge area being nationally recognized for its gypsum. Bricks, drainage tiles, and sewer pipes were produced from extracted clay deposits in multiple locations including Lehigh, Oskaloosa, Panora, Sheffield, and What Cheer.

Industrial growth coincided with a modest population increase. In 1890 Iowa recorded 1,912,297 residents, and by 1910 the number had increased to 2,224,771. Yet between 1900 and 1910, a multidecade decline in population began, concentrated in rural counties. Some Iowans decided to seek their fortunes on the Great Plains, in prairie Canada, or in irrigated lands in the American West. A typical newspaper advertisement encouraging an Iowa agrarian exodus read in part:

> Mr. Farmer: You can get rich raising alfalfa in the Big Horn Basin [of Wyoming]. If you will go with me on the next excursion I will show you many farms where there is now enough alfalfa in stack, grown this year, to repay the owner the purchase price of the land, and in many cases far more than the original cost of the farm. You can homestead 40 or 80 acres of this land under the Government Canal, repaying the Government actual cost for water in ten yearly payments without interest. Seed this farm down to alfalfa and stock it with hogs, a few milk cows and some chickens, and you have an easy living the rest of your life.[17]

Adding to earlier federal land disposal measures, the Kincaid Homestead Act of 1904, which granted 640-acre plots to settlers in northwestern Nebraska, and five years later the Enlarged Homestead Act, which increased the maximum permissible allotment to 320 acres of nonirrigated land in parts of the West, also contributed to the outflow. Although

lands beyond Iowa's borders were regularly pitched as economic para-
dises, many were not. Real-estate promoters and railroads together with
Washington lawmakers and bureaucrats encouraged farmer relocation.

Agrarians who remained in Iowa typically made improvements
without going heavily into debt. (They may have increased their indebtedness with land purchases.) Not only did they have outbuildings
repaired and constructed, but they remodeled or built new houses. "A
notable feature of the building trade in this part of the state this year is
the unusual number of farm houses being erected," observed the Council Bluffs *Evening Nonpareil* in 1908, "and most of them are modern up-
to-date residences, containing plumbing and some electric lights." The
naming of farms became popular, for example "Happy Acres," "Pleasant
View," and "Quietdale."[18]

IOWA AND ITS RAILROADS

Iowans embraced railroads early on, and their enthusiasm was understandable. Public roadways were nearly always unimproved, virtually
impassible during the spring thaw and rainy periods throughout the
year. The result was a vicious and viscous gumbo that created quagmires
and body-jarring ruts. Prolonged dry conditions meant dusty roads, and
wet-weather ruts and potholes often remained. Attempts in the late 1840s
and 1850s to construct plank roads for short or intermediate distances,
which Canadian projects had inspired, resulted in only a modest mileage completed in the Midwest and Iowa. These roads were built on a
graded roadway using heavy wooden planks laid across parallel wooden
stringers and were mostly abandoned after a few years. They became
weakened—even dangerous—from usage and decay, and repairs proved
time consuming and costly.[19]

Long before a railroad appeared on Iowa soil, intermittent talk burst
forth about welcoming the iron horse. As early as 1836, Dubuque resident
John Plumbe Jr. proposed an "Oregon Rail Road," a transcontinental
line that would extend from Lake Michigan through his hometown and
westward to the coast. Beginning in the mid-1840s, considerable discussion took place about building Pacific-bound railroads. Somewhat later,

scattered residents in Louisa and Marion Counties discussed an ambitious scheme: the Fort Wayne, Lacon & Platte Valley Air Line Rail Road.
Why the interest? This Platte Valley proposal, incorporated in Iowa in
1853, was "fully empowered to construct a Railway, from the Mississippi
river opposite New Boston [Illinois] through Wapello, to Council Bluffs
City." The hot-air scheme soon collapsed. Three years earlier, Iowans had
seen the first railroad organized in their state, the Davenport & Iowa
City Railroad. Enthusiasm for this fifty-five-mile project produced only
a paper reality. Its backers later supported the Mississippi & Missouri
Railroad, the first carrier in the state, and after 1866 the western extension of the Rock Island.[20]

In the decade preceding the Civil War, a web of iron rails began to
take shape in the Midwest. By 1853, the upstart city of Chicago showed
signs of emerging as a railroad Mecca—"the hub of the universe"—
having been linked the previous year to the East with the arrival of the
Michigan Southern and Michigan Central Railroads. It did not take long
before the Galena & Chicago Union, initial component of the Chicago
& North Western Railway (North Western); Chicago & Rock Island
(C&RI), core of the Rock Island; Burlington under several corporate
banners; and the Illinois Central Railroad (IC) pushed toward the Mississippi River and Iowa. In 1854 the C&RI became the first railroad to
reach the "Father of Waters" and two years later the first to bridge that
mighty stream. The Hawkeye State fortunately lay in the path of the most
direct routes from Chicago to the Pacific Ocean. In the 1860s, east–west
railroad construction erupted in the state, and subsidiary roads installed
hundreds of miles of track: North Western had the Chicago, Iowa &
Nebraska and Cedar Rapids & Missouri River Railroads; Rock Island
used the Mississippi & Missouri Railroad; Burlington employed the
Burlington & Missouri River Railroad; and IC utilized the Dubuque &
Pacific and Iowa Falls & Sioux City Railroads. They rushed to reach the
Missouri River. The former three headed for Council Bluffs and a connection with the Union Pacific (UP), eastern component of the initial
transcontinental railroad, while the latter sought Sioux City, also expect-
ing to tie in with the UP. The North Western won the race in 1867, and
its two rivals reached the Bluffs in 1869 and 1870. A hope for the future

scope of railroads in the state appeared in an 1869 issue of the *Cedar Falls Gazette*: "Iowa needs for her proper development, an east and west line of [rail] road through each tier of counties, and then connected at intervals of every forty miles by lines running north and south. Until she is thus gridironed she cannot have too many roads, and until then the projection and agitation of new railroad enterprises will not and ought not to cease."[21]

Following the Civil War, line construction exploded. Iowa claimed 2,683 route miles in 1870, 4,779 in 1880, and an impressive 8,366 in 1890. In sections of the state, the railroad map resembled a plate of spaghetti, and more lines were yet to come. Although the cataclysmic depression of 1893 to 1897 stymied building, trackage increased by the end of the century, standing at 9,366 miles in 1900. Soon the final wave occurred. A decade later, 9,755 miles laced the state. Route mileage peaked at 10,019 in 1914, two years before the national total reached its zenith. Iowa ranked fourth nationally in mileage, trailing the states of Texas, Illinois, and Pennsylvania. On the eve of World War I, no one in the Hawkeye State allegedly lived more than thirteen miles from a railroad station. By 1920, however, a slow decline in mileage had begun; the state's total that year slipped to 9,842 route miles and five years later to 9,756.[22]

After 1900, a portion of the trackage installed in Iowa came from newly completed shortline companies. (Shortlines are small, independent railroads and should not be confused with branch lines of trunk roads.) This was not a first-time phenomenon; similar independents had appeared decades earlier. In 1875 the Farmers Union Railroad, projected as a trans-Iowa carrier, opened a narrow-gauge (three-foot) line with cheap (and dangerous) strap-iron attached to wooden rails. It stretched the dozen miles from a sawmill on the Iowa River west of Liscomb northeast to Conrad and Beaman. Following the accidental death of promoter John Tripp, an Albion businessman who had laid out the Liscomb townsite and wished to stimulate its growth, the little pike disappeared in 1878. It gained the distinction of becoming the first railroad in the state to close. The second abandonment involved the tiny Ottumwa & Kirkville Railroad (O&K).[23] Opened in 1882, this road served residents of the inland Wapello County village of Kirkville (1880 population of 280), area farmers, and the nearby mines of the Wapello Coal Company. The O&K built approximately 3.5 miles of track to the southwest of Kirkville to connect at the Comstock Switch (renamed Kirkville Station) with the Keokuk to Des Moines line of the Rock Island. It used eight miles of trackage rights over that carrier to reach Ottumwa. When the mines shut down in 1890, revenues plummeted, and a year later the O&K ceased operations. Although the population of Kirkville had soared to 714 in 1890, it dropped to about 400 by the end of the decade. A more durable independent, the eight-mile Crooked Creek Railway & Coal Company that commenced operations in 1876, linked Lehigh with an interchange with the IC at Judd. Although constructed to a slim width, the road was standard gauged four years later. In the mid-1880s, Crooked Creek affiliate Webster City & Southwestern Railroad constructed a short extension to Webster City, while the Tabor & Northern made its debut at the end of the 1880s. These little roads were a harbinger of more to come.24

After the turn of the twentieth century, a host of sunset era short-lines appeared. The first was the Muscatine North & South Railroad (MN&S) that opened in 1899. This twenty-eight-mile road connected Muscatine to a southern interchange with the Iowa Central Railway at Elrick Junction. The MN&S failed financially in 1903, and a year later it was reorganized as the Muscatine North & South Railway. At last, in 1913, this reenergized railroad reached Burlington, its intended destination; the MN&S now spanned the fifty-five miles between its two terminals. Next appeared the smallest steam road in the Hawkeye State, still far larger than the 2.5-mile pioneer Iowa interurban Tama & Toledo Electric Railway & Light Company, one of the nation's tiniest. In 1901 the eight-mile Manchester & Oneida Railway connected the two places in its corporate name. It allowed Manchester, seat of Delaware County, to end the monopoly of the IC, connecting it at Oneida with the Chicago Great Western (Great Western) and the Milwaukee Road. The Newton & Northwestern Railroad (N&NW) became much more impressive. Following a 1902 consolidation with two small coal haulers, Boone, Rockwell City & Northwestern Railway and Boone Valley Coal & Railway Company, the recently organized N&NW built an impressive eighty-mile extension. This construction created a 102-mile railroad that joined Newton with Rockwell City, and in 1904 through service began between these two county capitals. Just as the N&NW had an involved corporate genealogy, so did the Chicago, Anamosa & Northern Railroad, commonly called the CAN. The company indirectly traced its history back to the Iowa Midland Railway, organized in 1870. A year later, this projected transstate road opened between Lyons (Clinton) and Anamosa, a distance of sixty-eight miles, but failed to build additional trackage. Confronted with ongoing financial problems, the Midland became a North Western property in 1884. Anamosa area residents retained railroad ambitions—in 1903, they backed the organization of the CAN, launched by the Dubuque-based real-estate, insurance, and loan business of Peter Kiene & Son. Two years later, the Kienes-owned Midland Construction Company completed a twenty-mile line from Anamosa to Coggon and an interchange with the IC. Management hoped to reach Quasqueton and Waterloo. After much struggling, the CAN in 1912 finally arrived in Quasqueton, making for a thirty-five-mile operation. But the shortline never built beyond that Buchanan County town and suspended operations three years later. The Iowa Northern Railroad became the last true agricultural shortline during this period. Opened in 1914, this five-mile pike extended north from Dyersville, located on the Great Western and IC, to New Vienna, a village of 188 residents. Financed largely by farmers in the New Vienna area, the Iowa Northern survived for only a few months. Inadequate funding and dreadful track conditions forced this woebegone road to suspend operations. Legal complications, however, prevented rails from being lifted until 1919.[25]

A distinctly different late nineteenth and early twentieth-century Iowa shortline was the Davenport, Rock Island & Northwestern Railway (DRI&NW). Rather than being a traditional carrier, it developed into an important terminal and bridge property. It began in 1884 as the Davenport, Rock Island & Railway Bridge Company and by 1900 connected Davenport and Clinton, a distance of thirty-four miles. When the company spanned the Mississippi River between Davenport and East Moline, Illinois, with its Crescent Bridge, its value and strategic importance soared. Unlike other Hawkeye State shortlines, the DRI&NW became jointly owned by two trunk railroads, Burlington and Milwaukee.[26]

Nearly a dozen electric railroads in Iowa paralleled the growth of the sunset steam shortlines. This was the time of national interurban

This image captures the first Chicago, Anamosa & Northern Railroad train to enter Quasqueton in Buchanan County, Iowa. Completed in 1912, this thirty-five-mile carrier experienced a short life, paralleling similar Hawkeye State shortlines built during the twilight years of railroad construction. In 1917 the CAN became junk. *(Author's collection.)*

mania. Several of these roads could best be classified as rural trolleys: the eleven-mile Albia Interurban Railway (1907–1908), eight-mile Cedar Rapids & Marion City Railway (1892), and three-mile Oskaloosa-Buxton Electric Railway (1907). Others took on the characteristics of contemporary steam railroads—in fact, three began as such.[27] These freight and passenger operators included the eleven-mile Mason City & Clear Lake Railroad (1897); sixty-mile Waterloo, Cedar Falls & Northern Railway (1897–1914); sixty-one-mile Inter-Urban Railway (1902–1906, later Des Moines & Central Iowa Railroad); twenty-seven-mile Cedar Rapids & Iowa City Railway (1904); sixty-five-mile Clinton, Davenport & Muscatine Railway (1904–1912); one hundred forty-seven-mile Fort Dodge, Des Moines & Southern Railway (née Newton & Northwestern, 1905–1916); twenty-one-mile Charles City Western Railway (1911–1915); and thirty-two-mile Iowa Southern Utilities (later Southern Iowa Railway, 1910–1914). At its peak, the Hawkeye State claimed 526 route miles under wire.[28]

SUNSET CLUSTER

Residents of the southwestern quadrant of Iowa never saw an interurban,[29] and at the start of the twentieth century they had access to just one steam shortline. Yet the Tabor & Northern served a limited territory. There had been another shortline: the Clarinda & St. Louis Railway (C&StL). In 1879 this locally backed company built a twenty-one-mile link between Clarinda and a Wabash connection at Roseberry, Missouri. A year later the Wabash took control, but that relationship did not save the line; the C&StL entered bankruptcy in 1886. The receiver tried to keep the road going but failed. The last train ran on December 19, 1889, and soon the track was dismantled. Sadness reigned in Clarinda and along the naked roadbed.[30]

The southwestern Iowa region was no railroad desert, though. By the early twentieth century, a half-dozen Chicago roads served Council Bluffs, making it a great railroad center. In 1867, following the arrival of the North Western, the Burlington-controlled Council Bluffs & St. Joseph Railroad, later part of the Kansas City, St. Joseph & Council Bluffs Railroad (KCStJ&CB), became the second railroad to reach this rail-oriented city. Soon came the Burlington and Rock Island. In 1879 the Wabash, led by financier Jay Gould, offered an alternative albeit much longer route from the Windy City via Moberly and Brunswick, Missouri. Then the Milwaukee (1882), IC (1899), and Great Western (1903) entered the Bluffs. The Burlington had the most pronounced presence—in addition to its original trans-Iowa stem, the company by the 1880s had installed a web of lateral branch lines. It had as objectives to fend off the system building of Jay Gould, who wanted his Wabash to tap Iowa's agricultural and coal traffic, and to increase feeder traffic. There was still another explanation for this expansion at the end of the 1870s: Iowa lawmakers in 1878 had made major adjustments to the earlier Granger Laws, lessening control over freight rates. Burlington president John Murray Forbes believed that this action made it safe "to satisfy the reasonable demands of the region naturally tributary to the main line of road." Common with contemporary industry policies, branches were incorporated as separate companies, with the Burlington acquiring their first-mortgage bonds and often much of their stock. After completion, they were leased.[31] The Burlington system built northward from Creston to Fontanelle (later extending west to Cumberland); Red Oak to Griswold; Hastings to Avoca and southward from Creston to Hopkins, Missouri (later greater St. Joseph, Missouri); Villisca to Clarinda and subsequently to Burlington Junction, Missouri (lengthening its St. Joseph line to the Missouri communities of Corning and Bigelow); Red Oak to Hamburg; and Hastings to Sidney. In 1880 the Burlington absorbed its KCStJ&CB affiliate. Sixteen years later, the Burlington enlarged its footprint when it acquired the Humeston & Shenandoah and in 1899 the connecting Keokuk & Western Railroads. In 1901 the Burlington streamlined its corporate structure by absorbing these various properties.[32]

The Rock Island also served a number of western Iowa communities, although far fewer than the Burlington. During the late 1870s, it constructed several branches radiating from its trans-Iowa line. At Atlantic the Rock Island built north to Audubon and southwest to Griswold, and at Avoca it ran north to Harlan and south to Carson. Following conferences between these two roads, the Rock Island did not seek to penetrate the realm of the Burlington directly.[33]

The western quadrant of the Hawkeye State became known as the Iowa Bluegrass County. Ridges and valleys characterize the terrain, especially near the Missouri River, where glacial windblown silt forms the Loess Hills. This landscape protrudes several hundred feet or more above the adjoining land features; it is not that gentle, undulating prairie found elsewhere in the state. Although the Bluegrass County was ideally suited for livestock raising, there existed fertile lands along its meandering and shallow streams, making for productive crop cultivation. It did not take long before corn replaced wheat as king. During the mid-nineteenth century, Euro-American settlers entered this region, and the population increased steadily. By 1900 Pottawattamie County (Council Bluffs) emerged as the leading center with 54,336 residents. The closest counties in head count, Page (Clarinda) and Cass (Atlantic), tallied less than half that of Pottawattamie, with 24,187 and 21,274 respectively. Although Council Bluffs–Omaha became prominent centers for business, other places established their own service areas; Atlantic, Clarinda,

Creston, and Red Oak dominated. If the viability of a town's Main Street gave a good indication of the general health of a community, it was readily evident in these four county seats. Small industries developed and flourished both there and in a number of smaller communities, which might have a creamery or flour mill. Commercial agriculture, however, remained the economic mainstay of the region, and rail transportation did much to make it possible.[34]

Even though a contemporary map of western Iowa suggests that trunk railroads offered adequate transportation, residents often believed otherwise. Most of all, there were those deplorable public roads. In 1904 less than 2 percent of Iowa's 102,448 miles of roadways were improved with gravel or broken stone. Not until 1911 would workers pour the state's first rural section of concrete pavement. No wonder there was this seasonal exaggeration: "Roads were as deep as they were wide." No one disputed this characterization; after all, Iowa was one of the mud-road states. An observer about 1905 commented: "It seems absurd that in a state so wealthy and prosperous, so advanced in education and intelligence the entire agricultural economy and the basis for practically all business activity should be left to the mercy of bad weather on account of roads which would be a disgrace even to a barbarian." Any trip with animal-powered conveyance was a challenge irrespective of weather-related conditions: "A trip of 10 miles was a long journey, and to travel 20 miles was a full and hard day's work." That logic led railroads, especially in the trans-Chicago West, to employ the team-haul principle, placing stations the distance farmers could travel to town and still return in one day.[35]

In the early years of the century, *Red Oak Express* readers were hardly shocked to see such reports about local road conditions:

> This week a farmer WALKED 4 miles to town with a basket of produce.
>
> This week a farmer's wife drove to town with her butter, and most everybody in town heard of it because it was about the only country butter received here the past week. Verily the bad roads have well nigh cut off the country from the town, and the town from the country.
>
> Bad roads have hindered the marketing of produce, stopped the delivery of the rural mails and put a damper on business.[36]

In a twist on the typical bad roads story, "Mud—Mud—Mud" appeared in a contemporary issue of the *Clarinda Herald*:

The knee deep mud which has prevailed the past week in Page county has been a good thing for the ground, but has kept people from seeing each or coming to town. Those who traveled have largely done so on horse back, and some of the farmers have "hoofed it" to town. The rural mail carriers have been hit perhaps hardest of all. Out of Yorktown on Tuesday one carrier made his route by walking fifteen miles. The other man rode his, but only part of the way. The frost went out of the ground just in time to let the rain and snow all filter in, and put the ground in best condition for a record hay crop this year.[37]

Iron horses and electric cars were the answer to contemporary road problems of "bottomless pools of rich, black Iowa mud." Automobiles and trucks were in early stages of development, and the "good roads movement" had yet to take hold.[38]

Quadrant residents fussed and fumed about service and rates. Their concerns centered on the impact of single-carrier monopolies. Take Clarinda—this Page County seat had multiple Burlington lines, radiating in all directions. Passengers and freight could travel north to Villisca on the Tarkio Valley line and connect with the east–west main stem; go east and west on the Keokuk, Shenandoah, and Red Oak secondary main line that provided another main stem link at Red Oak; head south on the Nodaway Valley branch (via Braddyville) to St. Joseph; and take the Tarkio Valley line southwest (via Northboro) to that same destination. The public could endure poor passenger service. If there were double-daily passenger runs, one might be a mixed freight train ("hogs and humans"). The latter, because of switching chores, commonly failed to meet published schedules, supporting that oft-repeated expression "to lie like a timetable." H. H. Scott, vice president of the Clarinda Commercial Club, expressed a widespread concern about the Burlington freight monopoly: "We came to the realization of the fact that, without competition in railway facilities, it was useless for us to try to get factories to come here." Scott's statement echoed the overstated views published a few years earlier by another Iowan, Delaware County judge A. S. Blair: "Study of our state railroad map will satisfy anyone that there is no town in the state of any importance that has but one railroad, and none of any considerable size or importance that has but two roads and that all cities of any size and importance have three roads and upwards with six or more outlets." Judge Blair added, "These facts, satisfy us that it is the railroads that build up towns."[39]

There were inland communities that desperately sought just a single railroad connection. College Springs in Page County and Grant in Montgomery County exemplified this longing: both were established trade centers, more than crossroad villages. College Springs, as its name implies, was home to a four-year institution of higher education, the United Presbyterian–sponsored Amity College. By 1900 the town population had reached nearly seven hundred, and college enrollment held steadily at about two hundred students, including those from out of state. The two communities, too, had distinct business sections. Grant, with approximately four hundred residents, boasted a modern gasoline-powered flour mill, a state-of-the-art blacksmith shop, and an attractive Methodist Episcopal Church.[40] Before the iron horse arrived in College Springs, the disadvantages of railroad isolation were felt in Grant, Elk Horn, Kimballton, Macksburg, Morton Mills, and Treynor. This involved more than personal travel—arguably the most troubling financial factor was a higher per-mile charge for overland drayage compared with the cheaper per-mile cost of rail transport. An inland community business was usually not large enough to justify the inventory carried by a counterpart in a railroad town, resulting in merchants unlikely to carry a sufficient stock and variety of goods. They also probably had to charge more for their merchandise. These factors hindered their competitive position.

Just as their neighbors in urban areas sought flanged-wheel transportation, farmers wanted convenient access as well. There was grain and livestock, mostly cattle and hogs, to send to market. With railroad access, farmers could bring in western feeder cattle to fatten before sending them off to packing plants. Such a practice potentially meant considerably more money in their pocketbooks. When rails became available, elevators and stock pens soon appeared.

The response to what was considered inadequate railroad coverage, explained in part by a competitive void, led to the construction of multiple shortline carriers. Steam power ruled, yet carriers might open or later operate with electricity. Steelways could be expanded and linked, creating routes that sliced the quadrant north and south, east and west. Eventually, residents welcomed the Atlantic Northern & Southern; Iowa & Southwestern; Creston, Winterset & Des Moines; and Iowa &

Omaha Short Line Railroads. The Des Moines & Red Oak Railway was only on the pathway to running. Before that project collapsed, workers had graded a portion of its route and assembled ties and bridge timbers along a never-to-be railed roadbed. Although the completed shortlines came late and failed early, they collectively had a positive economic and social impact on their service territory and reflected the excitement for railroads, steam and electric, prior to the triumph of internal combustion vehicles and networks of good roads.

RAILWAY AGE MATURES

When the Railway Age dawned in Iowa and elsewhere, states and territories needed to respond to this revolution in transportation. Lawmakers created incorporation statutes, delineated how private property could be taken for public use, and enacted other public-interest measures. In the 1870s, Iowa launched its Board of Railroad Commissioners, which had the authority to gather pertinent information in response to complaints about discriminatory rates, poor service, and similar matters and attempt to rectify them.

By the later part of the nineteenth century, an expanded legal code explained how Iowa would manage a railroad company that wished to abandon a line or to dissolve itself. It fell on commissioners to make these decisions. One provision focused on ownership of abandoned rights-of-way that had been taken through eminent domain. Although the law evolved regarding the length of time the rail line had been left idle, this land ultimately reverted to the original owners. As for the abandonment of a piece of trackage or an entire railroad, regulators held hearings and made their rulings binding. Such was the action taken for these four operating sunset cluster railroads. Following the federalization of strategic steam and electric railroads during World War I, Congress passed the Transportation Act of 1920 (known also as the Esch-Cummins Act) and altered the procedure. Under this federal measure, whenever a request for permission to end service occurred, formal abandonment could only be decided by the Interstate Commerce Commission. Except when the railroad was wholly intrastate, a state commission acted merely in an advisory capacity. This process usually took longer than when state authorities had a greater responsibility, as would be the case when the Atlantic Northern shut down during the Great Depression. The timing of this landmark legislation was good; economic historians customarily date the decline of railroads from about World War I.

Most states have a complex railroad history, and Iowa is no exception. Its railroad story understandably has focused on trunk roads. The smallest roads, particularly those that emerged after the turn of the twentieth century, have been largely overlooked by professional historians, history buffs, and railroad enthusiasts. This has been a shortcoming of transportation history. Much can be learned from studies of these inconspicuous and nearly forgotten shortlines. Just as human beings are unique, so too are railroads, including sunset-era carriers.

TWO

ATLANTIC NORTHERN &
SOUTHERN RAILWAY

CASS COUNTY

CASS COUNTY, SITUATED IN WESTERN IOWA, EMERGED AS THE
focal point of the sunset cluster railroads. Atlantic, the county seat, became the headquarters and operational hub for the largest and the longest lasting of these shortlines: the Atlantic Northern & Southern Railway (AN&S).[1] It also was the first of these shortlines to partially open.
On New Year's Day 1908, a special train made an initial trip over the seventeen miles between Atlantic and Kimballtown. Following completion
of a thirty-eight-mile extension from Atlantic to Villisca on December
29, 1910, the railroad floundered; five months later it entered receivership. As the result of a bankruptcy reorganization in 1913, the AN&S
was broken into two independent companies. The Atlantic Northern
Railway (AN) connected Atlantic with Elk Horn and Kimballton, and
the Atlantic Southern Railroad (AS) linked Atlantic with Grant and
Villisca. The former functioned until early 1936, but the latter survived
for less than two years.[2]

Atlantic was thriving at the time the AN&S celebrated the ceremonial hammering of the final spike on the Villisca extension. In addition
to serving as county capital, it benefited from a diverse economic base.
Leading businesses included the Atlantic Brick and Tile Company, Atlantic Canning Factory, and Atlantic Mill and Elevator Company. These
firms all relied on rail transport. Atlantic's population stood at 4,560,
resembling the size of two nearby county-seat towns, Clarinda and Red
Oak, which also undertook contemporary shortline construction.[3]

The coming of the iron horse to greater Cass County had sparked its rapid development. As the result of the acquisition of the Mississippi & Missouri Railroad (M&M) by the Chicago, Rock Island & Pacific (Rock Island) in 1866 and its arrival in Council Bluffs three years later, which forged a Chicago–Davenport–Des Moines connection with the Union Pacific–Central Pacific transcontinental routes, area residents gained access to the exploding national network of iron rails. Completion of the main line led to the founding of Atlantic, officially incorporated in 1869, and several smaller communities in the county. In 1879 the Rock Island expanded its local services by installing a twenty-five-mile branch northward to Audubon, and a year later it opened a fifteen-mile appendage southwest to Lewis and Griswold. Then there was the land grant Congress had awarded the M&M in 1856 as part of the Iowa Land Bill. This measure, administered by state lawmakers, gave the railroad more than 480,000 acres, including portions of Cass County. The Rock Island aggressively marketed this windfall: "CHEAP FARMS" and "CHOICEST & MOST DESIRABLE LANDS IN THE STATE OF IOWA." Settlers were attracted to the rolling landscape with its black loam soil underlaid with sandy clay, "some of the richest farming regions of Iowa." They eagerly purchased agricultural lands and town lots. Population of the county jumped from 1,612 in 1860 to 5,464 in 1870 and soared to 16,943 a decade later; the federal census in 1900 recorded 21,274 inhabitants.[4]

Even though Atlantic and Cass County were hardly railroad starved, residents of Atlantic and the neighboring county-seat towns of Clarinda and Red Oak wanted to end the domination of a single carrier. When the first segment of the AN&S opened, the *Atlantic Telegraph* remarked, "For a number of years past the citizens of Atlantic have from time to time talked with more or less enthusiasm among themselves about building a north and south railroad which should connect this city with either the Northwestern [*sic*] or Burlington railroads, or both, and thus give the city what all agreed we most needed, a competing line with the Rock Island." The newspaper continued, "That the completion of this road will mark the turning point in Atlantic's history, that it may give new life and a brighter outlook for the city's future is the earnest hope of all and the firm belief of many of its citizens." It closed with these thoughts:

"In conclusion let us all hope that the new road may prove a bond which shall unite and make Atlantic better acquainted with our neighbors on the north and make them better acquainted with Atlantic, and may this better acquaintance prove mutually beneficial to the citizens of all the communities through which the road runs is the sincere wish and firm belief of all interested."[5]

LITTLE DENMARKS

Cass County claimed residents who hailed from various parts of the country, primarily the Midwest, but also from Europe and the British Isles. Danes were the largest foreign contingent in the immediate area. By 1910 their numbers reached approximately three thousand residents. Census records, however, might list their nationality as German, as some immigrated from the quasi-independent Slesvig-Holstein duchies of the Danish kingdom. But during the Second Slesvig War of 1864, Prussia defeated Denmark, causing it to lose this portion of South Jutland that constituted two-fifths of its total land area and 40 percent of its population. Slesvig-Holstein became part of Germany, the Prussian-dominated nation-state created in 1871. The approximately two hundred thousand affected Danes were distressed about becoming Prussian and soon German subjects; military-age males, for one, wanted to avoid the Prussian or German army, as did their families. Understandably, this disastrous war triggered a surge of migration. More Danes, though, left their native country for other reasons, including poverty, overpopulation, land scarcity, religious freedom, and the chance to prosper in the New World. Niels Christian, who immigrated from West Jutland to Iowa, "wanted to go to America where there were many more opportunities—where he may one day own a large farm, with lots of machinery and livestock. America was on the move, and he wanted to be a part of it." Although families migrated, unmarried adults, mostly young males, became the dominant migrant group. Unlike Old Europe, the New World was a place for self-starters. After this initial outflow, chain migration followed into the early decades of the twentieth century, interrupted by World War I and largely ending with the National Origins Act of 1924.[6] Elk Horn, located in Clay Township of Shelby County and near the Cass County line, became the epicenter of Danish settlement. It emerged as a recognized community in 1867 when the federal government established a post office. Growth followed. In 1901 the town was platted and nine years later incorporated. The arrival of the AN&S in 1907 triggered that response, and by 1910 its population stood at 382; a decade later it climbed to 589 and was 98 percent Danish. Elk Horn became recognized as an enlightened place. "It is, in point of progressive tendencies, very near the head of Shelby County municipalities," observed a contemporary writer. "It is the result of the best thought and devotion of a sturdy and patriotic band of Danish pioneers." As early as 1878, the village had the first Danish Folk High School in the United States, which morphed into the Elk Horn Lutheran High School and College. Even though this combination school, college, and seminary attained only modest enrollments, it was unusual for a small community to have such an advanced educational facility. Initially Danish culture flourished. In 1880 appeared *Dannevirke*, a native-language newspaper, although it subsequently relocated elsewhere in the state. An orphanage was also established. Danes in Elk Horn usually assimilated quickly into American life. Those in neighboring Kimballton, three miles to the north, were more likely to preserve their Danish culture. Yet it was not unusual to see the Danish flag and the Stars and Strips flying side by side. Went a Scandinavian saying: "Love the old country like a mother and love the new country like a bride." It should not be overlooked that after the Prussian victory, Denmark was not the same place. "The Danes had witnessed the sad decline of their country after the traumatic events of 1864, when the Prussians occupied a large portion of Denmark," notes historian Arthur Herman. "Why look back with nostalgia to an old country that was not longer there?"[7]

Kimballtown, which became the northern terminal of the AN&S, emerged as the second Danish community in the area. It received a considerable number of residents from the Limfjord area of West Jutland and from Aero, an island in the Baltic Sea. Located in Sharon Township of southeastern Audubon County, Kimballtown, too, was situated close to the Cass County line. In 1883 Hans Jensen Jorgensen settled at the site and obtained a post office. The village grew and achieved incorporation in 1908, shortly after the coming of the railroad. Its population reached 241 in 1910 and 382 a decade later. Like Elk Horn, it was 98 percent Danish. Jorgensen remained a civic booster, donating land for the first school and church, backing construction of the Commercial Hotel, and helping to launch the enduring Landmands National Bank.[8]

Residents of these "Little Denmarks" were energetic, forward-looking, and Lutheran, although Baptist, Mormon, and Seventh-day Adventist Danes had settled early on in Elk Horn and environs. Yet differences involving specific religious and cultural beliefs existed between members of the overwhelmingly Lutheran majority. The majority in Elk Horn adhered to the conservative Inner Mission wing of Danish Lutheranism, accepting a literal interpretation of the Bible and stressing the importance of repentance. These pietistic believers also sought greater assimilation based on the notion that becoming Americanized would allow them to better spread their religious views. Residents of Kimballton generally embraced the more liberal Grundtvigian Lutheranism, following Danish theologian, poet, and philosopher N. S. F. Grundtvig. Their view of Lutheranism stressed the importance of the Apostle's Creed. Elk Horn had its Inter Mission followers and Kimballton the Grundtvigian disciples. Dancing, drinking, and Sunday labor were forbidden by the former but not the latter. These were the "Holy Danes" and the "Happy Danes." In 1894 the pietists launched the Danish Evangelical Lutheran Church in North America (or North Church) and merged with another conservative Lutheran group to create the United Danish Evangelical Lutheran Church (or United Church), leaving the Danish Evangelical Lutheran Church in America (or Grundtvigian Church) within the homeland denomination. The schism led to specific community destinations for new immigrants. "Elk Horn attracted those for whom purity of their faith was of paramount importance, while a large number of people who wanted to maintain the cultural ties to their Danish roots were attracted to the Kimballton area," noted one study. "However, the very fundamental differences which lay behind the church split in 1894, and the bitterness which resulted from the battle over the church property in Elk Horn, caused the two populations to develop reservations about each other, despite their common ancestry." Still Danish Lutheranism embraced the sanctity of labor and community, a worldview that advanced both Elk Horn and Kimballton. Not insignificantly, the non-Danish multicounty population accepted these people in their midst; after all, they were white, protestant, and mastered English more readily than most other non-English-speaking immigrants.[9]

A NORTH–SOUTH RAILROAD

For years, town, village, and farm residents who lived along what became the AN&S discussed railroad construction. Some thought that a line should be built beyond what became the fifty-four-mile Kimballton, Atlantic, and Villisca corridor. It might extend northward to Sioux City and southward to St. Joseph and Kansas City, a future segment of a great north–south road linking Canada with the Gulf of Mexico.

There had been earlier efforts to turn talk into reality for a localized north–south railroad. Hope emerged in 1902 for an electric interurban capable of handling both passengers and carload freight between Atlantic and Villisca. At least two Montgomery County townships considered a tax levy to aid construction of what was called the Villisca, Grant & Atlantic Railway. That March, a Grant representative told the Villisca newspaper: "Hear Ye! Hear Ye! to whom it may concern and others, and know all men, etc. Our goodly city is to have another railroad, and whereas we have had at least seven during the last 30 years, none of which have made an appearance and in view it is hereby ordered that further procrastination shall cease to be a virtue." The piece continued: "It is hereby ordered that a 5% tax be voted for said purpose and that said tax or any part thereof shall not become payable or due until the old-fashioned steam whistle of the engine at the depot in Milford [original name of Grant] shall be distinctly heard at the mayor's office." In June, Douglas Township (Grant) passed the ballot measure by a vote of 138 to 21, and soon surveyors were in the field locating a line in the vicinity of Grant and Morton's Mills. Yet the project fizzled. "We wonder what has become of our new Electric Road," commented one journalist. "We fear that it took on too heavy a charge of electricity and exploded." Nevertheless, Grant area residents retained a burning desire for a railroad whether steam or electric.[10]

After the Panic of 1903 had run its course, renewed proposals for interurban projects sprouted throughout much of the nation, including in Iowa. In November 1906, Clarence Ross and Charles Judd of the Engineering, Construction & Securities Company (EC&SCo) became involved with the building of the first leg of the AN&S, and they planned it as an electric road. Ross, who headed the tiny Chicago-based firm, had his eyes on municipally owned electric-light plants in Atlantic and Red Oak. He made acquiring the former facility a condition for constructing an interurban northwestward from Atlantic to Kimballton and perhaps beyond. What he first sought, though, was to build a twenty-five-mile electric railway between Red Oak and Atlantic. Although the Red Oak plan fell through, he and Judd, who served as chief engineer of the EC&SCo, realized that residents of Elk Horn and Kimballtown, Atlantic boosters, and area farmers wanted a railroad, and they would build one—electric or not. At first, expectations ran high for an interurban. Although Atlantic's city council approved the sale of the municipally owned power plant to the Ross firm, eligible voters needed to concur. They did not, defeating the purchase by a three-to-one margin. During the formative years of the twentieth century, support for public ownership of utilities remained strong; consumers repeatedly embraced "gas and water socialism," and that included electric plants. Commented the *Telegraph*, "But the talks on the streets plainly indicated that opposition to the sale of the light plant did not mean opposition to the building of an interurban road, by any means." Ross and Judd worked closely with the dynamic Hans Rattenborg, a thirty-five-year-old Atlantic realtor and land speculator who had earlier in his career manufactured and sold lighting rods for which he held a patent. Rattenborg became the "general field and right-of-way man and his work has proved that no mistake was made in the choice for the position." Ross, Judd, and Rattenborg were joined by Atlantic banker J. A. McWaid, Elk Horn banker John Petersen, Kimballton businessman Martin Esbeck, and other "progressive men" to drum up support for what emerged as a traditional steam shortline designed initially to serve Danish country and enhance Atlantic's trading area. "None of these men had ever had any experience in railroad building but they were willing to take a try at it."[11]

RAILS NORTHBOUND

Enthusiasts for an Atlantic-based railroad took action. Although the initial focus of construction centered on what became the shorter northern section, Kimballton was not expected to be the final endpoint. Manning (in southwestern Carroll County) and not Sioux City would likely be reached. It offered interchanges with three trunk roads: Chicago & North Western (North Western), Chicago Great Western (Great Western), and Chicago, Milwaukee & St. Paul (Milwaukee). On December 26, 1906, backers did an essential part of preliminary work by incorporating the AN&S under the laws of Iowa. The company had an authorized capital stock of $500,000 ($14,604,375 in current dollars) and a flexible description as to nature and intent. On January 7, 1907, the first stock subscription occurred, and soon fundraising began in earnest. On Saturday evening, February 2, 1907, a mass meeting took place at the opera house in Atlantic. There was band music, promotional speeches, and most importantly, "many stock subscriptions taken." Enthusiasm reigned. "The road now seems almost certain of construction."[12]

When the completed AN&S opened, Clarence Ross explained in a letter to the editor of the *Villisca Review* how the railroad had been financed. He offered the philosophy of its supporters, including those who earlier had backed the Kimballton line: "I beg to say, the idea, as in the case of the northern end, was to build a 'People's Railroad' to be owned and operated by the people and for the people." Ross did not mean an actual "people's" or "farmers'" railroad. The AN&S had not been built in the fashion of the Farmers Grain & Shipping Company and Fairmount & Veblen Railway in the Dakotas or of the few other bona fide self-help carriers where supporters participated in the actual construction. The AN&S more resembled the Dan Patch Line, the future forty-two-mile Minneapolis, Northfield & Southern Railway. In 1911 sparkplug Marion Willis (Will) Savage said, "The Dan Patch Electric Railroad is truly a People's Railroad, built by the people and for the people." He meant that mostly small investors had made its construction possible.[13]

Sales of shares of common stock became the core money-raising approach. This widely employed method of financing a shortline railroad yielded an encouraging response. By late February 1907, Atlantic supporters had contributed $62,000 ($1,746,326 in current dollars), those in

Elk Horn and vicinity $50,000 ($1,408,327 in current dollars), and in the Kimballton area $42,000 ($1,182,995 in current dollars). Funds did not immediately fill company coffers. "Par value of the shares is $100 [$2,817 in current dollars], five percent to be paid on demand," explained the *Atlantic Messenger* before the subscription process began. "The fund for this payment will be used for the surveys and other preliminary expenses. Twenty per cent will be due when first five miles are graded and ready for the rails; twenty-five per cent is due when the first ten miles are graded and fifty per cent when fifteen miles are graded and rails laid ready for the rolling stock." The report added, "This plan is certainly equitable and will commend itself to all prospective stockholders whether they invest much or little." Also commonplace were right-of-way donations and the exchange of stock for these hundred-foot-wide strips. In one instance, the company resorted to condemnation proceedings because of a quirky landownership agreement, which was resolved with a stock and cash settlement. Since the board of directors realized that stock subscriptions would be inadequate to pay for construction, estimated at approximately $300,000 ($8,449,965), property tax levies were sought from Clay Township (Elk Horn) and Sharon Township (Kimballton). Both measures passed overwhelmingly and generated $35,000 ($985,829 in current dollars). Included in the ballot measure was the standard deadline for completion. For tax-generated monies to be paid, a train needed to reach Kimballton by the stroke of midnight on December 31, 1907.[14]

The spring of 1907 saw line locators undertake two surveys. The preferred survey revealed that there would be a shortfall in funding. While the first dozen miles from Atlantic posed no costly construction issues, the hilly country outside Elk Horn and Kimballton meant that significant cuts and fills would be necessary, making the final five miles of grading more expensive. Notably, Creamery Hill outside Kimballton had to be avoided, necessitating the placement of grade west of the impediment. When eastern bonding firms appeared unlikely to decide to acquire the company's first mortgage bonds within an acceptable time period, the board opted to sell them locally.[15]

The AN&S forged ahead. On July 1, 1907, the building contract was let to Niels Bennedsen and Thorvald Jensen, who formed the Kimballton-Elk Horn Construction Company (née Kimballton Concrete Bridge & Culvert Company). Fifteen days later ground was broken, and grading commenced. Inadequate financing, however, continued to haunt the company. Officers, including President Rattenborg, sustained the project by giving their personal security on a $48,000 note ($1,351,994 in current dollars) and likely received first mortgage bonds in exchange. This money paid the contractor and satisfied bills for materials and transportation. Rattenborg went so far as to sell 11,500 fence posts at thirteen cents each from a farm he owned near Stuart, Iowa. He invested the resulting $1,495 ($42,109 in current dollars) in AN&S stock.[16]

By early autumn 1907, funding still posed concerns. A panic struck Wall Street, sharply interrupting the prosperity of the new century. Triggered by weaknesses in the banking system, this fragility quickly led to bank failures, rising unemployment, and uneasiness about the nation's economic health. This financial crisis exacerbated existing money worries for the AN&S and halted construction. The approaching deadline to reach Kimballton loomed, but fortunately money materialized. The board asked the 702 stockholders to advance funds on their shares. Most agreed—they contributed an estimated $30,000 ($844,996 in current dollars) and in returned received company stock.[17]

Building resumed. Workmen toiled on grading, bridges, and culverts, including a sizeable trestle over Indian Creek. On November 1 the company acquired a used locomotive to assist in tie and rail laying. This work began on November 15, with about one hundred men laboring on the freshly graded right-of-way to install relay rail. The steel weighed sixty pounds to the yard, similar to what other regional shortlines used.[18]

Excitement spread as tracklayers approached Elk Horn. On Christmas Day, 1907, the construction train, pulling a carload of coal, steamed into town amid great joy. "The business houses were decorated with flags and bunting, like as if it were the 4th of July, and a large banner stretched across the track bore the words 'Welcome to Elkhorn.'" The workers were dutifully honored, "marched from the railroad to the college grounds. There they were served a turkey dinner by the ladies of the community." Such public recognition frequently occurred as cluster carrier communities commemorated the arrival of the first train.[19]

Elk Horn was not the endpoint. Kimballton, three miles distant, still needed to be reached, and time was expiring. As of December 30, workers neared their goal but faced another half-mile. They sped up construction by placing just enough ties on the roadbed to support the locomotive. However, track still had not officially entered the town the next day. Could completion be achieved by the imminent deadline? The answer was yes. Local officials extended Kimballton's southern boundary to meet the railroad, and the locomotive and short construction train arrived around midnight on New Year's Eve. At that hour it was too late to celebrate, but anxiety levels eased.[20]

The Kimballton line remained unfinished. There was much to do before it could be expected to become a steady revenue maker. The track and roadbed required major attention, and it took months before the line was placed in an acceptable condition. During this time, numerous minor derailments occurred. Trackage had to be extended into Atlantic, but the Rock Island temporarily delayed that construction because of the need to cross its Audubon branch. On January 11, 1908, the AN&S received permission, and eight days later workers finished the yards. Acquisition of additional rolling stock became another priority. Clarence Ross arranged the purchase of a used combination baggage and passenger coach (combine). This was a good investment that long served the property. By 1909 the company had accumulated some equipment: two locomotives (American Standard 4-4-0 types),[21] two combines, three boxcars, and five flat cars. Support facilities, including cement-block depots in Atlantic, Elk Horn, and Kimballton, needed to be finished by the Elkhorn-Kimballton Construction Company and multiple sidings installed. An inspection by the Iowa Board of Railroad Commissioners also had to be completed and approved. Nevertheless, the board of directors, joined by backers, made a special trip on New Year's Day, 1908, from Atlantic to Kimballton and back. The trip consisted of two borrowed Rock Island coaches and several freight cars. Highlights included a "delicious (noon) dinner" for about one hundred guests who boarded in Atlantic, and speeches "carried on the rest of the afternoon." This memorable occasion produced "general jollification." Decades later the daughter of George Jorgensen Jr. related, "The town celebrated all day and most of the night!"[22]

The need to recruit employees increased the workload of President Rattenborg and other officials. Local residents took nearly all of the jobs, including those in train, maintenance-of-way, and office duties.

It was a joyous day in early 1908 when more than seven hundred investors in the Atlantic Northern & Southern Railway held their first shareholders meeting. Many gathered near the newly completed combination depot and office building in Atlantic. The locomotive is a classic 4-4-0 American Standard, a type the company used until it ended operations. *(Image provided by the Museum of Danish America, Elk Horn, Iowa.)*

Apparently, few if any had much railroad experience. The first general manager, however, had served as the Rock Island station agent in Atlantic, and some of the outside construction workers may have continued with the company. None of the railroad brotherhoods had members who worked for the AN&S, and no one in the industry or elsewhere considered that odd.[23]

When the AN&S received the green light from the railroad commission on February 14, 1908, regular freight and passenger service commenced. The company dispatched two daily-except-Sunday mixed freights and, if needed, extra movements. According to its September 1909 schedule, trains left West Atlantic at 7:00 a.m. and 1:10 p.m. and

Kimballton, Iowa.

In about 1909, passengers in Kimballton await the train to Atlantic. The depot is made of locally produced cement blocks, and the Danish Lutheran church stands out prominently in this postcard view. *(Image provided by the Museum of Danish America, Elk Horn, Iowa.)*

arrived in Kimballton at 8:40 a.m. and 2:40 p.m. They departed from Kimballton at 9:00 a.m. and 3:30 p.m. and returned to West Atlantic at 10:10 a.m. and 5:30 p.m. It took nearly one and a half hours to make the seventeen-mile trip. No wonder some patrons referred to the AN&S as the "*Awful Noisy & Slow.*" Service resembled that of an interurban not in speed but in frequency of stops. Before reaching Elk Horn and Kimballton, trains called at Harrisdale, Smith Lake, Gates, and Hansen Heights. These places lacked depots and agents but had sidings and stock pens and might have waiting shelters. Smith Lake, located six miles from Atlantic, featured a picnic grove and swimming area that became a seasonal destination for area residents, and later a Rothschild Grain Company elevator. Hansen Heights also had an elevator, and its office served as a waiting room. If passengers asked a crew member to make a special stop at a farmstead or road crossing, the conductor probably obliged. At scheduled stops (and perhaps elsewhere), students heading for high school classes boarded and detrained. These riders continued to use the rails on the Kimballton line for more than a quarter century.

Although the first leg of the AN&S was only seventeen miles long, passengers often traveled shorter distances. This ticket allowed a thirteen-mile trip from Kimballton to the Harrisdale neighborhood. (*Author's collection.*)

AN&S trains, too, carried express (becoming an agency of the United States Express Company that operated over the Rock Island), and locked pouches and sacks of US mail.[24]

Freight traffic resembled that of other sunset cluster carriers. Outbound shipments were predominantly livestock and grain; inbound shipments were coal, lumber and other building materials, farm machinery, and assorted less-than-carload (LCL) merchandise. Shipments of cattle and hogs, however, dominated. In fact, the first train from Elk Horn, which took place on January 25, 1908, carried livestock, and three days later a similar movement left Kimballton. In 1911 this business strengthened when the Farmers Shipping Company, located in Kimballton, opened as a cooperative association to manage livestock transport and sell agricultural supplies.[25]

Developing patronage on the AN&S produced limited profitability. Not long after operations began, the general manager reported that "the business [is] in fine shape and the road is more than paying for its operations." About this time a representative from R. G. Dun & Company, the commercial credit reporting agency, likewise thought well of the emerging railroad: "He thinks that the new Atlantic Northern & Southern

Two members of the Harris family, Lloyd and Reta, joined by Julian and Bess Motz, stand atop an AN&S locomotive at the Harrisdale siding. The date is unknown, but probably around World War I. No. 604 appears to be in the "out-of-service" category. (*Author's collection.*)

Railroad will be a great success." A year later, another account retained that optimism: "It has since been in operation and is daily increasing its revenue and is now earning $1,000 [$29,218 in current dollars] per month above expenses." This assessment is misleading. In 1909 net earnings stood at $7,172 ($209,554 in current dollars), but property taxes and interest payments on bonds produced a deficit of $1,935 ($56,537 in current dollars). As of June 30, 1909, the road had cost $268,110 ($7,833,749 in current dollars) or $15,771 ($460,803 in current dollars) per mile, typical for contemporary Midwestern shortline construction.[26]

Although the AN&S was no money machine, it sparked a boom in Elk Horn and Kimballton. As with other sunset roads, new and expanded businesses appeared. This vitality was seen in the variety of individuals who served both places. Each town had a postmaster, minister, physician, bank president, and teachers. Elk Horn also had a veterinarian. Both communities claimed an elevator, lumber yard, hotel, telephone exchange, and a variety of flourishing retail stores. Kimballton boasted a cement plant, brickyard, a second bank, and an automobile dealership and repair shop. Its thriving cooperative Crystal Springs Creamery Company, launched in 1890, became a signature institution, and by 1909 it claimed about one hundred fifty farmer members. Noted the local correspondent for the *Audubon County Journal* in July 1909, "Cement walks are making a wonderful improvement in our little city. Many other improvements are also being done which is making Kimballton look like a new place."[27]

RAILS SOUTHBOUND

Although talk continued about extending AN&S rails northward to Manning, the focus of conversation (and action) involved penetrating the fertile farmlands southward from Atlantic through Grant and Morton's Mills to Villisca. The Ross and Judd team again participated, as did Hans Rattenborg. Apparently for health reasons, Rattenborg stepped down from the presidency following the January 1908 meeting of the board of directors and assumed the vice presidency. Later, though, he resumed his duties as president. These men were keenly aware of the long-standing desire by farmers and especially Grant residents to have

convenient access to a railroad. They sought another interchange partner—the Chicago, Burlington & Quincy Railroad (Burlington), whose
Chicago–Omaha–Denver main line served Villisca. Yet Judd admitted
that the Rock Island had treated the AN&S well: "In justice it may be
said that it did for us voluntarily what many another railroad company
might not have done under competitive pressure."[28]

The economic arguments for expansion seemed compelling: "If seventeen miles of road could make itself self-sustaining, under the given
conditions, fifty-five miles, even under the same or similar conditions,
would be self-sustaining if due only to the reduced cost per mile of operating, there being certain charges which could not be materially increased in the longer line and certain not in proportion to the length."
There was more. A second interchange outlet would increase traffic and
rate divisions, and there were existing towns to serve and the possibility
of creating new ones.[29]

With the Kimballton line operating, fundraising became the focus
of extension supporters. This work centered on soliciting stock subscriptions from Atlantic, Villisca, and projected on-line communities, most
of all in the largest of these—Grant, located in Douglas Township of
Montgomery County. In June the *Villisca Review* reported that Judd and
Rattenborg appeared successful with their canvassing that inland town.
"They have so far sold 150 shares. The amount asked [in Grant] is $50,000
[$1,460,920 in current dollars] and there is assurance that that amount
will be raised without great difficulty." Next came stock solicitations in
two southern Cass County townships, Bear Creek and Noble, and also
in Washington Township of Montgomery County. "This work," related
Ross, "occupied the summer and fall of 1908."[30]

Although sales of stock purchase agreements went well in Grant,
they lagged elsewhere. "When it became evident that enough stock could
not be sold to make the road possible," explained Ross, "the people who
had done the most in subscribing for stock were first to suggest the voting
of taxes in the various townships and cities." The quest for public tax dollars occupied much of the winter of 1908–1909 and the following spring
and summer. This approach to raising construction money resulted in
impressive election victories in the townships of Douglas, Noble, and
Washington and also in Atlantic and Villisca. The ballot petition in Bear

Grove Township surprisingly failed to receive the required number of names, "so close as to make it uncertain," and no election occurred. The victorious outcomes contained standard provisions: 5 percent of taxable property for a five-year period and a completion date mandate before payment. In this case, the hour was set for midnight on December 31, 1910.[31]

The next step involved acquisition of approximately thirty-seven miles of the newly surveyed right-of-way. Most land titles were obtained for an exchange of stock. The estimated face value of these stock transactions reached between $20,000 ($584,368 in current dollars) and $25,000 ($730,460 in current dollars). Several landowners went to court demanding "fair compensation," and in time cash payments settled these disputes.[32]

Notwithstanding efforts to have construction begin quickly, Ross and Judd were not in a financial position to oversee this much anticipated work. By fall 1909, stock subscriptions amounted to about $110,000 ($3,214,025 in current dollars), and tax assistance stood at approximately $96,000 ($2,804,968 in current dollars). Additional funds were still needed, estimated at more than $100,000 ($2,921,841 in current dollars). Ross and Rattenborg, often joined by a board member, traveled widely to sell AN&S debt, making calls in Chicago, Kansas City, Philadelphia, and St. Louis. They failed, however. Finally, Ross journeyed to New York. "With a fair acquaintance in addition to introductions to bankers and brokers," relates his written account, "I felt reasonably sure of success, but I returned fully convinced that to sell the bonds there or in any other money centers at that time was an absolute impossibility." The probable reasons were twofold: the economy remained in recovery from the recent panic, and small agricultural roads were generally not considered investment worthy. The solution was to find local buyers for these mortgage bonds—and this ploy worked. The company received subscriptions for more than $100,000 ($2,817,590 in current dollars) and individual guarantees for $25,000 ($704,397 in current dollars) more.[33]

The AN&S used bond sales effectively. Some $50,000 ($1,408,795 in current dollars) of these securities were exchanged for construction materials. By spring 1910, in the words of Clarence Ross, "[these] bonds

As Christmas 1910 approached, a leased Hurley Track-Laying Machine sped up construction on the Atlantic to Grant portion of the thirty-six-mile Villisca extension. (*Author's collection.*)

made it possible to see daylight ahead for at least the construction of the main line, without sidings or equipment." The construction contract was let to Shughart & Barnes Brothers of Des Moines; graders began work on July 15, 1910, exactly three years to the day from when the first earth was turned on the Kimballton line.[34]

Charles Judd oversaw the engineering of the Villisca extension. A map of the completed line reveals a zig-zag configuration. Because of cost considerations, expenditures were held to the lowest possible level, averaging approximately $15,000 ($422,638 in current dollars) per mile. Judd determined that the maximum gradient would be 2 percent and the maximum curvature 6 degrees, and he succeeded. The challenging part extended between Atlantic and Grant with its "five summits." South of Grant, the line generally followed the West Nodaway River and was less hill and dale. Judd admitted that the route north of Grant could have been better. "By increasing the cost materially these [grades] could all have been eliminated on the present location." The one major bridge, crossing the Nodaway at Grant, should ideally have been a steel span of 125 to 150 feet in length; cost cutting resulted in a 476-foot-long concrete one. The rock bottom of the river made it impossible to install an even cheaper pile trestle. Judd expected line improvements would eventually occur: "They will come with time, but with them also will come heavier traffic and, it is hoped, the money with which to modernize the road."[35]

Once work gangs appeared, steady progress occurred. These men, many of whom were Greek and Italian immigrants, toiled from both ends of the line, and by mid-November 1910 they had completed most of the grading. Bridge and culvert work, too, had reached the final stage. Next came the tracklayers, and their work advanced rapidly. The Atlantic to Grant portion benefitted from a rented Hurley Track-Laying Machine that recently had been used by the Rock Island. This self-propelled wonder led a string of flatcars and automatically placed ties and sixty-five-pound rails in the correct position on the graded right-of-way. The machine could move one to two miles a day and required approximately thirty-five to forty men for peak efficiency.[36]

In contrast to the nail-biting that occurred when track building neared Kimballton, the southern extension was finished ahead of schedule—but not by much. The workers, who moved northward toward Grant, did a remarkable job when confronted with the midnight December 31 deadline. Without the assistance of the Hurley machine and using ties and rails supplied by horse-drawn wagons, they installed fourteen miles of track in fourteen days. Unusually good weather helped make this possible. These men, whose numbers had been increased, outdid themselves on Christmas Day, completing nine thousand four hundred feet in eight hours; trackmen considered a good day's work to be seven to eight thousand feet. The south-end force, together with its counterpart working from the north, received a bonus of time and a half for over four thousand five hundred feet laid daily. If tracklaying progress became stalled or slowed, threatening the loss of tax money, a group of Grant boosters announced in mid-December that they would "close their places of business and go to work on the railroad." On Christmas

This professionally made photograph, taken a few miles south of Grant on the afternoon of December 27, 1910, captures celebrants at the silver spike ceremony for the Villisca extension. The three men seated (left to right) are Clarence Ross, Hans Rattenborg, and Charles Judd. In the upper right-hand corner is the boom end of the Hurley Track-Laying Machine. *(Image provided by the Museum of Danish America, Elk Horn, Iowa.)*

Day, Grant residents breathed a sigh of relief as their town became connected by rail to Atlantic. The following morning, the crew headed south toward a grand meeting; two days later the AN&S was declared officially completed. The estimated cost totaled $800,000 ($22,540,725 in current dollars).[37]

Unlike what occurred when the three other sunset cluster roads achieved construction goals in Clarinda, Macksburg, and Treynor, the completion of the AN&S resembled the most famous event in nineteenth-century America: the wedding of the first transcontinental rails at Promontory, Utah Territory, on May 10, 1869. Two thousand five hundred copies of a souvenir edition of the *Villisca Review*, published on January 5, 1911, featured this banner headline: "Silver Spike Driven

Opening A. N. & S. R. R." There were descriptive subheadings: "Tuesday, December 27, '10 Was Great Day For Railroad Boosters"; "President H. S. Rattenborg Starts Silver Spike Into Tie at 37 minutes Past 3 o'clock in Presence of Nearly 3000 People."

Blessed by ideal winter weather and a large, enthusiastic gathering that included most of the residents of Grant, the festivities focused not on long-winded speeches but on driving that ceremonial silver-plated steel spike. President Rattenborg, his wife and daughters, Clarence Ross, Charles Judd, and members of the board of directors wielded a heavy maul and struck (or struck at) the spike. Once it was in place, Rattenborg suggested that the crowd sing "My Country, 'Tis of Thee," and "everybody joined in fine shape." Soon there was the blowing of steam whistles: "[They] sounded over the hills and across the well-groomed farms and they must have made themselves heard in Atlantic. They started to blow at 4:10 and for thirty-five minutes there was great rejoicing."[38]

Both before and after the driving of the last spike, Grant residents and those involved in the construction celebrated. This was not surprising; Grant was one of the largest inland towns in Iowa without a railroad, and finally there was the AN&S. The Masonic Hall became the site of two "splendid suppers." On Christmas Day, members of the southbound track force and other guests took their meals in shifts because of limited space: "There were 153 railroad men who were seated at the tables and the serving began at 6 o'clock." Following the spike ceremony, the northbound workers also assembled in the hall. Beginning at five o'clock and lasting late into the evening, approximately one hundred fifty workers and officers and about fifty others "were cordially received and liberally fed." During that event, Clarence Ross gave a brief speech and presented an engraved loving cup to the community. It measured about a foot high, and contained this inscription: "To the Citizens of Grant from the South End Construction Crew, in Memory of Their Loyalty in the Completion of the A. N. & S. R. R., Atlantic to Villisca, Iowa, December 27, 1910." Said Ross: "Out of their meager wages they have contributed handsomely toward this token of remembrance and have authorized me to present to you in their name this loving cup." The next day it appeared in the front window of the George Cary Drugstore, "and is the pride of all Grant people."[39]

TROUBLES

The completed AN&S opened to great excitement and expectations. Unfortunately, it immediately stumbled. Setbacks were largely anticipated; the track structure remained in a raw state, and a variety of betterments were required for the railroad to become fully functional. Even prior to the spike ceremony, the grading contractor Shughart & Barnes Brothers had filed a mechanics lien for $79,144.74 ($2,229,974.75 in current dollars). The initial bill had totaled more than $129,000 ($3,634,692 in current dollars), and the company had already paid the firm $50,000 ($1,408,795 in current dollars). To worsen matters, the anticipated Atlantic tax payments had become entangled in a legal dispute. And shortly after the completion of the southern extension, the passenger coach assigned to the Villisca line burned in the Atlantic yards. There was also the public embarrassment of a daytime excursion made by Atlantic boosters on January 6, 1911. Due to the unusability of several coaches borrowed from the Rock Island (the result of frozen and then burst water pipes), the train consisted of an AN&S coach and two boxcars. Riders jokingly referred to the latter as "side-door sleepers." The round trip proved exceedingly slow and jarring because of dismal track conditions and problems with the coach. It became "an unruly affair which came uncoupled several times during the trip." When the train finally reached Villisca at one o'clock, the coach had "about room enough to accommodate the ladies of the party." Male passengers, including dignitaries, guests, and band members, sat on benches in the boxcars. This Villisca special, however, cannot be considered a disaster, as "fully three hundred people made the trip and while the accommodations were poor, the people didn't do much kicking." Then Hans Rattenborg resigned suddenly. The publicly stated (and correct) explanation: "Ill health is the only reason for his retirement at this time." To restore his wellbeing, he traveled to Colfax, a central Iowa community known for its mineral water treatments. President Rattenborg had gone through the stress of the recent construction, and he experienced constant financial and operational worries about the railroad.[40]

Rumors immediately spread about the fate of AN&S. There was speculation that the Great Western would acquire the road—it allegedly had its eyes on the livestock, grain, and town expansion traffic in the area. It could do so by connecting its Omaha line at Manning to Kimballton, a distance of approximately twenty miles. The Rock Island presumably had the same goal. The Burlington also may have wanted the property: "[it] is envious of the competition which will be afforded by the new line and that it hopes to gobble up the road and thus completely control stock shipping and other businesses in southern Cass and in Montgomery counties."[41]

The new year would not be a happy one. Service began slowly on the Villisca extension. By mid-January, the AN&S had not yet established a regular schedule, "but [it is] aiming to get a train through each day and carrying some freight." By the end of the month, the inaugural shipment of livestock, consisting of five cars of hogs, left Grant for Villisca. Freight and passenger activities increased once the line received the blessing of the Board of Railroad Commissioners. Coinciding with the developing traffic, the company found itself short of funds. Employees could not cash their end-of-January paychecks at the Iowa Trust and Savings Bank in Atlantic. "It is said that the trouble is only temporary and the road will have money enough in a few days to meet the checks." This embarrassing experience was a harbinger of more to come.[42]

Money needed to be found to keep the fragile railroad functioning. Patrons of the Kimballton line responded; they had contributed about $61,000 ($1,718,730 in current dollars) by early February. "Almost all of the money raised has been subscribed by Danish people in the northwestern part of Cass and the southwestern part of Audubon counties." Rattenborg, who had regained his health and the presidency, raised about $65,000 ($1,831,433 in current dollars) in additional funds, largely from Danish farmers. He and other supporters next turned their fundraising efforts along the Villisca line, centering initially on the Grant area. By the end of February, about $12,000 ($338,111 in current dollars) had been raised in that community—far short of the overall goal of $50,000 ($1,408,795 in current dollars) for the extension. Villisca still remained to be canvassed. Fortunately, the parties owed seemed to have been kept at bay. "The creditors are disposed to hold off and see if there is a chance for the road to pull out before taking actions," observed one source in mid-February, "as with the appointment of a receiver they would fare much worse than they will if the road pulls itself out of its difficulties."[43]

While the AN&S struggled to remain afloat, a nasty flare-up erupted among workers. The trigger was the nonpayment of overdue wages to seventy-five to one hundred former graders and tracklayers who had built the southern extension. This unrest furthered soiled the company image. On March 2, 1911, these men demanded their money. They were "held up" by several boarding houses and restaurants in Villisca. As of March 1, their credit had been exhausted, and many began to go hungry. They were desperate and confronted Clarence Ross and Charles Judd, who happened to be in Villisca on business. A standoff followed, and the unpaid workers remained "very much incensed." According to a newspaper report, "It is said even that some of the desperate gang of laborers suggested that a rope be secured and that other dire things to be enacted to the defenseless men." Calmer members prevailed, but Ross and Judd, who feared for their safety, took refuge in the Fisher Hotel. One group then barricaded the interchange between the AN&S and the Burlington "with a pile of ties and declared that no more trains should be run until they were fed." These men kept an around-the-clock vigil on their hastily created blockade, making certain that no train operated over AN&S rails. They occupied some nearby empty boxcars for shelter and relied on "market men and store keepers to furnish them with the bare necessities." Negotiations between the railroad and protestors resulted in an agreement that food and fuel would be provided and money for the claims would come as soon as possible. The Villisca confrontation meant lost revenue; a sizeable amount of livestock from Grant, in one case, awaited transport via the Burlington interchange. To worsen matters, the wage dispute briefly spread to other employees. At last, on March 8, the confrontations ended. Back payments were arranged, and operations returned to normal.[44]

Although the wage disputes reached resolution, the financial crisis remained ongoing, worsening as the weeks passed. The company sought to prevent a receivership, but by April matters had reached a critical stage. Yet there emerged an intriguing proposal. It came from George Adams, president of the Iowa & Omaha Short Line Railroad

(I&OSL), the twelve-mile railroad that linked Treynor with the Wabash for a short connection to the Council Bluffs gateway. This little pike was also near a recently opened extension of the Omaha & Council Bluffs Street Railway (O&CBStRy). Funding to rehabilitate the AN&S would be provided, though Adams must be named receiver. This marked the beginning of a complex relationship between the AN&S and a syndicate consisting of the I&OSL and domestic and foreign investors. At this point, the board of directors discussed noncourt control possibilities. One involved raising additional money, focusing on supporters in Atlantic and along the Kimballton line. The other involved the possible breakup of the railroad, severing the Villisca extension from the original segment. "The difficulties which have beset the road have been many," reported a newspaper in late April, "and the condition of the road's affairs presented such a complication of technicalities that it was impossible to reach an agreement that would satisfy all claimants." An unfounded rumor spread that the Rock Island and Burlington would buy the property, the former buying the north end and the latter the south end. Then came the decision of the board: "A plan is now on foot to reorganize the company, putting it on a new basis and boosting it again." That meant receivership. On May 2, 1911, a district court judge signed a degree placing the railroad under his control and indicating that he would name a receiver within thirty days.[45]

A new chapter in the history of the AN&S was about to begin. On May 21, 1911, the railroad fell into the hands of a court-appointed receiver, and the future looked uncertain. This individual, E. S. Harlan, was a logical choice. Harlan served as company treasurer and understood the multitude of financial challenges it faced. No one believed that the railroad would be abandoned. It would be reorganized or at least sold to another carrier or carriers.[46]

COMMUNITY DEVELOPMENT

Before, during, and after the receivership, the AN&S helped its two most populous towns flourish. For Atlantic, it "has been a large factor in the industrial development of the city." The company payroll for approximately seventy-five hometown employees had a positive impact on the

A. N. &, S., DEPOT.
VILLISCA IOWA.

It was not unusual for a shortline railroad company to acquire a house near trackside to serve as a depot. The AN&S did just that in Villisca. *(Montgomery County History Center.)*

local economy. As the southern extension struggled, a Red Oak reporter observed in spring 1912 that "Villisca has not had a fair trial at the railroad but still has made more advancement the past year than in any previous one year in her history." While residents benefitted from their rail connection to the north, they were distracted for months by the grisly ax murders of two adults and six children on June 10, 1912. This never-solved case became a national sensation. When the AN&S earlier had reached Elk Horn and Kimballton, it spurred local commercial and residential growth and expanded cultural and social activities.[47]

On the south line, the largest community and oldest incorporated town, Grant, boomed. "The town of Grant, it is claimed, has about doubled in population [by 1915]," reported the Board of Railroad Commissioners. "At this point there are: an elevator, lumber yard, postoffice, hotel, bank, implement house, poultry house and two stores." Grant had other betterments: a sizable stockyard near the recently erected depot and water tank, a "new automobile garage," a large, $20,000 ($524,371 in current dollars) three-story brick school, and the *Grant Chief*, which printed its inaugural issue on April 6, 1911. Grant had also expanded its boundaries to accommodate more private dwellings. "The town has taken on new life during the past year," commented a Red Oak visitor in October 1911, "and with many new business buildings and homes and with most of the older ones repaired and painted, with the streets kept in good shape and with a smile of contentment up on every face." Later the *Villisca Review* lauded the process that it saw. "Grant is very much on the map since they have the railroad. They claim the best [base]ball team in southwest Iowa, a fine Chautauqua, a winter lecture course, a commercial club, a band, [and] a newspaper." With railroad service, the town became an active livestock selling and shipping center. A widely advertised public auction held on November 6, 1913, called for the sale of sixty Guernsey and Jersey cattle. "Nothing over 5 years old, a lot of fresh ones; registered Guernsey bull, great breeder. Everything you want from a calf up to 5 years old." Grant was full of life and optimism.[48]

Morton Mills (née Morton's Mill), four miles south of Grant, emerged as more than a sleepy crossroads settlement. It burgeoned with the arrival of AN&S rails, although on a smaller scale than its neighbor. Early on the W. B. Prather general store building was physically moved, relocated "from the corner down next to the railroad track which will make it more convenient for handling freight." "Wide-eyed" individuals quickly acquired land parcels at trackside to establish their businesses. In October 1911, E. E. Lehman of Corning selected the location for a grain elevator and coal shed, and construction began almost immediately. It didn't take long before the community had stock pens, a blacksmith shop, an implement house, a poultry house, a lumber yard, a hotel, two stores, a combination restaurant and meat market, and a bank. Then there was the matter of a post office. For years prior to rural free delivery (RFD), Morton's Mill had a tiny post office located in the general store. When the Post Office Department established an RFD route in the area, this facility closed. But in 1913, the post office was reestablished: "Until some arrangement can be made for hauling mail on the A. N. & S. Railroad, the mail will be carried to Morton Mills by a rural carrier out of here [Villisca], but it will be addressed with the name of the post office

This postcard view looking east from the Atlantic Southern tracks reveals Main Street in Morton Mills. In the distance is the recently completed Disciples of Christ Church. (*Author's collection.*)

instead of to the Villisca route." When the railroad received a contract to handle mail, RFD service ended. The village also took pride in having a depot. The newly organized Morton Mills Boosters Club raised funds to help pay for this structure, and it did what it could to improve the town. This included promoting an annual tent Chautauqua, a popular form of entertainment and venue for political and cultural presentations. In hundreds of communities, this was the most exciting time of the summer. Morton Mills took pride in claiming that it was the smallest place in America to host a seven-day event—"it was a good Chautauqua town." A landmark achievement for this up-and-coming community came on February 14, 1914, with dedication of the newly completed Christian Church (Disciples of Christ) building. The previous one, located outside Morton Mills, had burned, and the congregation decided to rebuild in town. The press described the replacement structure as "one of the finest country churches in Iowa."[49]

The AN&S spawned new settlements. In an era of closely spaced, agriculturally supported communities, another crossroads trading center, Sciola, sprang forth because of the railroad. Situated four miles south of Morton Mills and seven miles north of Villisca, a local farmer who had received a financial settlement from the railroad so that tracks could pass through his land donated a half-acre for the aborning village. Development followed, and optimism about its future reigned. Even before the railroad opened, the Villisca paper enthusiastically but in an exaggerated fashion described the village with the headline: "Sciola On The Boom."

> The A.N. & S. Rail Road is already having its effect on the city of Sciola, and that metropolis is rapidly pushing to the front. It has adopted a motto: 'Watch Sciola Grow,' and the citizens there are talking of forming a booster club, and they may later pave the streets. The first move was made by the Stoddard Lumber Company of Villisca, which has purchased of J. A. Whitney a tract of ground just across from the Sciola store and will erect an office and lumber sheds there, where a stock of building lumber and material will be kept when shipments can be made by rail from Villisca. Just across the road on B. R. Mayhew's ground a sign reads that the Green Bay Lumber Company will have a branch office there just as soon as the new railroad is completed, but the location of the yards has not been decided upon. On the west side of the right of way, just west of the Sciola store, Turner Bros. of Red Oak are going to erect a good sized elevator, and lumber hauled from Villisca Monday is now on the ground. It is expected that cement work will be started about Friday.[50]

Although never incorporated, Sciola during the railroad years ultimately boasted more businesses than a general store ("the main building in town"), lumberyard (only one opened), and grain elevator. In addition to a small depot, the village featured a combination barbershop-restaurant, blacksmith shop, implement shed, and stock pens.[51]

Sciola also served residents in the Tenville community, which consisted of about fifty people clustered around a country store approximately a mile west of the AN&S tracks and others living in the immediate farming area. Located several rail miles south of Sciola, this site briefly came to life near the end of railroad service. Known as "Tenville Siding," it became a "new station" in January 1914, yet a depot was never built and only sidetracks were installed. About this time, individuals from the vicinity formed their own booster club; these "hustling, up-to-date" backers planned to make their neighborhood a "thriving business center."[52]

Tenville nevertheless remained a stillborn village. The only successes at trackside were a grain elevator, wagon scale house, coal shed,
and stock pens. Local promoters did organize a cooperative store based
on the English Rochdale Plan, and they named their endeavor the Nodaway Valley Improvement Association. Stock shares were sold, but the
project collapsed soon after the railroad suspended operations at the
close of 1914. The store, although built, never opened. Town lots were
staked out but never recorded. Efforts to establish Tenville came too
late—supporters did not realize that town creation had essentially run
its course in Iowa and virtually all of the Midwest.[53]

Even with the opening of the AN&S, town founding between Atlantic and Grant sputtered. This twenty-two-mile stretch of line consisted
of three scheduled stops all located in Cass County: Marker, Galion, and
Lyman. Initially Marker had only a siding and stock pens, but toward
the end of railroad service a general store opened. Galion and Lyman,
on the other hand, developed more commercial businesses, and each
sported a small depot.

Eight miles south of Atlantic, the Galion site (sometimes listed as
Seven Mile) came alive with the arrival of the railroad. There had been
a country store about a mile away, but its owner relocated his business
nearer to the tracks, likely having his building transported there physically. Soon a grain elevator and stock pens appeared near the depot. The
place may have contained a few houses, but with the lifting of the rails,
Galion faded rapidly. In the mid-1930s, a visitor described the abandoned
townsite: "Today, all that time has not erased of Galion are the gradually
filling excavations where buildings had stood."[54]

Lyman (called New Lyman), three miles south of Galion, was only
modestly larger. This hamlet was also dominated by a general store that
had been relocated. George Gerloch, who had moved his business "many
times," left what became "Old Lyman" for the railroad site on the Simon Sunderman farm about three-quarters of a mile to the south. A
1912 photograph reveals that two additional businesses stood near the
Gerloch store, and one was likely a blacksmith shop. A grain elevator,
stock pens, depot, German Evangelical Church, and a few houses made
up this infant community. Allegedly, the place also had two creameries.
When the railroad died, so did most of Lyman. Within several years,

Gerloch returned to the original Lyman, situated on two well-traveled roads, and opened a store and a gasoline filling station. He also acquired the depot and had it and his store moved. "Caterpillar tractors did the hauling of the buildings." When a railroad left, adjustments, even radical ones, occurred.[55]

Residents and patrons of existing and startup communities along the Villisca extension benefited from good passenger train access, generally superior to what the Burlington and Rock Island provided on their neighboring branch lines. Except on Sundays, the company offered double-daily service. Take Morton Mills: southbound trains arrived at 7:30 a.m. and 2:25 p.m. and northbound ones at 8:50 a.m. and 4:45 p.m. On Sundays a single passenger train arrived at 10:50 a.m. on its way to Villisca and returned at 4:45 p.m. Track conditions and equipment issues surely altered these announced times.[56]

Before the coming of the AN&S and in other places that lacked a railroad, consumers customarily found higher prices in stores of inland towns, villages, and hamlets. That changed. Patrons of businesses in Morton Mills, for example, pleasantly discovered that they usually paid lower "Villisca prices" when they shopped locally. They no longer needed to travel ten or more miles to make less expensive purchases. Thanks to the railroad, the variety and perhaps the quality of goods increased. Another benefit was cheaper prices for lump coal, the dominant heating fuel—by rail, prices might drop by 25 to 50 percent per ton.[57]

A STRANGE TWIST

Enter the Shaw syndicate, technically the English-based Berkdale Company. George Adams of the I&OSL served as the front man for a group of business, financial, and railroad men who became deeply involved with the bankrupt AN&S. The foremost American participant was Leslie M. Shaw, one of the most recognized figures in Iowa. Early in his adult life, this uprooted New Englander moved to the Hawkeye State, where he graduated from Cornell College and the Iowa College of Law. Shaw established a thriving legal practice in Denison and launched several area banks. A popular orator, gold standard advocate, and Republican workhorse, he became his party's nominee for governor in 1898. Shaw won and served two terms. Not long after Theodore Roosevelt ascended to the presidency, he selected this Iowan as secretary of the treasury, impressed with his "ability to captivate his audience while explaining financial issues in an understandable manner." After leaving office in 1909, Shaw remained in the East and continued his involvement with financial institutions both there and abroad.[58]

The precise origins of the syndicate's plan are unclear. At the time the AN&S slipped into receivership, the syndicate's apparent objective involved using the I&OSL corporation to construct a 150-mile passenger and freight interurban between Council Bluffs and Des Moines and using the AN&S as an electrified or steam-powered feeder. The core route would incorporate the I&OSL and extend eastward through Atlantic and other communities, roughly paralleling the Chicago–Omaha line of the Rock Island. Trackage rights over the Inter-Urban Railway would provide entry into the Capital City. The syndicate believed that the Rock Island was vulnerable to traction competition, especially for passengers, and planned to create a better alternative route. As it said about the Rock Island, "it owns a crooked line from Des Moines to Council Bluffs." In fact, Rock Island management realized that its way west from Des Moines was poorly engineered; there were rumors in 1912 that the company "is planning to extend its line from Winterset to Council Bluffs on a direct survey and thus gain over fifty-five miles over its present route."[59]

Although accounts vary, the syndicate planned to pay about $400,000 ($11,270,362 in current dollars) for the AN&S. By December 1911, this seemed likely to happen. The Council Bluffs *Nonpareil* reported on the front page of its Sunday edition the latest activities and speculations under the headline "Developments in Big Iowa Railroad Deal." It discussed a recent trip made by Leslie Shaw to the state, including stops in Des Moines and Council Bluffs. Two prominent individuals, F. M. Hubbell of Des Moines, who headed Equitable Life of Iowa, and G. W. Wattles, president of the O&CBStRy, apparently agreed to serve on the board of directors. Hubbell was the leading businessman in Des Moines and arguably in Iowa. He had invested heavily in several start-up narrow-gauge steam railroads and managed them with considerable success. In 1884 Hubbell had organized and continued to control the profitable Des Moines Union Railway, a terminal company the syndicate could use.

Shaw expected London financiers to play a principal role in the financing, specifically in the purchase of the I&OSL and AN&S together with
construction between Treynor and Des Moines and possibly between
the Neoga area and the O&CBStRy. The work would also include the
much-discussed expansion of a line from Kimballton to Manning. The
total estimated cost stood at whopping $5,000,000 ($140,879,530 in current dollars).[60]

Journalists speculated on another participant in the plan to take
over the AN&S and I&OSL—one not involved in the Shaw syndicate.
It was Edwin Hawley, one of the most powerful and secretive railroad
magnates in the nation. "Even in his day he was probably the least known
and most feared of all railroad executives," observes railroad historian
Frank P. Donovan Jr.[61]

Why would Hawley desire two Iowa shortlines? Although he controlled the Minneapolis & St. Louis (M&StL) and Iowa Central Railroads (consolidated in 1912), he sought to strengthen his railroad empire,
which by 1911 included the Toledo, St. Louis & Western (Clover Leaf),
Chicago & Alton (Alton), and Missouri, Kansas & Texas (Katy) Railroads. The M&StL already connected Winthrop, Minnesota, with Storm
Lake, Iowa, and Hawley wanted to enter the Omaha and possibly the
Kansas City gateways from the north. With construction southwest from
Storm Lake, the M&StL could use the I&OSL to achieve such goals. If
the Shaw railroad succeeded in reaching Des Moines (which Hawley
could likely capture), the M&StL would have another way to access the
Omaha gateway. The AN&S might somehow be used to gain entrance
to St. Joseph and Kansas City and could include the gestating Iowa &
Southwestern Railway (Ikey). Without question, Hawley had the skill
and financial wherewithal to expand his holdings as he saw fit.[62]

What appeared to seal the immediate fate of the AN&S took place
at the receiver's sale held in Atlantic on September 28, 1911. No agent of
Edwin Hawley participated; there was no reason to at this time. George
Adams won with a bid of $402,000 ($11,326,714 in current dollars). There
were other bids, but none for the entire railroad. Atlantic banker J. A
McWald, who represented first mortgage bondholders of the Kimballton
line, bid $65,000 ($1,831,434 in current dollars) for that trackage, and
former president Hans Rattenborg bid for it as well. His offer was much

higher at $156,000 ($4,395,441 in current dollars). There were three bids for the Villisca line. The first two were for $100,000 ($2,817,590 in current dollars), coming from Shugart & Barnes Brothers, and $165,000 ($4,649,024 in current dollars) from Abeles & Taussig. Both had sizable claims against the company. The final bid was a surprise. It amounted to $220,000 ($6,198,699 in current dollars) and came from Neil MacDonald of New York City. He was associated with Clarence Ross and Charles Judd—these men wished to protect their financial interests. Apparently, MacDonald, Ross, and Judd thought seriously about the Ikey stretching from Villisca to points in northwestern Missouri, or they knew of or suspected Hawley's interest. Although there had been talk of splitting the AN&S, the judge, who now oversaw the bankruptcy, was not interested in that alternative. It appeared that the Shaw syndicate would take ownership. Following court procedures, Adams deposited a certified check for $5,000 ($140,879 in current dollars) to show good faith.[63]

Numerous twists and turns followed the sale. The challenge for the Shaw syndicate was raising money, which depended on the sale of $5,000,000 worth of bonds. This became an ongoing quest, and one that lacked an easy resolution. Based on a London cable, John Hess, attorney for the I&OSL, told the press in mid-March 1912 that no money would be immediately forthcoming: "I am able to appreciate the position of the Englishmen. They are simply 'playing safe' in the deal and there were a few formalities that have not been closed up."[64]

Delays continued. In late April 1912, the court allowed the syndicate additional time to honor its bid. Leslie Shaw left for Britain and Europe to work with his partners and contacts on bond sales. By mid-May he had yet to report on the success or failure of his mission. The general consensus was that the necessary funds would materialize. Shaw and his associates publicly expressed optimism. "They never felt the slightest doubt about their being able to swing the deal." The syndicate won another thirty-day extension. Finally good news arrived—on June 26, Hess learned that contracts for the bond sale through a Brussels financial house had been signed, and soon funds to complete the sale would be at hand. Another short continuance was granted. On July 16, still no money. The syndicate posted a $5,000 forfeiture bond, and the court briefly extended the deadline. The judge, whose patience was wearing thin, issued an ultimatum. If the money, which he reduced to an initial payment of $25,000 ($679,920 in current dollars) was not received by July 27, he would order the road resold on August 1.[65]

Two of the three largest creditors, Abeles & Taussig and Shugart & Barnes Brothers, applauded the court's ruling. Kimballton-Elkhorn Construction Company, which was owed $150,000 ($4,079,523 in current dollars), did not initially participate, possibly because it was experiencing a reorganization and would soon morph into the Jensen Construction Company. Abeles & Taussig claimed $54,571.97 ($1,537,614.60 in current dollars) and Shugart & Barnes Brothers $71,113.36 ($2,003,683.34 in current dollars). In the complaint filed by their lawyers, they told the court: "It has been almost a year since the first sale order was made. The roadbed, rolling stock, etc. of the A. N. & S. is [sic] depreciating in value rapidly. The receiver has issued a number of receiver's certificates and these have had to be sold at a discount. They are drawing 8 per cent interest." These parties worried about what the railroad owed them. If the Shaw deal went through, they would recoup most or all of their investments. They may have had an alternative motive for filing this court document, as revealed later, and Robert Abeles would be the acknowledged beneficiary.[66]

The judge and others involved in the AN&S surely realized that behind-the-scenes interests were battling the Shaw syndicate. The perpetrators were the Burlington and Rock Island Railroads, each of which had established connections in British and European financial circles. The Burlington, part of the powerful Hill Lines since 1901, had greater influence than the Rock Island, controlled by the faltering Reid-Moore interests. How they specifically sought to stymie the Shaw interests is not known, but journalists sensed their activities. "The Iowa railroad syndicate did not want the Shaw syndicate to succeed," explained a circulating press story. "The [Shaw] syndicate was tapping territory which the Iowa roads covered and coveted." Explained another published report: "In the financial fight to gain possession of the Atlantic Northern & Southern, Iowa people are witnessing one of the greatest struggles that has been thrown on the railroad map of Iowa." It continued: "The Atlantic property, as a railroad, is perhaps insignificant in comparison

with the big systems. It is the principles that are involved. The Iowa railroad systems do not want the syndicate to succeed." More so than the
Rock Island, Milwaukee, and North Western, the Burlington fought to
protect its service territory.[67]

As the case dragged on, another (albeit limited) reprieve for the
Shaw syndicate occurred. A substitute judge gave the organization a
two-day extension for meeting the $25,000 installment deadline. Again
it failed to deposit the funds. Yet the indulgent judge granted still another
brief extension. Somewhat dramatically, the former governor personally
appeared before the court and handed over the required money, sav-
ing the day for the syndicate. A few weeks afterwards, another $25,000
was deposited, but more than $300,000 ($8,159,046 in current dollars)
remained to be raised. A month later, attorneys for Shugart & Barnes
Brothers, joined by a representative for Robert Abeles, filed a writ of
prohibition with the Iowa Supreme Court. This tactic was designed to
prevent the district court from allowing the syndicate additional extensions. The filing contained strong language: "This postponement has
long since exceeded its discretion and powers," "clearly illegal," "false
statements," and "illegal advantage."[68]

The legal battle appeared unending. In a key ruling on December
14, 1912, the Iowa Supreme Count announced that it lacked jurisdiction
and sent the case back to the district court. Shaw interests took heart
and continued to believe (or hope) that adequate funding could be arranged. Shaw, though, was not that sanguine about acquiring the bond
money. "There is at present a stringency in the foreign and Canadian
money markets due to wars and rumors of war." This was the time of the
First Balkan War, which had erupted in early October 1912 and would
last until mid-1913. Until conditions in continental Europe improved, the
syndicate needed to tap domestic sources.[69]

The quest by the Shaw group to acquire the AN&S continued. Even
though in early 1913, the court revealed that it wanted the railroad resold,
appeals for extensions by the syndicate might continue for the foreseeable future. This would not happen. The rebidding, which occurred in
late February, failed as a result of "the absence of the required forfeit
[certified check] in the case of the Shaw bid and insufficiency of the

other bids." The judge set a new date for March 21, 1913. Again failure. The explanation: "None of the bids were sufficient considering receiver Harlan's estimate of the value of the railroad property and not in the best interest of the creditors, if accepted." Editorialized one newspaper, "If anyone is trying to keep up with the legal and other movements of the Atlantic Northern & Southern, except perhaps the running of trains on that line, it must keep them busy."[70]

The rebidding process seemed unending. In early May, another one took place, and Leslie Shaw apparently gained the AN&S with a much-reduced bid of $294,000 ($7,808,462 in current dollars). The court accepted on May 19. Robert Abeles offered $120,000 ($3,187,127 in current dollars) for the Villisca line, but no one bid for the Kimballton trackage. Under terms of the sale, Shaw had until June 2 to finalize his winning offer. That never occurred. In a welter of events, receiver E. S. Harlan was deposed for financial irregularities, and Atlantic attorney W. A. Follett became his replacement. Follett, working with the judge, announced that the railroad would be split into its northern and southern sections, and bidding would take place on June 10, 1913. Abeles won the Villisca line with a bid of $98,000 ($2,602,820 in current dollars). The Kimballton line went to its first mortgage bondholders for $87,000 ($2,310,667 in current dollars). The judge scheduled August 8 as the date when final transfers and deeds would be given for the two properties. However, it took until February 5, 1914, before the tangled affairs of the AN&S finally passed from court jurisdiction.[71]

At last rumors of an AN&S takeover ceased. Coinciding with the final bidding, Shaw had withdrawn from the contest, concluding that obtaining adequate financing was an impossibility. It is not clear how much money he lost personally in his quest to create a mini-Iowa railroad complex, but it may have been in the range of $50,000 ($1,327,970 in current dollars). Reported a newspaper account, "Leslie Shaw and a syndicate spent nearly two years in trying to secure and failed after having forfeited several large cash options to the courts." Not to be forgotten was Edwin Hawley. He may have had his eyes on the AN&S and I&OSL, but on February 1, 1912, he died suddenly of a heart attack. The big expansion plans of the M&StL had forever ended.[72]

This rare, blurred, undated photograph made from a glass plate negative captures either a northbound AN&S or Atlantic Southern train crossing the West Nodaway River immediately south of Grant. *(Montgomery County History Center.)*

ATLANTIC SOUTHERN RAILROAD

The Atlantic Southern Railroad (AS), officially The Nodaway Valley Route or, as locals dubbed it, the "Aunt Susie," experienced a troubled and short operating life. The company dispatched trains from August 9, 1913, to December 31, 1914, although it continued for a few days in early 1915 to "clean up business on the property." When the railroad stopped, more than one hundred employees needed to find new jobs; it retained a few watchmen for several years to protect against fires and thefts. Its tortured demise devastated supporters and had a negative impact on its service territory, affecting especially the former inland towns of Grant and Morton Mills.[73]

One individual personified the Villisca line. It was St. Louis tie dealer Robert Abeles, and his reign proved controversial. Even before the court legally transferred the 36.6-mile railroad to him, he assigned his rights to a new entity registered as the Atlantic Southern Railroad Company. For an investment of $172,000 ($4,568,216 in current dollars), he received $400,000 ($10,623,758 in current dollars) in stock and bonds. Abeles stated that he had secured the property free and clear of all financial obligations. He was correct. The bankruptcy judge stated that he would not issue a deed unless outstanding claims were extinguished. Others, including residents of the Grant and Morton Mills areas, disagreed. In July 1915, their representatives did so at a public hearing in Red Oak conducted by the Board of Railroad Commissioners. They contended that those who supported the construction of the Villisca extension had invested more than $300,000 ($8,452,771 in current dollars) in the form of stocks and bonds, tax levies, materials, and labor. Their contributions needed to be considered.[74]

Robert Abeles proved an able manipulator. He took $200,000 ($5,311,818 in current dollars) out of the company treasury and paid himself that amount for the Atlantic Southern. "Here is a clear case of dissipation of resources," argued the Board of Railroad Commissioners in its hearing report released on September 27, 1915. "Mr. Abeles should return $28,000 [$743,663 in current dollars] in cash to this company." It continued: "In addition to the $28,000 excessive cash payment, $200,000 in bonds were issued to Mr. Abeles without consideration, and should be canceled; or if these constituted the real consideration paid for the property, then Mr. Abeles should return the entire $200,000 in cash, which he received at the same time the bonds were issued to him." The Board wondered if these financial maneuvers were "a fictitious proceeding, and no cash was transferred actually to the company; and the stock was consequently issued in violation of the laws of this state in regard to the issuance of stock for cash; and also in violation of the articles of the incorporation of the Atlantic Southern Railroad Company, which provide that 'all stock shall be fully paid and non-assessable when issued.'"[75]

Did Abeles believe that it was more profitable to milk the Atlantic Southern and then junk it rather than operate it? The answer is unclear. He may have taken a wait-and-see approach, having that luxury of options.

The Abeles regime, which included brother J. D. Abeles, son Robert, and son-in-law De Roo Weber, touted various betterments, investing allegedly $40,000 ($1,062,375 in current dollars) in the railroad. These included acquisition of two used locomotives, one of which came from the North Western. "[It] has a large arc headlight," reported the *Villisca Review*. "It is also equipped with the electric appliances for lighting a train with electricity, but is not used at the present by the road." The company installed turntables in Atlantic and Villisca, the former designed "so that engines do not have to be run over to the Rock Island table at that place to be turned around, thus losing over an hour" and the latter "so the Q will not be bothered." It also added a telephone system and more right-of-way fencing and made emergency track improvements. State regulators, however, believed that by the time operations were suspended, the railroad had not been placed in good order.[76]

Hardly unique to the sunset cluster, the Atlantic Southern suffered from arguably poor operating procedures. While the skill levels of those individuals who conducted the day-to-day business are mostly unknown, the Board suggested they were sadly lacking. De Roo Weber, AS general manager, had earlier been a stenographer, not a railroader. In 1910 he served as vice president and general manager of the Abeles & Taussig Tie & Timber Company. In its hearing findings, the Board included this commentary: "At first the company operated six trains, two passenger and one freight each way daily; then they operated four trains daily, one passenger and one freight train in each direction; and then, about November 1, 1914, and for a period of two months, the company operated two trains, a mixed passenger and freight train in each direction, daily." The conclusion: "If two trains were all that the business justified, six trains were evidently an extravagance. There had been only a two month's trial of the two trains daily." There were other concerns, two of which involved annual expenditures for freight car rentals and money wasted on locomotive repairs. And this observation: "Frequent inexcusable delays, and other evidences of gross mismanagement were testified to by residents living along the line of railroad."[77]

Admittedly, the financials for the first six months of 1914 did not look promising. Freight earnings stood at $23,012 ($603,341 in current dollars), passenger at $11,521 ($302,064 in current dollars), and other income at $2,857 ($74,775 in current dollars). Although revenues reached $37,390 ($998,031 in current dollars), expenses totaled $47,791 ($1,253,010 in current dollars), leaving a sizable operational deficit. Soon the fate of the Abeles road was widely publicized. *Poor's Manual of Railroads* printed the announcement that the Atlantic Southern intended "to cease business December 31, 1914, claiming that they had been operating the road at a loss." Weber told a reporter that "the road could not be operated except at a continual loss and that the only thing to do with it is to tear it up and get as much as possible out of the sale of the material used in construction."[78]

When the Atlantic Southern petitioned the Board of Railroad Commissioners for permission to abandon, it failed to receive an unconditional green light. Regulators concluded that the trackage between Atlantic and Lyman could be retired, as it was expensive to maintain and generated little traffic. There was more. "That portion of the line is closely paralleled by the Rock Island Railroad on the west; and the Burlington (Cumberland branch) draws from it on the east. For these reasons we conclude that a justification, or public necessity, does not exist for requiring the continued operation of passenger and freight trains on that portion of the said line." The Board believed that abandonment of this section "will materially increase the earning power of the defendant company." The remainder of the line was different. It was in the public interest to maintain service, and Abeles should give it a fair trial. If operated properly, the railroad could be expected to pay expenses and generate a profit. As the Board later emphasized, "a railroad company after receiving public aid cannot abandon the operation of its property until it gives it a full, fair, reasonable trial. This has not occurred with reference to the Atlantic Southern."[79]

When word spread that the Aunt Susie planned to shut down at midnight on December 31, it immediately alarmed patrons. Preparing for the worst, freight users rushed to meet their needs. "The freight business during December was enormous, the people in the towns along the way shipping in their needed goods before the road closed down," reported the *Villisca Review.* "And the farmers north of here shipped all the live stock possible."[80]

No place was more concerned about the closure than Grant. At a March 1915 meeting held in the town, consisting mostly of local and Morton Mills citizens, discussion centered on how best to retain service. They agreed to have a professional study made before taking legal action. Several individuals were selected to solicit funds to pay an experienced engineer to ascertain the viability of the property. A goal of $2,000 ($51,918 in current dollars) was set to finance this initial step.[81]

The determination to save service between Lyman and Villisca remained strong. "The people of Grant and vicinity will fight Robert Abeles to the very last in an effort to compel him to operate the road," editorialized the *Grant Chief* in November 1915. Supporters took heart when the Board of Railroad Commissioners ordered the reopening of the twenty-one-mile section of line. Abeles refused. "We are ready to fight the matter out in the courts," announced his attorney W. A. Follett. "I do not believe there is a court on earth which will attempt to force a company to run trains at a loss." In a strategic move, Abeles transferred all the stock from the Atlantic Southern to himself to avoid the case coming before the district court in either Cass or Montgomery Counties. He soon filed suit in Polk County (Des Moines) to have the regulatory body's decision overturned. Abeles also became a plaintiff before the federal court. "By getting the case before the federal court," observed the *Red Oak Express*, "Abeles thinks to circumvent the people."[82]

Robert Abeles found outside support for his shutdown strategy. The trade publication *Railway Engineering* ran a short article, "Unfortunate Railroad Project," and agreed that the Atlantic Southern should be abandoned. "It soon became apparent [in 1913] that it did not pay to operate it. The track had never been ballasted; the rails were full of kinks; business was shamefully bad, and the cost of maintenance heavy, so the owners ran the last train on December 31, 1914, and closed operations altogether." The writer made this closing comment: "Railroad building in these days requires much careful consideration to insure success and the necessary support." In his mind, the Aunt Susie should never have been built.[83]

The battle over the fate of the Atlantic Southern stretched into 1916. That January, a spirited hearing took place in a federal courtroom in Council Bluffs. The proceedings included a presentation made by Mayor W. G. Hall of Grant. "He told of stores after the Atlantic Northern & Southern had been built, of elevators and lumber yards and other businesses which now are ruined by the absence of train service." Abeles representatives again drove home the point that profitability of the railroad would never occur, and they emphatically denied mismanagement. In early February, the federal judge made his ruling. He decided that the order of the Board of Railroad Commissions must remain undisturbed until such time as the resources of the state courts had been exhausted.[84]

In April the case resumed in Polk County District Court. It did not take long before the judge decided that Robert Abeles had the right to abandon the Atlantic Southern, agreeing that the road could never be profitable. This judicial opinion, of course, angered railroad backers. "Just how much the judge knows about railroad matters we are unable to say but in his opinion there's nothing to it, the road can't be made to pay, so the stuff [is] all off," editorialized the *Grant Chief*. "However, the people have a rather decided opinion that the state railroad commission knows more about railroad affairs, has a firmer grasp on infinite detail of managing a road, and knows better whether a line of road pays, than does the judge."[85]

The federal judge reentered the fray. Following the state court invalidation of the Board of Commissioners ruling, he held conferences in late June and early July 1916 with the parties involved. The judge subsequently decided that the Atlantic Southern could be abandoned. He pointed out that those wanting to save railroad service could purchase the property, an idea that was contemplated but did not happen.[86]

In February 1917, a swan song of sorts for the Villisca line came from the editor of the *Chief*: "One morning this past week, there came to our ears the joyful sound of a train whistling at the crossing near the depot. But alas, the train with its couple of flat cars was here simply for the purpose of hauling rails to Atlantic to be stored." There was more. "For a long time, men have been engaged south of town, tearing up the rails. When enough had been pried loose, an engine was sent down from Atlantic. The rails were carried down to the depot in a hand car, probably because the bridge across the Nodaway is unsafe for the locomotive to pass over."[87]

A feeble, last-gasp effort to save a portion of the Atlantic Southern occurred in May 1917. At a meeting held in Morton Mills, a group of area residents sought to raise $70,000 ($1,438,484 in current dollars) to rescue the line between Morton Mills and Villisca. Community backers learned that only a small portion had been generated in subscriptions. "The meeting broke up as joyfully as a slacker trying to join the Quakers in order to keep out of war."[88]

The legal actions taken by Robert Abeles proved victorious; he succeeded in overturning the action of state regulators. For Abeles, the process of dismantling occurred at an opportune time. After the outbreak of the European war in 1914, demand for scrap metal steadily increased. Rails and other salvageable pieces sold at premium prices. "Material is now said to be more valuable than when it was laid [on the AS]," reported one source. Rumors indicated that the steel from the abandonment, which consisted of rails, spikes, tie plates, and switches, yielded $165,000 ($3,980,696 in current dollars). A St. Louis scrap dealer apparently bought the materials, and some or all were destined for a shortline project in Arkansas. There were more assets to sell, including structures and about sixty acres of land. Abeles did not sustain a financial loss with the liquidation of "my railroad."[89]

ATLANTIC NORTHERN RAILWAY

Although dismemberment of the Atlantic Southern upset citizens who had finally gained railroad service, residents along the Kimballton line retained access to the iron horse for another generation. On August 13, 1913, Elk Horn residents John Leistad, S. C. Pedersen, and John Peterson filed incorporation papers with the Cass County Recorder for the Atlantic Northern Railway Company. Like most shortlines, it had a nickname: "Aunt Norie." At this time an appraisal was conducted. Two Des Moines railroad officials did this exacting work, and they estimated the value of this seventeen-mile railroad (18.7 miles with yard tracks and sidings) at $238,000 ($6,321,136 in current dollars).[90]

The transition from Atlantic Northern & Southern to Atlantic Northern would not be seamless. Adjustments had to be hammered out with bondholders and other legal matters resolved. Early signs, though, offered optimism. An October 1913 report indicated that "it was shown that the traffic on the line under the new regime is very satisfactory, and with improvements in the train service and otherwise contemplated, the road is believed to be on the road to prosperity." There remained strong community support, especially from livestock and grain shippers. "The Atlantic Northern has secured an enviable reputation as a stock shipping line," noted a newspaper in March 1915. That same year, 75 percent of taxpayers in the Elk Horn and Kimballton area agreed to a voluntary one-time contribution of 5 percent of the taxable value of their property to the company. These funds went for tie renewals, bridge repairs, bond interest, and the like.[91]

Operations lacked complexity. The company dispatched a daily-except-Sunday mixed train and other freight movements when required. It owned a secondhand American Standard locomotive and leased another. In addition to motive power, rolling stock as of 1915 consisted of just a single piece, a passenger (combine) car. Three years later the ICC reported one locomotive, three freight cars, and the combine. Rails remained light, fifty-six pounds to the yard.[92]

The federal government launched the US Railroad Administration in December 1917 to unsnarl wartime traffic, taking control of strategic steam railroads and electric interurbans. Shortlines like the Atlantic Northern were usually not included. As a consequence, these roads had to shift for themselves with no mandated priorities and reduced business. In 1918 the company sustained its largest ever loss, amounting to $12,660 ($221,601 in current dollars), but as in the past residents came to the rescue. In the fall of 1919, business interests in Elk Horn and Kimballton joined area farmers to raise sufficient funds to retire $100,000 ($1,523,417 in current dollars) of outstanding bonds, paying ninety-six cents on the dollar. Those who participated in this refinancing received stock for their contributions.[93]

The 1920s offered challenges. A postwar economic slump ravaged the country between 1920 and 1921, a downswing appropriately described as the "Forgotten Depression." Farmers especially encountered financial troubles: commodity prices plunged, crop surpluses mounted, farm foreclosures rose due to owners' inability to meet obligations from money borrowed against inflated land prices during World War I, and banks failed. Iowa led the nation in bank failures from 1921 to 1931 with an average of eighty-seven per year. These agricultural hard times continued throughout the decade and well beyond.[94]

The Aunt Norie mirrored national happenings within the railroad industry, particularly for agriculturally dependent shortlines. Although operating revenues fluctuated, they trended on a downward trajectory. In 1920 they totaled $52,654 ($692,694 in current dollars), but by 1925 they had dropped to $35,277 ($530,483 in current dollars). Revenues from the transportation mix remained largely constant. By categories for 1926, freight totaled $33,763 ($502,689 in current dollars), passenger $1,862 ($27,722 in current dollars), mail $1,113 ($16,571 in current dollars), express $1,171 ($17,434 in current dollars), milk $436 ($6,497 in current dollars), and "special service trains" $30 ($446 in current dollars).[95]

The company publicly worried about its future. In 1928 it placed a warning in the *Elk Horn Review* with the heading "*Time Changes Point of View of Railroad!*" Part of the copy read: "Time has changed things somewhat. A competitor has entered the transportation field and business that formerly went to the railroad is now being diverted to trucks. Perhaps these same patrons of trucks were the ones who enabled the railroad to be built." The concluding comments: "Down in your heart, Mr. Farmer, you want the railroad to continue operating. If this is the case then let the railroad have your business. Be a booster of the Atlantic Northern at all times."[96]

Deficits were managed. In 1929, the company acquired an old but reliable American Standard locomotive[97] "to be used solely for any emergencies arising." A year later, it conducted several pressing bridge and track repairs. In 1933 H. H. Fulton, a Lewis, Iowa, train enthusiast, made these comments in a short piece published in *Railroad Stores*: "Although it employes only ten people, the Atlantic Northern is so well

These photographs, taken in June 1933, show the final years of the Atlantic Northern
Railway. The venerable 4-4-0 locomotive handles several stock cars and a tank car in
Atlantic, revealing the company's usual freight traffic pattern. The Atlantic cement
block depot and office structure shows neglect, and the yards are largely empty and
choked with vegetation. In less than three years, abandonment will occur.
(*Courtesy of Railway & Locomotive Historical Society.*)

managed and has such loyal employes that it has shown substantial
earnings, even in depression times." Not true for the latter. Operating
revenues, which stood at $33,991 ($587,809 in current dollars) in 1931
plummeted to $16,650 ($338,242 in current dollars) two years later, and
net income dropped from $751 ($15,256 in current dollars) to a deficit
of $1,829 ($37,155 in current dollars). Coinciding with the Fulton commentary, the *Des Moines Register* reported its financial woes: "For some
time it [AN] has been operating at a loss, for the owner-customers are
not patronizing it. Trucks, busses, automobiles all have taken their toll
from Atlantic Northern's revenues." It added, "Recently a meeting was
called at Kimballton. Farmers, businessmen, stockholders, customers,

and possible customers were urged to patronize the road." Unless traffic increased, the consensus emerged that abandonment would be the only practical alternative.[98]

The end of service was not immediate. Revenues and expenses for 1934, however, proved disappointing: $17,171.97 ($337,375 in current dollars) for the former and $19,000.34 ($373,297 in current dollars) for the latter. The operating ratio stood at 110.65. Ironically, the last large movements occurred when the railroad handled carloads of construction materials for the building of Iowa Highway 64 in Audubon and Shelby Counties. When revenues failed to rebound, stockholders in September 1935 sealed the fate of the company by voting to shut down and liquidate.

On December 7, 1935, the ICC approved the abandonment petition. Since the railroad operated entirely within Iowa, state regulators needed to grant their permission to abandon. Approval came on January 6, 1936, the day the last revenue train plied AN rails. There was one last action to take. The Articles of Incorporation required a vote by two-thirds of the stock issued to officially dissolve. That approval came at a meeting held on January 21, 1936, in the opera house at Kimballton.[99]

It did not take long before the Board of Directors began selling off physical assets. The better of the two locomotives, acquired in 1929, went to the Manchester & Oneida Railway for $1,000 ($18,977 in current dollars), and a leading dismantler of Midwestern railroads, Hyman-Michaels Company of Chicago, acquired the rails, switches, and fastenings at the fair-market price of $12.51 ($237.41 in current dollars) per ton. Local farmers purchased the usable ties for fence posts at four cents apiece, right-of-way parcels were either sold or returned to former landowners depending on how they were acquired, and an oil firm bought the Elk Horn depot.[100]

As with most railroad abandonments, there was sorrow when the Hyman-Michaels "death train" worked its way slowly from Kimballton toward Atlantic. Residents had fought to build and to retain this rail artery, but the transportation picture had changed. Automobiles were ubiquitous, and trucks, traveling on an expanding network of all-weather roads, could haul grain and livestock to market or to elevators and stockyards located on nearby railroads. An attractive feature of truck transport was that farmers no longer needed to take their products to town or a siding since they could be picked up at farmsteads. If residents lacked access to an automobile, they might take a White Way bus to either Audubon or Atlantic. The Aunt Norie, which had been woven into the fabric of community life, had had its value greatly reduced. Its end failed to kill off either Elk Horn or Kimballton. Their populations remained stable: 513 in 1930 and 486 a decade later for the former and 378 to 349 for the latter. Mail service went from rail to motorized "star route." Then came that record-shattering winter of early 1936; blizzards and frigid temperatures caused a local coal crisis. A month after the railroad quit, the Elk Horn and Kimballton communities were reported to be without fuel. "Due to the recent abandonment of the Atlantic Northern there will be no means of getting coal to the communities until the roads are cleared." The loss of railroad service had been temporarily inopportune.[101]

A pleasant surprise came with the liquidation. Investors may have assumed that their shares were worthless or virtually so. The four hundred stockholders owned 1,113 shares with a par value of $100, which realized about 25 percent of face value. By early 1937 they received their checks, much appreciated remittances during the "Roosevelt Recession" years of the Great Depression.[102]

In the 1936 edition of the *Orange Quill*, the Elk Horn High School yearbook, student Emery Carlsen wrote, "The full effect of [abandonment] did not dawn upon the people until January 6, 1936, when the last train pulled out of Elk Horn. A group of people, a much smaller group than that which had cheered it on its first appearance, watched the train roll slowly out of Elk Horn 'round the bend; then they realized it was gone forever." He closed with these words: "The rumble of the wheels soon died away, but the memory will always linger in the hearts of those who were served so faithfully." With each passing year remembrances grew dimmer but never completely disappeared.[103]

THREE

IOWA & SOUTHWESTERN RAILWAY

RAILROAD PROBLEMS

ABOUT THE TIME OTHER SHORTLINES EMERGED IN WESTERN Iowa, Page County residents boasted having their own railroad, the Iowa & Southwestern Railway. Instead of referring to its official name, those who knew this Clarinda-based carrier often called it the "Ikey."[1] Resembling other sunset carriers, it lacked much mileage, being 17.4 miles in length. Still, the Ikey interchanged with two trunk roads: the Chicago, Burlington & Quincy Railroad (Burlington) in Clarinda and the Wabash Railroad in Blanchard.

Clarinda, the principal town on the Ikey and self-proclaimed "Queen City of the Nodaway Valley," was hardly railroad starved. A 1910 Iowa railroad map reveals that Burlington patrons had access to multiple routes for personal travel and for sending and receiving freight, express, and mail. There were two connections to the Chicago–Omaha–Denver main line, two branch lines to St. Joseph, and the former Humeston & Shenadoah and Keokuk & Western Railroads extended south and southeast of the Burlington's trans-Iowa stem. Residents of similar size communities in the state and elsewhere might have envied this extensive rail network.

Why did the railroad map displease Page Countians? Reasons varied. Most of the approximately four thousand residents of Clarinda, the seat of government since the county was organized in 1851, believed that they must liberate themselves from the "grasping," monopolistic powers of the Burlington. A similar feeling may have existed in Blanchard, founded in 1879 and incorporated a year later, where the Brunswick, Missouri–Omaha line of the Wabash served as its lone steel artery to the outside world. Clarinda citizenry fumed about freight rates and matters of service. The former issue, though, stood out. In locals' minds, freight rates stymied economic and population growth. Regulators had apparently failed to rectify the situation, and it would not be until 1910, when the Ikey was gestating, that the Mann-Elkins Act granted the Interstate Commerce Commission (ICC) extensive rate-making powers. Yet the public could not expect quick redress of rate-related grievances. Service complaints centered on freight equipment shortages and delays with inbound and outbound shipments. There was also dissatisfaction with infrequent and repeatedly late passenger trains, which often consisted of "old fashion" coaches. When the Commercial Club of Tingley, located about fifty miles east of Clarinda, complained repeatedly to the Burlington about the limited passenger service (one daily train each way) on the former Humeston & Shenandoah–Keokuk & Western route, "the officials came and did as one man puts it, 'just as we expected,'— nothing." This was but another example of the attitude of an impersonal railroad. Minor but annoying, the Burlington had long refused to install a telephone in its Clarinda freight office. A sign of corporate arrogance, it was claimed. Blanchard citizens, who in 1910 numbered 408 (on the Iowa side of Missouri border), were seemingly not troubled by rates. They did, however, complain that it was not easy to reach Clarinda by rail for business, shopping, or visiting. A trip involved changing carriers in Coin, five miles northwest of Blanchard, and this transfer was hardly seamless. It was necessary to walk three-quarters of a mile between the Wabash and Burlington stations, and more time was wasted when trains were late. To worsen matters, the Burlington offered only single-daily passenger service, and these movements were designed for riders who boarded in Clarinda. A journey between Blanchard and the county seat likely required an overnight stay in Clarinda. If a direct trip could be made over a single line offering a double-daily schedule, residents expected it to be more convenient, faster, and cheaper. Blanchard area denizens also sought a more direct route to eastern markets—the Chicago stockyards, for example. Just as other places nationally desired to end their status as inland communities, so did College Springs. In fact,

College Springs, which claimed a 1910 population of 626, held the dubious distinction of being the largest town in Iowa without a railroad.[2] This
one-time abolitionist utopia, known originally as Amity, had in the early
1880s missed out on the Clarinda, College Springs & South Western
Railroad, a Burlington subsidiary that built to the north and northwest
through Page Center and Coin. By the early twentieth century, residents
seemed desperate. "College Springs never needed a Rail Road worse,"
proclaimed the community's *Current-Press* newspaper. One reason was
its struggling Amity College, a four-year liberal arts school founded in
1871, which faced that pressing need to improve travel opportunities for
faculty, students, and visitors.[3]

AN INTERURBAN?

How could Page Countians solve their various transportation problems?
As hunger for interurbans soared after the turn of the twentieth century,
there was hope that an electric line would be built through Clarinda,
College Springs, and Blanchard. One rumor spread in 1906 that such a
traction project would connect Des Moines and St. Joseph and in the
process slice through the county. Although the route of the northern
section was not fully determined, it likely would extend to Clarinda. The
southern end, promoted by Alice Butler—an unusual role for a woman
in the interurban era—would operate between St. Joseph and Tarkio and
probably reach Clarinda. "Page County is wealthy enough, and thickly
settled enough," opined the *Current-Press*, "to make it an object for some
electric railway line or lines to engage in business here."[4]

Following the brief but disruptive Panic of 1907, the possibility of
building an interurban, albeit of modest length, improved. Optimism
came from a not unexpected source: the Engineering, Construction &
Securities Company (EC&SCo) of Clarence Ross and Charles Judd.
These men had learned through the Clarinda Business Men's Association
and other contacts of Page Countians' desire for an electric road to connect Clarinda with College Springs and Blanchard. Being "wide awake,"
they had already made their presence known in the region with their
involvement in several undertakings, namely the Oskaloosa-Buxton

Electric Railway, Albia Interurban Railway, and Atlantic Northern & Southern Railroad (AN&S). Ross and Judd made themselves temporary residents of the Hawkeye State. Judd and his wife Cora, for instance, rented a house on Twentieth Street in Clarinda.[5]

Backers of the Page County interurban met frequently with the EC&SCo to formulate a construction strategy and marshal public support. In spring 1908, citizens from College Springs and the surrounding area assembled in the Amity College chapel to discuss prospects with Judd. "We believe in a progressive and prosperous College Springs and the increased value of real estate in our town alone will build the road," commented an enthusiastic attendee. Residents took this position: "They are not very particular whether it be an electric or steam road or what towns get it, just so it runs through College Springs." That August, William Smith Farquhar, a prominent local farmer who in 1902 had founded the Farquhar Savings Bank in College Springs, checked out the recently completed Kimballton line of the AN&S. The College Springs editor believed that "it was through Mr. Farquhar that Messrs Judd, [Hans] Rattenborg [of the AN&S] and Ross were interested in the road from Clarinda to Blanchard."[6]

It is possible that Charles Judd or others at the Amity College meeting were aware of the recent remarks made before the Iowa Railway Club by A. E. Parks, an interurban enthusiast. He argued that "between main lines of steam railroads in territory that was reasonably densely populated, there was usually not sufficient additional business in sight to cause the steam lines to spur out 15, 20 or 30 miles and put on the mechanical appliances necessary to efficiently operate that spur." Parks believed that electric roads, built to high standards, would benefit steam roads by increasing their carload freight, especially livestock, and less-than-carload (LCL) traffic together with an enhanced passenger business.[7]

More talk about an interurban followed. Beginning in 1909, a growing consensus developed that it would run southwesterly from Clarinda through College Springs to Blanchard. Yet an alternative endpoint emerged. As early as 1908, there were discussions of an electric road connecting with the Wabash in Elmo, Missouri, an Atchison County farming community of several hundred residents. "It is the general supposition that if the road is built between Elmo and College Springs it will eventually go on through to Red Oak, thus giving Red Oak an outlet to the Wabash."[8]

Would Elmo be the destination? In January 1909, Charles Judd seemed favorably inclined. Compared to the projected route to Blanchard, this one was slightly shorter, the countryside was somewhat less rough, and lower construction costs were anticipated. "The Elmo line has the advantage of less rise and fall in grade, amounting to 244 feet," reported Judd. "It has more of level and light gradients and less of heavy gradients. It has less curvature per mile, and less yardage, but more bridging; the cost of right of way will be less."[9]

The Judd assessment for where the interurban should terminate was disregarded. Backers expected more financial aid from Blanchard because it claimed a significantly larger population, and there was strong desire for that community to be linked directly to Clarinda. Using this connecting point with the Wabash meant a less legally complicated intrastate endeavor.

A STEAM ROAD

Soon the Page County railroad project moved forward. As with other projected interurbans in the area, steam and not electricity would be employed. "The estimated cost for construction and equipment for steam service is about $300,000 [$8,765,524 in current dollars] and for an electric road about $75,000 [$2,191,381 in current dollars] more than this," circulated one report. Substantial savings indeed. Some backers thought the road might become a "wireless interurban," meaning that operations would be with internal-combustion equipment. Perhaps it would be a McKeen gasoline motor car, or it could be something more exotic. Already the Chicago, Rock Island & Pacific (Rock Island) had experimented (disappointingly) with a Ganz steam-powered motor car on its Winterset branch.[10]

In February 1909, talk turned to action. Page Countians were surely pleased when backers drew up incorporation papers for the Iowa & Southwestern Railway Company. Four months later, they filed this document with the county recorder, and on June 14, 1909, a charter came from the Iowa secretary of state. Businessmen in Clarinda, College Springs, and Blanchard, joined by a large contingent of area farmers, endorsed these transactions. Shareholders selected William Farquhar as their president. "He has been a resident of this county for over forty years; he has been one of the most successful farmers of the state and today is one of the best bankers and businessmen of the state." The foremost backer from Blanchard was board member William Dewhurst, co-owner of the Dewhurst and Boyle Hardware and Implement Company. The "mainspring from start to finish," however, was A. F. Galloway, cashier of the Clarinda Trust and Savings Bank, who served as corporate secretary and later as traffic manager and purchasing agent. Earlier in his career, Galloway had worked for the Burlington as its station agent in Clarinda.[11]

Progress advanced. Management engaged the EC&SCo to direct the solicitation of stock subscriptions. Farquhar, Galloway, and their associates authorized the firm to build the line "on a cost plus 10 percent basis," a common arrangement for railroad construction contracts. The *Current-Press* summarized the principal particulars of this document: "In the contract just signed they [Ross and Judd] are to receive ten per cent of the amount of stock subscription, ten per cent of taxes voted (if any), ten per cent of right of way secured by them. They stand all expenses of surveys, etc." Continued the account, "When enough money is raised to build the road they are to receive the contract to build the line, receiving ten per cent of the amount of money expended." Protection for investors was not neglected: "There are clauses providing for arbitration in case of difference of opinion between the directors and contractors."[12]

Optimism reigned. The *Clarinda Herald* put forth the case for the railroad: "Every business will be greatly increased, population will come, competition in railways will bring more factories, the value of the stock of every corporation now operating in Clarinda will go up. Can we afford it? Can Clarinda, with two and a-half millions of wealth, let College Springs, with her quarter million, build this road somewhere else. Enough said, we can't afford to lose it." The newspaper added this encouraging albeit misleading assessment: "A report, recently published in the [Des Moines] Register and Leader, shows that 98 per cent of the railroads in Iowa are on a dividend-paying basis. Some of these roads, too, are operating in a much poorer territory than that which our proposed road will enter here."[13]

There was the fanciful notion that north–south railroads, including the Ikey, would benefit from Gulf of Mexico traffic generated by the opening of the Panama Canal. At a "Big Railroad Meeting" held in Clarinda in mid-July 1909, a participant said: "When the Panama canal is completed, the north and south roads will become the main trunk lines. The opportunity Clarinda now has of getting on a main trunk line by helping to build this road from Clarinda to Blanchard, which eventually will go on to Tarkio and thence to St. Joseph."[14]

During the remainder of 1909 and throughout much of the following year, raising funds became the Ikey's preoccupation. Aided by energetic committee members, Judd, always a cheerleader, sought out stock subscribers: "Now is the time to put your shoulder to the wheel and push it along." The *Herald* had a dire warning: "If we lose this road two of our largest factories have said they must move elsewhere to secure better [rail]road facilities."[15]

The financial objective was to raise $150,000 ($4,382,762 in current dollars), half the estimate cost of building and equipping the road. Expectations ran as follows: Clarinda businesses and area residents would contribute $75,000 ($2,191,381 in current dollars), College Springs $50,000 ($1,460,921 in current dollars), and Blanchard $25,000 ($730,460 in current dollars). The Page County press provided continuing updates. The *Herald* printed an ongoing bar graph that showed the amount achieved. Both the *Herald* and the *Page County Democrat* listed contributing businesses and individuals and included the amount of their pledges. In Clarinda, the A. A. Berry Seed Company and the Lee Electric Light Company emerged as leading backers. Both firms expressed displeasure with the Burlington and were potentially the largest Ikey customers. In late January 1910, the *Herald* reported exciting news: "Ross and Judd now announced that Blanchard has taken her entire quota of $25,000 worth of stock, and that the very small amount still remaining to be raised in College Springs is assured." Added the newspaper, "that means the greatest part of the work is done."[16]

Approximately a month before the *Herald* report on stock subscriptions, Ikey advocates had received more positive news involving a special bond election held in Clarinda on December 21, 1909. The outcome surprised no one. A petition with hundreds of taxpayer signatures had asked City Council to place a limited tax issue before voters. The wording in part called for "collection and payment of a tax of five per cent upon the assessed value of taxable property in said city of Clarinda, Iowa. Said tax to be levied in the year 1910, upon the assessment of the year 1910. All of the said tax to be collected in the year 1911." It came with this limitation: "The entire line of railroad from the said city of Clarinda by way of College Spring to said town of Blanchard, to be completed for the passage of cars thereon by December 31st 1911." Although adult women in Iowa could not vote for officeholders until the ratification of the Nineteenth Amendment to the US Constitution in 1920, they could participate on tax issues if they or their husbands owned property. State law required a separate "Men's Ballot" and "Women's Ballot," but both counted equally. Females came to the polls in droves, voting 374 in favor and 72 against. The overall six-to-one victory margin of 828 to 114 ultimately generated nearly $33,000 ($964,208 in current dollars). "This is the greatest majority ever given a proposition of this kind in the experience of the promoters C. A. Ross and C. B. Judd, who have been concerned in many similar elections," noted a local editor.[17]

At the annual stockholders meeting, which attracted "a large crowd" in late January 1910, attendees sought immediate action. "Messrs. Ross and Judd were authorized and urged to go into the market with the bonds at once and thus complete the financing of the road at the very earliest possible date, so that work may start in the early spring." There was this upbeat comment: "The proper spirit was manifested all along the line."[18]

The rosy outlook at the January meeting did not mean that work gangs would soon shape the roadbed. Selling Ikey bonds became a challenging endeavor. In late July, *Herald* readers received an update about the financial situation. "The burden has been with the promoters to sell the bonds. Our bankers have been doing their part to help with the sale, and at times it looked as if the bonds were about sold when discouragements would come." Continued the report, "Money matters are not as free as they have been, and the buyers are slow to take up with these small railroad bonds." The writer still held out hope: "There is a prospect that our financiers will get to work along new lines and have all the money needed by the time the frost is out of the ground next spring." Within less than a month, the Ross-Judd team placed a large portion of this paper. Since survey work had been completed, it appeared that construction would start shortly.[19]

CONSTRUCTION

The process of shaping the Blanchard to Clarinda grade finally commenced. During the last week of August 1910, work began at multiple locations: Wabash interchange, between Blanchard and College Springs, and north of College Springs. The general contract was awarded to Shugart & Barnes Brothers of Des Moines, the firm involved with the Villisca extension of the AN&S. As was commonplace with canal and railroad building, it sublet short sections of the grading. The pace, though, did not move with lightning speed; only five miles had been completed by early November. Construction materials and a locomotive had been ordered, and fence wires and posts were starting to arrive in Blanchard "and will be placed in position as rapidly as possible." Company treasurer I. H. Taggart urged prompt payment of stock subscriptions, reminding investors that "rails must be paid for on delivery and the graders and bridge men also call for prompt cash payments."[20]

Grading progressed in a welcomed fashion. By December 1, 1910, the *Page County Democrat* stated happily that "fully 85 per cent of the grading on our new road project is now completed." It speculated that "this means that the work of finishing should be done in a short time, with good weather prevailing." The newspaper went on to report, "Some enthusiasts imagine they already here [*sic*] the Burlington conductors calling out 'Clarinda, change cars for College Springs and Blanchard.' It won't sound bad."[21]

Likely in anticipation of the coming of a new railroad outlet, Clarinda experienced an economic boom. "Our city is so full of factories now that the trouble is to get residence properties for the workmen," commented the *Herald*. "With our new additions to the city we will be able to provide residences for all who desire a home." It looked forward to a big town-lot sale at the end of October. "You want a home in town where you can have all the advantages that are to be had in a strictly up-to-date, live, hustling and rapidly developing little city like Clarinda is. You can't make a better investment than secure some of this land." The newspaper speculated that it might be possible to lure the Swanson Manufacturing Company away from Shenandoah. The firm would continue to have access to the Burlington and Wabash, and it would have the added benefit of a customer-friendly hometown carrier.[22]

At the close of 1910, Clarence Ross claimed progress. He announced that 80 percent of the grading and 90 percent of the cement and brick culvert work had been finished. Ross also indicated that "a great deal of the bridge construction is now completed." Yet not all of the right-of-way had been acquired. "There are two small tracts of right-of-way to be secured yet, [and they] are through two five-acre tracts and the land involved in [sic] less than an acre." As the new year began, Ross expected that with completion of the Villisca extension of the AN&S, the tracklaying crew he had organized would arrive shortly in Blanchard to start its labors. The crew's work in fact commenced on January 7 but lasted only briefly. These men probably returned to Villisca and waited to be paid for their labors. At the time, the *Herald* failed to speculate why the first train would not run between Blanchard and Clarinda for nearly a year.[23]

The reason was money. In April 1911, there was a published explanation for the long delay. "The grading for the new railroad is virtually completed [and] only a few minor places to be finished," commented the *Democrat*. "There will probably be no ties and rails laid for some time as the matter of working up finances to meet the expenses in grading this spring will be looked after. They have about $15,000 [$408,638 in current dollars] to raise and with the road bed completed and two miles of ties and rails on the ground the officials are in a good position to get this." Again, that perpetual optimism. Still, more than $15,000 was required to bring the Ikey to Clarinda.[24]

By October the financial situation looked much brighter. Neil MacDonald, a New York City investor connected with the Ross firm, gave real hope. He offered Ikey stockholders $100,000 ($2,817,591 in current dollars) "either wholly in cash, or in part in cash and part in rail contract."

Construction workers, teams, and equipment approach College Springs in 1911.
Onlookers watch these highly anticipated activities. (*Author's collection.*)

At the core of the proposal, MacDonald wanted "$70,000 [$1,972,313
in current dollars] of the bonds of said company and 25 per cent of the
capital when said rail credit or $50,000 [$1,408,795 in current dollars]
its equivalent in money is made available and the remaining $70,000 in
bonds and 25 per cent of the capital stock when the additional $50,000 is
paid to said company." Since the estimated cost to complete the road required $169,000 ($4,761,728 in current dollars), local supporters needed
to raise $32,000 ($901,629 in current dollars). The remaining amount
would come from the earlier Clarinda tax commitment. "The $32,000 is
the hill of difficulty which must be climbed and if it is not done all money
and effort heretofore expended will have been thrown away," remarked
the *Clarinda Journal*. A member of the Ikey board of directors opined
that the body sought "to secure a contract that will protect the rights of
the stockholders and keep the road out of the hands of the C.B. & Q. and
its friends." Several weeks later, the board formally approved a version of
the MacDonald financial deal.[25]

Construction workers did not immediately tackle completion of the
Ikey. In a November 16, 1911, letter to the *Current-Press*, William Farquhar assessed the situation. He indicated that engineers had begun setting

stakes for several bridges and that "bridges will be more likely than anything else to delay tracklaying." Farquhar continued, "We can afford to
spend a few hundred dollars in preparation as we are now doing but we
cannot afford to begin the real work of construction until the money to
complete is pledged. When the work is begun there must be no delay
for lack of money or for any other cause." His closing words: "Now that
the long, long hoped for Railroad is so nearly in sight it behooves every
resident of College Springs, Blanchard, Clarinda and all along the line
to make one last effort to make it a reality."[26]

Page Countians responded to the financial needs of their emerging
railroad. With additional money in hand, the right-of-way became an active construction zone. By mid-November, it seemed probable that rails
would reach Clarinda by the end of December. "As many as two dozen
teams from College Springs and around Blanchard are donating hauling
of the big pilings used in the construction of the railroad," reported the
Journal. "This certainly shows a commendable spirit on the part of the
farmers toward the new enterprise. The pile drivers are at work and the
road is being rapidly pushed forward." The core workforce consisted of
ninety or so outside laborers, likely including some who had been involved with the Villisca extension. Locals characterized these workers as
"Greeks" and occasionally in less flattering terms. (There was widespread
feeling that southern and eastern Europeans possessed low-grade intelligence, inferior to those from northern and northwestern Europe.) These
men focused on installing ties and rails. Ballast would be compacted dirt,
and later cinders were applied to soft spots. By the end of November, the
line advanced about three-fourths of a mile per day. All but two miles of
rail were sixty-pound newly manufactured steel from the Lackawanna
Steel Company, and the remainder consisted of used fifty-six-pound rail.
The ties were mostly "second class white oak, with some red oak and
cedar." Two pile-driving gangs stayed ahead of the tracklayers.[27]

Winter had come to Page County as the deadline of midnight, December 31, 1911, loomed. Seventeen days before the year ended, the work
train steamed into College Springs. "The work of laying the rails from
Blanchard having been completed and the train brought up a crowd of
people from the south county line and denizens of College Springs met
them with the band and loud shouting for joy." Finally, the community
had put an end to its status as an inland town.

CLARINDA!

"Onward to Clarinda!" An exciting climax to building the Ikey came as 1911 was about to end. On Friday evening, December 30, the track gang was only seven-eighths of a mile from the Clarinda town line. Both builders and observers expected that rail laying could be easily completed the following day, even though one of the two locomotives borrowed from the Wabash gave out due to a boiler leak. The company planned to run a free public excursion from Clarinda to Blanchard and back on Saturday afternoon. That was not to be. Shortly before midnight on Friday, the other Wabash locomotive derailed three miles northeast of College Springs while pushing two flatcars of rail toward Clarinda. Fortunately, "the Wabash kindly furnished a third engine." President Farquhar realized that the exhausted workers needed help. The temperature was near zero, and the air filled with blowing snow. He immediately called for volunteers, and about fifty College Springs men responded. Saturday saw feverish action. "The College Springs bunch put in the day laying ties, carrying steel, using the pick or shoveling dirt, carrying spikes and anchor bars, and even watering the engine." The relief locomotive's water tank was discovered nearly empty; the engine backed down to a mostly frozen creek, and a bucket brigade filled the tank. After about an hour, the locomotive steamed back to the work site. "Although the day was extremely cold and stormy, the College Springs boys were a happy bunch and when the train pulled into Clarinda, it was the College Springs crowd that made the most noise."[28]

When the work train reached Clarinda on that frigidly cold final day of December 1911, it was not only the College Springs volunteers who were joyful; locals also celebrated. The locomotive "let loose the whistle and let the people know that the Iowa and Southwestern was in. Soon there were hundreds of cheering spectators, and the town's factory whistles began to wail." The screaming noise was hardly an annoyance to most citizens: "The long and loud sounding of steam whistles, the notes of which were a sweet music to the ears of the people friendly to the road." There was a makeshift parade, not of floats and bands but of laborers. "It was an inspiring sight between 4 and 5 p.m., to see the long procession of workers on the C., C. S. and B. railroad marching up town in Clarinda, two abreast, 132 in number as they were counted from a

Journal office window, the work they had been doing in railroad building, completed, and they were about to be guests at a good meal as a sort
of celebration for what they had done. They went to different hotels to
eat." Happiness reigned. "The railroad shows what Page County pluck
and money can accomplish." The tax dollars were assured; Clarinda had
an alternative to the Burlington, and expectations ran high for the new
railroad.[29]

Bigger doings took place on New Year's Day. About noon a special
train, which consisted of borrowed coaches from the Wabash, arrived in
Clarinda. Riders from Blanchard, College Springs, and crossroad locations were aboard. At 2:00 p.m. the train departed Clarinda with more
well-wishers: "About 130 were loaded up from here and started on a free
railroad ride." (Another source counted 150.) After a brief stop in College
Springs and a short stay in Blanchard, the train returned to Clarinda,
taking one hour and twenty-five minutes. In Blanchard, restaurants were
"unprepared for the hungry gang as they were cleaned out in short order."
These excursionists were a friendly lot. "In one of these restaurants the
visitors helped in the serving of the food called for, being careful also to
see that the restaurant lost no money." The trip was considered a success. "It was really a pleasant and agreeable outing and everyone surely
enjoyed themselves as was evident by the mirth, wit and merriment prevailing reaching home."[30]

Will Millen, a Clarinda resident, went so far as to write the following verse. His literary efforts suggest the poor condition of the freshly
installed track.

'Twas on a winter evening
The snow was falling down
The Iowa and Southwestern
Came whistling into town.

The smoke was rolling high,
The rails of steel were laid,
The taxes on deposit
To the railroad will be paid.

The track is rather rolly
So "there's a reason" for the fact
That if we rode to Blanchard
We'd be glad to hoof it back.[31]

The first carload of Flour to reach College Springs by rail was one of

Shambaugh's S. P.

and was shipped over the Iowa and Southwestern railway from Clarinda, Jan. 30, 1912, for Pollock & Stanton.

Shambaugh's Sweet and Pure Flour

first at Ames, first at College Springs, and first in the bread and cake of the land.

Its Sold by your Grocer

In January 1912, the *Current-Press* in College Springs carried this advertisement for Shambaugh's Sweet and Pure Flour. The advertisement notes the flour's baking quality and that it was the first carload of flour to reach the town over Ikey rails. (*Author's collection.*)

The final construction spurt revealed strong community support. Pride was taken that the entire tracklaying was done in twenty ten-hour working days. Much more work remained to be done on the line involving leveling, tamping, and the like. The company also required support facilities, including turntables in Blanchard and Clarinda, depots in Clarinda and College Springs (it arranged with the Wabash to use its Blanchard station and agent), shelters, sidings, and several stock pens. Right-of-way fencing needed to be completed.[32]

FREIGHT AND PASSENGER SERVICE

Regular operations did not begin immediately; what developed was intermittent freight service. The February 1, 1912, issue of the *Journal* featured this advertisement: "The first carload of Flour to reach College Springs by rail was one of Shambaugh's S. P. and was shipped over the Iowa and Southwestern railway from Clarinda, Jan. 30, 1912, for Pollock & Stanton." Reported the *Democrat* not long after, "The new Iowa and Southern [*sic*] railroad has not yet opened up for transportation business but first of the week there were three carloads of stock shipped over it to the Wabash main line and considerable more will be ready soon."[33]

In early February the Ikey promised regular freight and passenger service as quickly as possible. Still, it was painfully slow in coming. Four months later the *Current-Press* commented that section crews continued to work on "putting the track in shape." It added, "Just as soon as the track can be completed the management will put on a regular train service, and then look-out, the Iowa & Southwestern will do business." Financial limitations and the overall poor condition of the track structure explain the lengthy delay.[34]

With funding in hand, the Ikey readied itself for an "official" opening. By July, carpenters were at work in Clarinda converting a former private dwelling into a depot and adding a freight and baggage section. These betterments "will make a very creditable improvement to the city." Nearby a company-owned residence became the home for the section foreman, and a small workforce installed the transfer track with the Burlington. Announced the *Herald*: "July 20th is the date set by the Iowa Railway Commissioners on which the new road may begin traffic."[35]

A local photographer captured an Ikey crew switching the Blanchard
Roller Mills, a business aided by the arrival of the town's second railroad.
(Larry Polsley collection)

After receiving the regulatory green light, service officially began.
Initially the Ikey operated only a single round trip passenger train between Clarinda and Blanchard. Fares were three cents per mile. Intermediate stops were made not only at College Springs but also at Finley
and Taggart between Clarinda and College Springs and at Dewhurst
between College Springs and Blanchard. The train consisted of a combination baggage and passenger coach and boxcar for LCL freight. "[LCL]
freight is being shipped over the road in goodly quantities. Poultry, butter and eggs are being received daily [in Clarinda] from the south." Then
there were carload movements. "A carload of groceries from Omaha
came in Tuesday [July 25, 1912], and on the track stands a car of coal for
the Lee Light Co. from Huntsville, Mo." Both arrived via the Wabash.
In mid-November 1912, Turner Brothers, grain and lumber dealers in
College Springs, described their rail activities. "[We've] shipped out of
here over 40,000 bu. of wheat, 2,600 bu. of oats, 1,500 bu. of corn, and
shipped in 29 cars of lumber, 9 cars of cement, 15 cars of sand, 20 cars of
coal, 2 cars of shingles, 1 car of telegraph poles, and 1 car of bricks since
the middle of July." Bread-and-butter traffic involved outbound grain and
livestock (cattle and hogs) and inbound lumber, rock, and coal. The latter
constituted the largest single commodity handled in 1914, amounting to
slightly more than 30 percent of all tonnage. US mail and express also

traveled over Ikey rails. Wells Fargo & Company, which operated over the Wabash, handled the latter, and it rented office space on Main Street in Clarinda to serve the public.[36]

The opening phase of the Ikey reflected the hope of its patrons. When the editor of the *Red Oak Express* solicited comments about its value to the community, he received several letters, all thankful and optimistic about the new shortline. C. A. Lisle, president of the Lisle Manufacturing Company, closed his response with these thoughts: "As to the future benefits to be derived from the new railroad, no one can give a definite or even approximate estimate but we already know in our own business that we are getting value received for our investment and have no disposition whatever to complain of the cost or to doubt the future efficiency of the road." Responded W. L. Pedersen, a piano and organ dealer: "I believe that the railroad will be a good thing for Clarinda. It has the support of every business man and the good will of every enterprising citizen." He concluded, "It is my opinion that this road will pay. While it may not pay a large dividend I do not think there will be any loss. It has helped to cement the three towns as one, has given College Springs a railroad which needed an outlet, and the benefit to them can hardly be estimated."[37]

To the delight of everyone who relied on the Ikey, passenger train frequency increased. On December 1, 1912, double daily (except Sunday) service became a reality, improving connections with both the Burlington and the Wabash. Salesmen ("commercial travelers" or "drummers") benefited greatly from additional trains. Lamentably, these trains frequently ran late. In October 1913, a College Springs writer commented that "traveling men hate to stop here as they never know just when they will get in nor when they can get out of town. People seem to think it is alright for it to be late once in a while but are not at all pleased with the way it has been running lately." The new afternoon southbound train usually allowed the US mail and Chicago newspapers, via the Burlington connection, to be delivered to College Springs and Blanchard in the evening. The November 1913 edition of *Russell's Railway Guide and Hotel Directory* listed daily departure at 5:30 p.m. with arrival in College Springs at 6:25 p.m. and Blanchard at 7:00 p.m. The morning daily-except-Sunday train left Clarinda at 6:20 a.m., reaching College Springs at 6:55 a.m. and Blanchard at 7:25 a.m. The northbound daily train departed Blanchard

A group of likely Amity College students and faculty board an Ikey train in College Springs for Clarinda on a cold winter day. The date is probably 1912. *(Larry Polsley collection.)*

at 10:00 a.m., arrived in College Springs at 10:40 a.m. and in Clarinda at 11:30 a.m. The daily-except-Sunday train steamed out of Blanchard at 6:20 a.m., reached College Springs at 6:55 a.m., and at 7:25 a.m. reached Clarinda. As this published schedule reveals, Ikey "varnish" moved slowly. Even at these speeds, the ride often jostled passengers. There were complaints from Blanchard residents about when they could travel, arguing that the timetable favored Clarinda and its business interests.[38]

No common carrier failed to dispatch special excursions. The first advertised extra on the Ikey took place on May 20, 1912, when Madame Ernestine Schumann-Heink, the Prague-born singer billed as "the greatest of concert contraltos," gave a well-received recital in Clarinda. A few months later, the railroad provided extra movements for those from Blanchard, College Springs, and intermediate points who wished to attend the week of Chautauqua programs in Clarinda. The featured attraction for the 1912 season was William Jennings Bryan, three-time Democratic Party nominee for the US presidency and soon to become US secretary of state. Clarinda bragged that it hosted the largest Chautauqua assembly in Iowa.[39]

There were individuals who used Ikey rails but did so without tickets. After the railroad opened, it was not unknown for Amity College male students to "borrow" handcars, usually kept unlocked at the nearby College Springs station, to make evening round trips to Clarinda. "The Opera House was a favorite entertainment spot." When the college closed its doors in May 1914, these nocturnal activities ceased.[40]

As on other shortlines, riders on the Ikey probably knew the crew members and others who worked for the company. The local depot agent was usually as well-known as a physician, preacher, or banker. These railroads frequently recruited locally; they were hometown affairs.

A likely representative of Ikey employees was John George. Tragically, he became an accident fatality—the only one in company history. On June 23, 1913, while firing on the morning Clarinda-bound passenger train, George apparently took a break from shoving coal near the Finley road crossing. While inspecting the undercarriage, he slipped and fell to the tracks, breaking his neck and dying instantly. George, who was fifty-one, married with children, and a Blanchard resident, had been employed by the railroad since operations began. "For a time he looked

A group of Blanchard-based Ikey section hands gather at trackside for their picture. The image reveals light rails and an unballasted roadbed. *(Larry Polsley collection.)*

after the engine, then was fireman and also looked after it nights, but for the last two weeks he had been firing only and this was to be a permanent job." George had not previously been a railroader but was a plasterer by trade.[41]

The common image of shortline railroads is that they created happy, family-type environments. That may have been largely true, but short-lines often encountered financial troubles. Pay disputes, most of all, triggered employee unrest and the occasional strike. The Ikey was no different. Unlike serious labor discontent on the Villisca extension, worker disruptions were sporadic and involved maintenance-of-way personnel. One flare-up occurred in April 1913. "The strike 'microbe' has struck the section hands on our division [College Springs] of the Iowa and Southwestern and they have struck for better pay and less 'cussins.'" The threat of strike breakers appeared. "It is reported that a gang of Dagoes or Greeks will be sent in here to take their places, but rumors are afloat that there will be several first-class funerals if they do." Fortunately, the unrest faded away. "Some in authority have resigned, the men have gone back to work and everything is now passing off as smooth as a June morning."[42]

BURLINGTON TROUBLES

While labor-management relations did not worry Ikey officials too much, they fretted about their relationship with the Burlington. The Chicago-based giant did not like this upstart railroad, just as it was not especially pleased about having shortlines in its midst. Fortunately for the Ikey, it had the accommodating Wabash as an interchange partner.

On January 21, 1913, the Ikey responded to the shortcomings of the Burlington. William Orr, founder of the Clarinda Trust & Savings Bank now serving as the railroad's general counsel and president, filed a formal complaint with the ICC about freight car interchange, reciprocal (or competitive) switching, and joint rates. If the Clarinda road was to survive, it required a hospitable connector in its principal freight sending and receiving terminal. Local support was overwhelming for the Ikey's cause. "We are glad to notice that the Iowa and Southwestern has taken steps to see that the Burlington does the square thing with us on the interchange of traffic, switching cars and joint rates on freight," editorialized the *Herald*. "Any man or company of men who have acted so contemptibly small as they have in so many things, deserves the censure of every fair minded man and if they wont do what is right we are glad to know there is a law to make them do what is right." This developed into a lengthy and stressful ordeal for the Ikey; it would not have a David versus Goliath ending.[43]

The legal fight was on. In late March, hearings on the case of *Iowa & Southwestern Railroad v. Chicago, Burlington & Quincy Railroad* began in Des Moines before an ICC examiner. J. H. Henderson, commerce counsel for Iowa Board of Railroad Commissioners, represented the Ikey. Grievances were substantial, and their impact severely damaged revenues. The company, for example, had to pass up eight carloads of clover seed for the Berry Seed Company because of discriminatory rate divisions imposed by Burlington, Milwaukee Road, and Chicago & North Western Railroads. The Burlington held fast in its determination to limit competition in Clarinda. In late 1914, the Ikey believed that the ICC had given it a victory on matters of switching and joint rates, but unfortunately rulings were unclear and promoted more litigation. The Ikey lodged similar complaints with state authorities. On August 15, 1915, these charges were resolved favorably, but they involved only intrastate movements. The ICC had yet to render clarifications.[44]

The Burlington did not need to worry about federal regulators—the Ikey was faltering. Unusually wet conditions in the spring of 1914 not only made Page County roads difficult if not impossible to navigate, but they caused the portions of the roadbed, especially fills between College Springs and Blanchard, to settle badly. The Arnold Cut proved inordinately troublesome, at times crumbling and burying the track. Because of poor management and financial limitations, cuts had never been cleaned or ditched since the line opened, and they were not sufficiently drained. These conditions disrupted service, forcing the railroad to return to a single round trip daily passenger schedule and delaying freight runs. Repairs took time and bled funds. And these fixups had unintended consequences. Where the tracks had been raised in places, the original gradient increased from 2 percent to nearly 3 percent. Not until June 13, 1914, would the Ikey restore normal passenger operations and improve freight service. "The company [is] now in better condition to give good and more regular operations."[45]

Early in 1915 the Ikey took pride with a sizeable revenue freight move. "A special stock train of eighteen freight cars loaded with one car of hogs and seventeen of cattle was conveyed over the Iowa and Southwestern Railroad to Blanchard and transferred to the Wabash road for the St. Louis market." The news story added, "The stock was to reach St. Louis in less than twenty-three hours. The special nearly reached passenger time. This is the largest single shipment from this section in a long time."[46]

DECLINE

While the report of a revenue-generating stock train was uplifting, financials were not, and legal troubles were brewing. Operating revenues for 1914 stood at $21,808 ($571,774 in current dollars), but expenses amounted to $26,524 ($695,420 in current dollars). In October 1914, two lien holders filed suit in federal court for the Southern District of Iowa at Creston for $20,200 ($534,371 in current dollars) to recover their charges for right-of-way grading and construction materials. After a court appraisal of the property, which placed its value conservatively at $194,000 ($5,036,039 in current dollars), a pivotal event took place on April 24, 1915. That Saturday afternoon at 3:30 on the north steps of the Page County courthouse, outside the sheriff's office and before a large crowd, the deputy marshal for the federal court officially held the sale of the Ikey. He received only one bid, that of C. C. Barnes of Des Moines on behalf of Shugart & Barnes Brothers and the Abeles & Taussig Tie & Timber Company of St. Louis. Both firms had earlier been heavily involved with the Villisca line. Barnes did not bid on the rolling stock but only on other assets, including track and right-of-way. He was not the sole creditor at the sale. There were others, including representatives of the Lackawanna Steel Company and the Wabash, who were willing to see if the Ikey could turn profitable. After all, this was a sale and not a sale. Under Iowa law, stockholders had a year to "redeem" their railroad. The official Ikey response was straightforward: it planned to pay off all creditors.[47]

Page Countians did not want the Ikey to fail. The railroad had a significant local role to play, and it had already benefitted its service area. "It is known that the business interests of Clarinda have been largely increased and advantaged by the road, even in its imperfect and interrupted operation of the past," editorialized the *Journal*, "that it has largely increased sales in different lines of trade and that it has been the means of enabling Clarinda to get better service on the other lines [of the Burlington] entering the city. The road, too, has been of vast importance to College Springs and Blanchard."[48]

If satisfying creditors was not enough for Ikey directors to worry about, Mother Nature seemed determined to sink the property. The summer of 1915 proved exceedingly wet. "One of the heaviest rains of the season came Sunday night," reported a College Springs resident in mid-July. "Three inches of water fell during the night, which washed out a number of bridges in this vicinity and made others unsafe. The Iowa and Southwestern railway was badly damaged in several places between

College Springs and Clarinda, which will stop our train service for a few days." The storm produced more rain in the Blanchard area. "Blanchard and vicinity was [sic] visited with a heavy rain Sunday night. About four inches during the night and the water is higher than it has been for several years." These deluges forced the company to suspend operations. Problems grew immediately after the storm, when several cars of stone and sand pressed the track deep into the mud. More rains followed. Noted the College Springs newspaper about a month later: "The Iowa and Southwestern which has been shut down now for weeks on account of washouts and wet weather is reported by men who ought to know that it will be running again inside of ten days." Through service remained closed until mid-September. "The Iowa and Southwestern have [sic] a force of hands at work in the Arnold cut towards Blanchard, which during the exceedingly wet weather caved off and buried the track in some places about four feet deep. Flat cars are loaded and the dirt hauled onto the grades where it is needed. . . . It will take a week if not more to clear it up so the trains can run through to Blanchard."[49]

Patrons worried. "The recent deluge, as other roads have suffered, and the people are quite anxious it [Ikey] should be put in shape to run when the wagon roads are bad, which is the time it is most needed." College Springs had no practical way to send out grain and livestock or to receive coal, lumber, and other bulk commodities. The company responded as best it could, but a lack of funds prevented it from hiring more men for repair work. In fact, the road owed back wages to its small force of maintenance personnel. The Ikey did receive encouragement from E. S. McClelland, general manager of the Tabor & Northern: "Local support of the I. S. W. Ry. will make it succeed."[50]

Notwithstanding an outside reassurance, the Ikey struggled. A red-letter day came on April 24, 1916, the deadline for the stockholders to redeem their railroad from creditors. Funds, however, were unavailable. Revenues had been drastically reduced due to the prolonged service disruptions caused by excessive rainfall. Passenger trains had been canceled, and freight movements had become intermittent. And there remained that uncooperative Burlington.

What took place on that fateful Monday in April came as no surprise. Prior to the deadline, directors of the Ikey had been in negotiations with representatives from Western Tie & Timber Company. This St. Louis firm had recently purchased the certificate of sale from Shugart & Barnes Brothers and Abeles & Taussig. Why did Western Tie & Timber take this action? Perhaps it believed that the Ikey could become a solvent enterprise or more likely could be sold to the Wabash. In all likelihood, Abeles & Taussig would have junked the railroad; after all, it had embraced that strategy with the Atlantic Southern. "Realizing this danger the stockholders unanimously voted in favor of turning the line over to any person or persons who would agree to rehabilitate and operate the road. The purchase of the certificate of sale by the Western Tie and Timber Co. took it entirely out of the hands of Abeles & Taussig and the danger of having the track torn up has been averted." There was hope. Reported one source: "The [new] owners of the line do not wish to operate the railroad and are willing to dispose of their holdings, preferably to local parties."[51]

The Iowa & Southwestern *Railway* was no more. The new company, Iowa & Southwestern *Railroad*, was incorporated on April 25, 1916, with the Page County recorder and soon with the secretary of state in Des Moines; this reorganization wiped out the initial stock. Investors and Clarinda taxpayers had made a financial sacrifice, yet they had been warned. "When the stock was sold for the building of the road instructions were given to the solicitors not to promise that the road would be directly financially profitable to the purchasers of the stock, but that it should be considered in the light of a donation." Some stockholders failed to recall that caveat, not anticipating what would happen with a change in ownership. There was the expected replacement of officials and directors, leaving only two Page County residents on the board of directors (A. A. Berry and C. V. Nichols). The new management suspended operations until details of reorganization could be finalized.[52]

Regular service did not resume. The Ikey remained alive—but barely. There would be no more passenger trains, and freight operations continued only intermittently. For 1916 the company handled just 9,131 tons of freight, mostly livestock, coal, and lumber, and generated a paltry $130.54 ($3,149.33 in current dollars) in revenues. In June the College Springs correspondent for the *Herald* observed: "We were all happily surprised to see the train pull in again last Monday afternoon, after a lay off of over two weeks. We certainly hope that matters may soon be arranged so that we may have our regular trains again." In the interim, an enterprising College Springs resident had a trailer built for his Model-T Ford so that he could haul mail, express, and light freight to Blanchard and Clarinda. In October the express business ended; Wells Fargo retreated to the Wabash depot in Blanchard, and Adams Express, which operated over the Burlington, continued to serve Clarinda.[53]

Western Tie & Timber wanted to forsake the Ikey. Since no grassroots movement emerged to regain local control, the two alternatives were a Wabash buyout or abandonment. By summer 1916, rumors spread that this St. Louis trunk road would acquire the property. "The purchase of the road will mean much for the Wabash company and they can depend upon the loyal support of the city of Clarinda and the intermediate territory," editorialized the *Democrat*. "It will also be a great help to Clarinda. Let's all boost." In October the *State Line Herald* in Blanchard reaffirmed that rumor. "It looks like the I. & S. W. Railway would yet survive the storm of financial difficulties." Speculated the newspaper, "While there is nothing official regarding the transfer of the short line to the Wabash, it is generally believed among railway circles that a contract for the sale has been made, and that it will only be a course of a short time that the Wabash will start work to reconstruct the system. The road bed is all that would serve the new owners. New engines, cars and other equipment would be necessary."[54]

Was the Wabash interested? Yes, but it would do its due diligence. The company had only recently emerged from bankruptcy, having been under federal court control since December 1911. It now had the wherewithal to purchase and operate the Ikey. The latter, however, would not be cheap, especially correcting the sagging roadbed and cuts. Not long before the Wabash officially exited bankruptcy on October 22, 1915, it engaged Chicago railroad consultant J. W. Kendrick, who had previously worked for the company, to study the shortline. He was not impressed. Kendrick concluded that the physical conditions were inadequate for minimal branch line operations, and its rolling stock was of junk caliber. He also condemned management: "The Company's records have been very poorly kept—in fact, most of them have been lost." Kendrick thought it foolish to have the Clarinda agent serve as its auditor

Railroad consultant J. W. Kendrick included this photograph of poor track conditions southwest of College Springs in his 1915 report on the Ikey to Wabash officials. *(John W. Barriger III National Railroad Library.)*

and blasted the absence of a roadmaster. "It is very wasteful to operate the property without supervision, as at present, for it is inconceivable that it can be so operated without incurring a loss more than sufficient to secure and pay for competent oversight." Any talk of extending the road to Tarkio was nonsense, with Kendrick seeing no merit in any "expand or die" argument. Still, Kendrick did not consider the Ikey to be an immediate candidate for abandonment. It needed to improve the Clarinda freight market, pursuing revenue possibilities from the Green

Bay Lumber and Clarinda Lawn Mower Companies. Formation of a subsidiary terminal company offered a better way to manage interchange problems with the Burlington.[55]

Wabash officials and likely Edward F. Kearney, the coreceiver who became president with the reorganization, surely read the Kendrick report. Proof of Wabash interest in the Ikey came on November 4, 1916. A party of executives and operating personnel, headed by Kearney, made a "thorough inspection" trip over the road. A dinner at the New Liderman Hotel in Clarinda, hosted by the Commercial Club, topped off the visit. "They expressed themselves as highly pleased with Clarinda. Several spoke of our city as one of the cleanest, nicest, little towns they knew of." That positive impression of the Page County capital failed to make the Ikey a Wabash appendage. Rehabilitation costs were probably too great for the anticipated business.[56]

ABANDONMENT

Although the Wabash never added the Ikey to its system map, backers of the road did not abandon hope that it could be saved. But they were only grasping at straws. A. A. Berry, the wealthy Clarinda seed company owner who likely represented both his hometown and the interests of Western Timber & Tie, thought that Louis S. Cass, "one of Iowa's greatest railroad men," might play a role in keeping the Ikey alive. Cass was one of three brothers who controlled the profitable Waterloo, Cedar Falls & Northern Railroad, the second largest interurban in the state. Berry invited Cass to visit Clarinda, and he accepted. In early January 1917, Berry showed Cass his hometown and the Ikey, and then his guest spoke to the Greater Clarinda Club. Cass told his audience that an electric railroad would energize the area and that operating costs would be much less than conventional steam power. He also said that "it was his candid belief that Clarinda could and would support such a railway." Cass's motivational talk promoted this editorial response from the *Democrat*: "To the people of Clarinda and Page county, opportunity is knocking at our door. Let's boost—all of us—and put our shoulders to the wheel and raise from those two streaks of rust, 18 miles long, an example of what Page county can do." These thoughts were badly out of date and hardly reflected reality. Cass nevertheless avoided getting involved in any attempt to electrify the Ikey. But an assistant, a "Mr. Bentley" who also addressed the gathering, commented that he had been studying conditions in Page County and would be willing to help convert the Ikey into an interurban. "Mr. Bentley is of a pleasant disposition—and under the able guidance of Mr. Cass has, no doubt, learned the lesson of what should and should not be done in promoting and operating an electric line."[57]

Rust had not fully encrusted Ikey rails. Occasional freight movements occurred. For a short time, a College Springs resident used a handcar to transport mail; later he acquired a Smith Form-A-Truck (a kit allowing a Model-T Ford to be converted into a truck) and fixed the truck with flanged wheels so that "he can handle the [LCL] freight business as well as the mail." Around the time the Ikey moved toward outright abandonment, Washington federalized all major steam railroads but excluded most shortlines. Because of two worthy customers in College Springs—a contractor who was building a school on the site of the defunct Amity College and a lumber yard addressing the critical need for coal—the US Railroad Administration ordered the Wabash to provide maintenance and service on an as-needed basis between Blanchard and College Springs. The eleven miles to Clarinda remained out of service.[58]

The saga of Ikey's decline continued. Rumors circulated that the Wabash would take over the Blanchard to College Springs trackage permanently. But was there any hope for restoring service between Clarinda and Blanchard? On the eve of World War I, there was talk of the property becoming a component in a 187-mile route between St. Joseph and Manning, Iowa. In May 1918, A. F. Galloway, who represented the Ikey, requested that the state railroad commission endorse the project and asked the Capital Issues Committee, a division of the Federal Reserve Board, for authority to sell $75,000 ($1,312,805 in current dollars) worth of bonds for debt relief and rehabilitation. Reported the Council Bluffs *Nonpareil*: "If the present stretch of seventeen and a half miles can be put in operation the remainder of the promotion will be carried out following the war." Hiram J. Slifer, a lieutenant colonel with the Twenty-First US Engineers, had made such a study before he went off to fight in France. A consulting engineer in private practice, Slifer possessed solid qualifications, having previous experience with three Granger roads:

North Western, Rock Island, and Great Western. He concluded that if completed, this north-south route, with its multiple interchange points, would be profitable, and he optimistically suggested that "annual earnings would be easily $4,800 [$98,638 in current dollars] per mile." Perhaps Slifer was correct, but the odds for success were astronomical.[59]

By early fall 1918, any realistic likelihood of a functioning Ikey had ended. The federal government wanted its rails, switches, and other metals. The Committee on Scraps of the War Industries Board (WIB) requested that Ikey steel be placed on the market. "Owning to the enormous demand for iron and steel and the shortage of scrap metal, it is becoming difficult to obtain adequate supplies for needs," explained W. Vernon Phillips, who chaired the subcommittee on scrap for the American Iron and Steel Institute that had close ties to the WIB. "Users of iron and steel who did not get priority allocations are eagerly seeking supplies, and every effort is being made to increase the supply of scrap." The Ikey complied. A local company, Clarinda Iron & Metal Company, would collect the scrap and ship it to the US Arsenal in Rock Island, Illinois. The public response? "While the people along the line of the 'Ikey' will be sorry to see the rails go," surmised the *Herald*, "they see in the act the one comforting consideration that it may help win the war." Others surely disagreed, most of all College Springs residents.[60]

Physical abandonment began in October. Under normal conditions the dismantling would have been a mundane process, but the fall of 1918 was different. Military service had eliminated many able-bodied males from the local labor pool and so did the deadly outbreak of the Spanish influenza pandemic. The deadly plague hit western Iowa especially hard. Mounting infections and deaths forced the closing of most businesses, churches, and public institutions, including schools and the State Hospital for the Insane in Clarinda. What to do? One effective response was to hire healthy high schoolers. "The contractors who are tearing up the old road needed the boys, as the boys needed the coin for spending money; so the work has been mutually satisfactory," a reporter noted. Since schools were shuttered, teenagers were available, although a few contracted the virus.

The rail removable process started near the middle rather than in Clarinda or Blanchard. Salvaged materials went north to the Burlington

In late 1918, a dismantling crew takes time off from its rail removal work between College Springs and Blanchard. Most of the men are probably local farmers. (*Larry Polsley collection.*)

and south to the Wabash. A truck was employed. "The rubber tires are taken off and the truck then placed on the railroad track, which they fit perfectly, with sufficient play to allow for the wobbly condition the track is in," observed the *Herald*. "The truck draws its load easily, carrying as high as 24 rails to a load, 650 lbs to the rail total 15,600 lbs to the load, or nearly six tons, with the help of a specially built trailer behind. This is a larger load than can be pulled over the dirt roads by the truck." Added the newspaper, "American ingenuity cast about to find some way of keeping out of the mud."[61]

Ikey steel came too late to assist the war effort; it did not help either the home front or the military in Europe. The rails delivered to the Burlington fell into the possession of the American Trading Company of New York City. Their fate was a customer in Shanghai, China. Those stockpiled in Blanchard went to another metals dealer.[62]

Around the time of the Ikey's opening, College Springs merchants and others line up for a photograph to be converted into a picture postcard. This "New Business Row," located along the westside of the main commercial street, suggests a prosperous community. A massive fire in 1901 had forced the rebuilding of most of the business district. *(Larry Polsley collection.)*

The Iowa & Southwestern Railway was a bitter disappointment to its backers; it operated for only five years. As with other sunset cluster railroads, the Ikey made positive contributions to Page County. The construction phase pumped thousands of dollars into the local economy. Clarinda and College Springs each experienced population growth and business and residential expansion with the arrival of service. Blanchard, though, saw less development, "adding a little to what was already there." In 1913 the Clarinda *Herald* ran a story, "New Building Operations," saying that "contractors, carpenters, masons and teamsters all are agreed that there are now more building operations going on than ever before. Constructive work is at premium and it is coming to a point where the person who wants work done has to wait his turn." That same year the progressive climate prompted the town to replace its mayor-council government with a city manager, becoming the first municipality west of the Mississippi River to adopt the council-manager structure. This allowed local government to operate on businesslike principles. During the railroad years, College Springs enjoyed its golden age. Even though Amity College folded in 1914, residents saw a variety of new businesses, including a grain elevator and a "first-class" restaurant. In August 1912, a Clarinda editor brought his readers up to date on their neighbors to the southwest. He spent a few moments at the elevator watching workers load two boxcars with grain, and he continued his stroll along the main commercial street. (Following a massive fire in 1901, this rebuilt street became known as "New Business Row.") The editor encountered prosperous establishments, both old and new. "Mr. A. M. Abbott has a large double store and does a big business in furniture, hardware and undertaking. He keeps four regular men busy waiting on his customers." He enjoyed chatting with R. A. Hawthorne, who recently had moved to town from Maywood, Nebraska, and opened the Amity Store, which "handles books, stationery, man's furnishings, and talking machines and his stock will undoubtedly appeal to the discriminating buyer." In his conversation with R. Steel Finley, a real-estate agent, "Mr. Finley says that since the new railroad has been built there are a number of well to do families thinking of locating at the Springs." Such glowing accounts ended as the Ikey declined and died.[63]

FOUR

CRESTON, WINTERSET &
DES MOINES RAILROAD

AN EMPTY CORRIDOR

AS THE TWENTIETH CENTURY BEGAN, THE RAILROAD MAP OF Iowa revealed an obvious empty corridor between Des Moines and Creston. This general region to the southwest of the Capital City had long been considered a desirable place for new construction. Although railroad promoters and builders had not overlooked the area, their efforts for penetration had been mixed. In the early 1870s, residents of Creston, Winterset, and intermediate points had unsuccessfully backed the St. Paul & Southwestern Railroad. This paper entity hoped to build between these two Iowa towns. A few years later, local boosters had boomed for naught the Bedford, Winterset & Des Moines Railroad, designed to link the communities in that company's corporate name. And additional schemes popped up intermittently.[1]

One important step to address the void occurred in the 1880s. Between 1882 and 1884, the Des Moines, Osceola & Southern Railroad (DMO&S), a narrow-gauge (three-foot) road, opened between Des Moines and Osceola, seat of Clarke County, and later extended south to the coal-mining community of Cainsville, Missouri. This construction resulted in 111 miles of line. In 1888 a reorganization created the Des Moines & Kansas City Railway (DM&KC), the "Blue Grass Route of Iowa."[2] Theodore Sherwood, DM&KC general passenger agent, underscored the long-standing need for railroad service in this general territory. "Heretofore the region which stands sponsor for our highly esteemed title [Blue Grass Route] has been almost entirely shut out from the Capital City by the 'high protection wall' of long, circuitous, and tedious routes. As a result, the thrifty inhabitants of the live towns of the richest part of Iowa have been cut out of the commercial and social intercourse which should exist between the two." The DM&KC, widened to standard gauge in 1896, entered the orbit of the Keokuk & Western Railroad and soon the Chicago, Burlington & Quincy Railroad (Burlington), the dominant road in southern and southwestern Iowa. Sometime after the DMO&S appeared, the Wisconsin, Iowa & Nebraska Railway, known as the "The Diagonal" and subsequently folded into the Chicago Great Western Railroad (Great Western), sliced through the region. Yet it failed to serve any county-seat town, having principal stations in East Peru (Peru), Lorimor, Talmage, Shannon City, Diagonal, and Blockton. For a large population, neither railroad solved the problem of reaching Des Moines directly.[3]

AN INTERURBAN DREAM

With the advent of the Interurban Age, the possibility of enhancing connections to the state capital increased. Such alternatives were hardly surprising. Traction enthusiasts in the Hawkeye State nearly always sought more than rural trolleys reminiscent of the cheaply built lines found along country roads in New England and parts of the Midwest and South. Instead, backers wanted their properties constructed to the more demanding specifications of steam roads. Quality branch lines would be their models. As expressed by an Iowa editor, the idea was for promoters "not building a line that follows the contours of the country, up hill and down hill, but a line as straight as the crow flies, and at a grade that might as well do for a trunk line where the heaviest engines and the longest trains are to be pulled." This strategy required mostly private rights-of-way that would permit heavy-duty motors to pull freight equipment interchangeable with steam carriers. In this way bulk commodities could be shipped and received. The result would be "electric steam railroads."[4]

As the century began, it appeared that residents of Creston, Macksburg, and Winterset would have an interurban. Omaha promoter Lyman

Waterman sought to make reality the proposed Creston Electric Light, Railway & Power Company (CELRy&PCo). This approximately forty-mile road would connect the Burlington main line in Creston with a branch of the Chicago, Rock Island & Pacific (Rock Island) in Winterset. The firm would also provide electricity to Creston, Winterset, and customers along the route. By February 1901, the CELRy&PCo still needed to secure franchises in Creston and Winterset and rights-of-way along certain country roads in Union and Madison counties. Financing likewise needed to be completed. J. S. Polk, president of the Des Moines City Railway, expected to have a Capital City–based interurban connect with the CELRy&PCo in Winterset, a distance of about thirty-five miles. There was also the expectation of an electric railway tying Creston with Mount Ayr, seat of Ringgold County, approximately twenty miles south of Creston. This led to the incorporation of the Des Moines & Southern Electric Company. Coinciding with these plans, a rumor circulated that the Burlington would build from Creston through Macksburg to Winterset and then to Des Moines. This had become a popular corridor.[5]

By mid-1902 prospects for a Creston to Winterset interurban looked encouraging. Franchises had been granted, and financing allowed surveys to be completed and building to begin. The Collins Construction Company of Chicago won the contract for grading and installation of track and electrical equipment. Early on, the interurban's primary investors revealed their optimism when they incorporated the Iowa Land and Townsite Company. The firm acquired forty acres in Union Township of Adair County for what would be the stillborn town of Leith (later spelled Leath City).[6]

Yet the CELRy&PCo sputtered and died. An internal leadership squabble led to a reshuffling of officers. By 1903 Lyman Waterman had left the company, turning his attention to the Mount Ayr project. The proposed Des Moines to Winterset interurban scheme also collapsed, causing questions about a Winterset franchise. Management issues and financial shortfalls led to the end of construction, although some grading had occurred north of Creston.[7]

The electric dream did not fade away. Shortly before the Panic of 1907, interurban enthusiasts in Des Moines began to contemplate seriously lines to the southwest, including a sixty-five-mile line to Creston. Residents of the intermediate territory began to consider similar construction. The Capital City enjoyed excellent steam road service in most directions; beginning in 1902, it had the electric passenger cars and freight trains of the Inter-Urban Railway (IUR) operating to Colfax and four years later to Perry and Woodward. In 1907 Des Moines benefitted from the electrified Fort Dodge, Des Moines & Southern Railway (FtDDM&S) to Ames, Boone, and Fort Dodge. Later, that company offered similar service to Rockwell City, Webster City, and Lehigh. A contemporary map published in a Des Moines newspaper showed multiple proposed interurban lines radiating out of the city. These included not only the one to Creston but others to Chariton, Ottumwa, Waterloo, Webster City, and Audubon. The IUR was projected to extend its Colfax line to Marshalltown and its Perry line to Jefferson.[8]

What was the steam railroad situation for Creston, Winterset, and the intermediate village of Macksburg? The Des Moines & Kansas City and Great Western both had missed Creston, the former by thirty-three miles and the latter by about a dozen miles. Still, the 6,924 residents of this vibrant Union County seat had access to the busy Chicago–Omaha–Denver stem of the Burlington and two branch lines: north and west to Greenfield and Cumberland and southwest to Bedford and St. Joseph, Missouri. It also boasted the Burlington's division headquarters together with a large roundhouse and repair facility. Crowed a local realtor: "CRESTON has a fine Water Works System, Sewerage, Gas, Electric Lights and Electric Power for machinery day and night. Miles of paved streets. Splendid Schools and Churches. Two Daily Papers and a Federal Court house. It is a healthy and good place to live in." If a railroad from Creston to Des Moines were built, Winterset would likewise benefit. This seat of Madison County with a 1910 population of 2,818 suffered from mediocre rail service, being at the end of a forty-two-mile Rock Island branch that ran east to Carlisle and north to the Capital City. The closest station to the Great Western, East Peru, was about fifteen miles distant. Macksburg, a farming community of about two hundred residents southwest of Winterset, never had a railroad.[9]

Even though the preliminary construction in northern Union County had failed to achieve an interurban, advocates by 1907 felt

A vibrant Creston, dominated by the Burlington Railroad, is visible in this 1908 view of the station and surrounding area. In the background (*upper right*) is the smokestack for the roundhouse and shops complex. (*Author's collection.*)

encouraged. More planning suggested that a functioning electric road between Creston and Des Moines remained a realistic possibility. "The line is fifty-eight miles of construction and sixty-four miles of operation, the understanding being that we use five and seven-tenths miles of the Des Moines City Railway's tracks for passenger terminals in Des Moines," related a backer to the *Creston Advertiser-Gazette* in August 1907. "We have deeds and contracts over eighty per cent of the right of way already secured; also franchises in Creston, Macksburg and Winterset." Reported another source, "Creston people are much elated over the prospects and are confident that the road will go through." Although the newly incorporated Creston, Winterset & Des Moines Electric Railway (CW&DMER) was estimated to cost a hefty $1.8 million ($50.7 million in current dollars), supporters considered it a winning proposition. "Our total tributary population, as estimated, is about one hundred and sixteen thousand people. The total tonnage produced in the territory tributary to our line is three hundred and seventy-six thousand tons, of which approximately two hundred and fifty thousand tons is [*sic*] available for haul, either long or short." Enthusiasts bragged that "it will build and operate entirely upon its own private right-of-way, 100 feet wide." The CW&DMER would accommodate steam-road rolling stock, freight equipment that electrics Inter-Urban and FtDDM&S presently handled. Supporters did not miss the point that these two interurbans generated solid revenues, and Des Moines showed indications of becoming "a good interurban city."[10]

Excitement spread, being particularly strong in and around Macksburg, this inland community that physician-founder Dr. Joseph Hughes Mack Jr. had laid out in 1873 and incorporated three years later. "Some of the people around Macksburg are very much elated over the prospects of the interurban railroad," noted the Macksburg reporter for the *Winterset Madisonian* in January 1908. "They know personally of the benefits the people have in sections where there are trolley lines. Liberal subscriptions are being offered [because] a railroad through this section will benefit every farmer within five miles of the line, to the extent of one dollar per acre every year for the next twenty years."[11]

While farmers and villagers might express excitement for the CW&DMER, meaningful financial support was essential for the road to be more than another "hot-air" proposition. It seemed that all the railroad talk so far was just that. In February 1908, supporters took heart when the press revealed that F. M. Hubbell, the powerful Des Moines businessman who controlled the city's streetcar system and the Des Moines Union Railway, indicated he would subscribe $5,000 ($146,000 in current dollars) to the project. Members of the Des Moines Commercial Club also announced their approval, planning to raise $250,000 ($7.3 million in current dollars). The road was expected to be a boon to Capital City businesses. "It will enable women shoppers to come to Des Moines, make purchases and return the same day. It will enable merchants of the southwestern towns to telephone orders to Des Moines wholesale and jobbing houses and get goods delivered immediately. It will bring many people from this section of the country to our theaters. The benefits will be reaped by men in every field of business." News also came that Winterset interests had agreed to buy $30,000 ($876,000 in current dollars) worth of securities, and commitments would be "substantial" in Creston. "PROGRESS, ADVANCEMENT, MODERNISM" became the slogan for the ongoing crusade.[12]

More encouraging news followed. In late September, the *Des Moines Register and Leader* revealed that avowed interurban enthusiast Leslie Shaw, former Iowa governor and US secretary of the treasury, had endorsed the undertaking. So had Charles Wolf, described as a Parkersburg, Iowa, capitalist; this banker and land speculator planned to commit $60,000 ($1.75 million in current dollars). At best this was wildly optimistic speculation. Newspaper readers may have expected "dirt to fly" momentarily, but that did not happen.[13]

Early in 1909, less welcomed reports came from a Des Moines meeting of interurban backers. Apparently efforts to arrange for the disposal of construction bonds had fizzled. A recent state law, which had tightened the sale of securities, may have deterred investors. Moreover, fallout from the Panic of 1907 had made bonding houses more cautious. Creston attorney Richard Brown, who became heavily involved in the Creston project, speculated that these two events "will necessitate a much larger amount of money being subscribed by the people locally than was previously asked for."[14]

The financial situation prompted CW&DMER backers to rethink their goals. "The company is seriously considering the road in sections, either building from Des Moines to Winterset, or from Creston to Macksburg," observed the *Creston Semi-Weekly Advertiser*, "the plan being to complete the road in two or three years." For this to happen, individuals who had already subscribed to stock would need to approve the new arrangement, since the original proposition called for building the entire road at one time.[15]

The news worsened. "The Creston Road Is Abandoned," proclaimed the *Des Moines Capital* in March 1909. Even though "the project was practicable," backers concluded that the financial obstacles were too great. Subscriptions had lagged, and franchises awarded by local governments in Creston, Macksburg, and Winterset would shortly expire; perhaps they could not be quickly renewed.[16]

Reports of the demise of the CW&DMER proved premature. In April 1909, proponents circulated an open letter that offered promise. "This road is owned and controlled by your own neighbors and fellow citizens who are determined to build the road. All they need is the continued loyal support of those who have befriended the undertaking in the past. We have not been talking much noise, but we have been quietly and persistently at work." And they continued to be. By July these interurban hopefuls revealed that the Engineering, Construction & Securities Company (EC&SCo) headed by Clarence Ross, already active in the region, had agreed to participate. Why become involved with such a small-time company? Again, the likely explanation: "It would be impossible to interest Eastern capital in the proposition." The EC&SCo had successfully coordinated the building of the steam-operated Kimballton line of the Atlantic Northern & Southern (AN&S) and recently opened interurbans based in Oskaloosa and Albia. The Ross firm had already encouraged communities monopolized by a single rail to build interurbans or steam shortlines, and it continued to offer its multiple services. "A survey gang will be put to work soon to complete the survey commenced and well progressed about a year ago and as the facilities of the Judd & Ross Company will permit construction work."[17]

UNDER STEAM

Involvement by the Ross firm did not mean the interurban would quickly take shape. Plans changed dramatically. The Des Moines interests had retreated, expressing greater interest in a projected hundred-mile electric road between Des Moines and Red Oak via Winterset and Greenfield. This left backers of the CW&DMER to Creston, Macksburg, Winterset, and the surrounding countryside. "The incorporators are wealthy farmers living along the right-of-way," reported *Railway World*, which was true to a large degree. Leading the project were Richard Brown of Creston, president; Jerry Wilson, Macksburg, first vice president; M. F. Harris, Winterset, second vice president; A. S. Lynn, Orient, secretary; and W. W. Walker, Macksburg, treasurer. "The new organization has nothing to do with the old organization, which has been wholly abandoned." Newsworthy was the announcement that the project would be a conventional steam road, and construction would begin between Creston and Macksburg and later continue to Winterset—Des Moines would not be an immediate objective. An interurban, even if constructed to the cheapest standards, would involve more than rails alongside a public road or on a graded right-of-way; it would require a pole line and overhead wire, electrical substations, and a source of electricity either from its own generating plant or supplied by an existing power company. A steam road, on the other hand, could be less costly, perhaps built for as little as $10,000–$12,000 ($292,000–$350,000 in current dollars) per mile, and secondhand locomotives and other pieces of rolling stock were readily available at reasonable prices from railroads and used equipment dealers. Or it might become a "wireless interurban" of sorts, using gasoline motor cars for passenger, mail, and express service and steam for freight operations. In 1911 the *Electric Railway Journal* reported such an intent.[18]

The new approach appeared workable. In October 1909, a Winterset journalist wrote that "between Creston and Macksburg nearly every farmer benefitted by the road has agreed to subscribe to stock and it is thought that the financing of the proposition will not be difficult." Backers must have been encouraged with happenings not far to their west, namely the opening of the AN&S between Atlantic and Kimballton not long before. The local press was impressed that this steam shortline "has been entirely paid for by farmers and business men in towns and country along the route." Another editor spurred on the undertaking: "Success to the new railroad from Creston to Winterset. Success to any new railroad in Iowa."[19]

Support in Creston blossomed. Civic-minded residents continued to express remorse that the Union County metropolis had missed a chance to have a Burlington competitor. "May she never again let slip the opportunity that was hers when the Great Western was permitted to go right past her door, without so much as passing the time of day," observed a visiting Council Bluffs *Nonpareil* reporter in November 1909. A new spirit of community pride and purpose had developed in Creston. "A booster movement is on foot that bears the aspect of determination and success in its every line. The booster club is to be incorporated. The thousand dollars [$29,218 in current dollars] is to be placed in the treasury by popular subscription, and, thus armed the boosters are going up to look for factories and things for their town—thus instead of waiting for the good thing to come along and then try to raise the needed funds in a haphazard way."[20]

Another factor played into the desire for a booster club. Likely in the minds of these uplifters were memories of the severe negative economic impact that a bitter locomotive engineers strike in 1888 had inflicted on their community. Once members of the Brotherhood of Locomotive Engineers, who had been joined by firemen and switchmen, returned to their posts after losing their wage demand, a rapid recovery failed to occur. Then the deadly Panic of 1893 struck, resulting in five more difficult years. A diversified economy would mitigate the effects of the dominant Burlington payroll.[21]

In 1910 the Creston to Winterset project made some behind-the-scenes progress. Stock solicitation dominated activities. "Work is progressing very satisfactorily," opined the *Winterset Madisonian*, "though little has been said or done to attract newspaper attention." By September Creston journalist Paul Junkin revealed "that all subscriptions necessary to finance the road as far as Macksburg had been secured and that the contract for that portion of the road would probably be let this winter."[22]

On September 16, 1911, backers of what was now the Creston, Winterset & Des Moines Railroad (CW&DM) filed articles of incorporation with the Iowa secretary of state. This document authorized capital stock of $500,000 ($14 million in current dollars) and gave the company the now-common right to operate "in whole or in part by steam, electricity, gasoline, or other such motive power as shall be adopted by the Board of Directors." Reports speculated that by summer 1911, construction would begin between Creston and Macksburg. Even though the area press had earlier announced that stock subscriptions had been completed with approximately four hundred investors, financial matters remained to be finalized. In July a Creston reporter wrote that "the sale of stock at Macksburg was completed this week, [and] the solicitors will go into Union township [Adair County], where there is $1,500 [$42,263 in current dollars] yet to raise." He added: "It is expected that two weeks will be required in that territory, and after bringing the subscriptions up to the required amount there, the solicitors will move into Spaulding township [Union County]." Stock subscriptions would not be the sole source of financing. In October special elections were held in Union Township and Grand River Township (Macksburg) where voters overwhelmingly approved a 5 percent property assessment for five years. Supporters expected that a combination of stock subscriptions and tax money would make first-mortgage bonds attractive to investment houses, thus completing the financing.[23]

The slow advance of the CW&DM continued. Local funding was in place, at least for the Creston to Macksburg leg, and chief engineer Charles Judd proclaimed unequivocally that construction would begin in the foreseeable future. "Macksburg is about to get a railroad—a hope deferred from time to time during the past forty years," proclaimed the *Madisonian* in January 1912. In the spirit of unbridled optimism, the newspaper declared: "If the road is built to Macksburg, it is certain to be built on to Winterset and Des Moines."[24]

CW&DM management still needed to juggle financial matters. It had to sell bonds since subscriptions to stock were payable only when the bonds had been placed. This became a challenge, in part because neither the Burlington nor the Rock Island wanted the road built. Not wishing to lose a valuable slice of territory, these railroads likely pressured bonding houses in Chicago and New York to avoid these offerings. Their actions were reminiscent of their response to the Shaw syndicate. Forced to be resourceful, the CW&DM, likely at the suggestion of Clarence Ross, launched a subsidiary firm, the Iowa Bond and Security Company. It marketed the 6 percent gold-first mortgage notes, targeting mostly Iowans. Although some prospective investors may have become skeptical when several recently opened Hawkeye State shortlines encountered money reversals, success followed.[25]

Finally, in August 1912 the CW&DM let the construction contract. Following the announcement, supporters "held a jollification meeting," reported an area newspaper. "Enthusiasm is manifested by every one there over the prospect of securing a road." The company had raised $135,000 ($3.67 million in current dollars) from stock and taxes and generated $144,000 ($3.9 million in current dollars) from bonds. Now the pressing concern was that the track reach Macksburg by midnight on December 31, 1912, to become eligible for township tax payments.[26]

Under the supervision of Charles Judd, the twenty-one-mile route between Creston and Macksburg became a construction zone. Because of his unpleasant experiences with Shugart & Barnes Brothers, Ross engaged a St. Joseph, Missouri, contractor. Laborers were mostly assembled from the area. A Des Moines newspaper included this recruitment advertisement: "100 MEN WANTED for track laying on the Creston, Winterset and Des Moines Railroad at Creston, Iowa. Spikers and wrenchmen $2.25 per day, common labor $2.00; first class board at $4.50 per week. Railroad fares allowed by company on surrender of railroad agents receipts." Onlookers soon watched hefty steam traction engines pull earth-moving equipment to shape the right-of-way together with approximately fifty assisting mule teams. Workers built three wooden deck bridges (including a substantial one over the occasionally treacherous Grand River), installed concrete and brick culverts, and unloaded fifty-six-pound "relay" rails, ties, and other materials at Burlington sidings in Creston, Spaulding, and Orient. Tracklaying began on the east side of Creston near the fairgrounds, a location that became the "Creston Transfer," and proceeded northward on the west side of the Cumberland branch through the village of Spaulding (1910 population of one hundred). At Burlington Crossing, a mile north of the Union-Adair County line, the track gang turned eastward, progressing through the Zion community (failed Leith City townsite). Shortly it entered Madison County. Before rails could reach Macksburg, graders faced a steep ascent coming out of the Grand River Valley and a massive clay ridge immediately west of Macksburg. This route through Blue Grass Country was not flat as a floor.[27]

Charles Judd traveled to Chicago to acquire secondhand rolling stock. He found two American Standard (4-4-0) steam locomotives that could be used in the building process and later serve as motive power for the completed road. This engine type provided what the CW&DM needed (as it had for the AN&S and Iowa & Southwestern): acceptable speed over a cheaply built track. A steam-powered ditcher and two center and two side-dump cars were also purchased, essential for taming that challenging terrain outside Macksburg. A used passenger coach (combine) and several freight cars were part of these equipment acquisitions.[28]

Public Auction Sale!

Of Lots at Macksburg, Iowa.

I will sell at Public Sale

Wednesday, November 13th, 1912

Sale Begins at 10:00 a. m.

150 Lots in the Town of Macksburg, Iowa

Macksburg is in the southwest part of Madison county. It is the terminus of the railway now being built from Creston. It is the farthest from competition of any town in the state, being thirteen miles from Lorimor, seventeen miles from Winterset, twenty miles from Creston, and twenty-two miles from Greenfield.

In consequence of this large territory, and being located in the richest farming district in Iowa, it is safe to say that it will be a town of several thousand within the next two years.

Now is the time for those looking for locations for business of any kind to get in on the ground floor. The railway will be completed January 1st.

The lots to be sold are divided into business, resident lots and acreage. The business lots are conveniently located to the depot; the resident lots and acreage are further back on high, slightly land.

Also, an EIGHT ROOM HOUSE, conveniently located to business center, with good Barn, Wells and Outbuildings.

I am the sole owner of this property, which is unencumbered and in consequence will be sold without reserve at bidders' prices; also, the 160 acres on which these lots are located, and in consequence can satisfy anyone wishing a location.

We have arranged for a suitable tent in which sale will be held in case of bad weather.
Take the C. G. W. to Lorimor; C. R. I. & P. to Winterset; or C. B. & Q. to Creston or Orient.

TERMS---This property will be sold on contract; One-fourth cash on day of sale; balance in three annual payments at six per cent.

For further information, apply to GUY BARKER, Des Moines, Iowa, or ADAM BUSCH, Macksburg, Ia.

S. K. NOLAND, AUCT., 401 Clapp Blk. Des Moines, Iowa.   **Capt. E. G. BARKER, Owner**
W. W. WALKER, Clerk,
Cashier National Bank, Macksburg.

On November 6, 1912, the *Winterset Madisonian* published this advertisement promoting a town-lot auction in Macksburg. The promoter sought to exploit the approaching rails of the Creston, Winterset & Des Moines. Although residents had convenient access to the auction site, it is not clear how prospective buyers would reach Macksburg from railroad connections at Lorimor, Orient, and Winterset. (*Author's collection.*)

As the CW&DM took shape, excitement grew along the route, the greatest of which was in Macksburg. Even before residents heard the shrill whistle of a steam locomotive, development accelerated. Taking advantage of the advancing rails, E. G. Barker, who owned 160 acres of farmland that adjoined the town, vigorously promoted the sale of 150 lots at a public auction scheduled for November 13, 1912. Handbills and newspaper advertisements told of the exciting future of Macksburg: "It is the farthest from competition of any town in the state, being thirteen miles from Lorimor, seventeen miles from Winterset, twenty miles from Creston, and twenty-two miles from Greenfield." The promotional copy continued: "In consequence of this large territory, and being located in the richest farming district in Iowa, it is safe to say that it will be a town of several thousand within the next two years." The auction apparently went well. The Fullerton Lumber Company, which operated multiple yards in western Iowa, became involved in local real-estate transactions, prompting a Macksburg resident to comment: "It looks as if one could certainly get lumber at the right price." There also existed excitement in Des Moines. As the *Register and Leader* believed, "the line must eventually serve as another spoke in the wheel of commercial feeders, which it is hoped will radiate from Des Moines."[29]

A FUNCTIONING RAILROAD

The red-letter day for the CW&DM came on December 31, 1912. In order to meet the deadline imposed by township voters, construction workers, numbering at times around two hundred men and toiling in day and night shifts, pushed the steel rails toward Macksburg. "Splendid weather" aided their heroic efforts. By December 20, the track-laying gang neared West Macksburg, site of ongoing earth-removal work and technically within the town's corporate limits. In order to win the race with the calendar, the final few miles were built to the barest standards, reminiscent of when the AN&S had battled the clock to reach Kimballton. "The latter part of the road is not graded at all, only the surface dirt taken off so the track could be laid and the train pass over it," related a local writer. Helped by this drastic shortcut, the first train arrived at the hastily installed West Macksburg siding at 4:30 p.m. on that last day of 1912. There was no driving of a ceremonial spike, only relief that rails had reached Macksburg. The following day, New Year's 1913, there was community recognition of the virtual completion of the railroad. "Crowds gathered around the engine and two coaches as they landed on the prairie near here and the New Year's celebration began in earnest."

Richard Brown and other officials of the road became "grand celebrities." A smaller commemoration took place in Winterset. "Winterset citizens have watched the building of railroad with the greatest of interest."[30]

Much remained to be done on the CW&DM, however. Track, especially the final section, had to be reworked. The cut on the westside of Macksburg needed to be completed and depots in Creston and Macksburg, support facilities, and sidings readied. Yet on Friday, January 4, 1913, "the first passenger train" took directors and additional riders from Macksburg to Creston. Before the railroad could become a certified common carrier, an examiner from the Iowa Board of Railroad Commissioners needed to make a favorable inspection. Fortunately, approval came quickly. By June 30, 1913, the company had spent more than $235,000 ($6.2 million in current dollars) on its physical plant and rolling stock or approximately $11,000 ($309,935 in current dollars) per mile, somewhat less than most contemporary Midwestern shortlines.[31]

Another memorable day occurred on February 4, 1913. The CW&DM officially issued its first public timetable, listing the schedule between Creston and West Macksburg (the mile of track into Macksburg, a few blocks north of the public square, remained unfinished, as did the depot, engine house, and turntable). If patrons expected frequent, speedy trips on the two daily-except-Sunday mixed trains between its terminals, they were surely disappointed. The morning "accommodation" left Creston Transfer at 7:00 but did not reach the end of the line until 9:05 a.m., struggling up the West Macksburg hill. There were intermediate stops at Spaulding, CB&Q Crossing, Ramsbottom, Zion, and Wilson. The afternoon mixed from Creston operated on a slightly faster schedule, leaving at 3:00 and arriving in West Macksburg at 4:50 p.m. The morning run from West Macksburg departed at 9:30 and steamed into Creston Transfer at 11:00 a.m., and the afternoon train left at 5:00 and reached its destination at 6:20 p.m. Ballast scorching it was not; speeds averaged about ten miles per hour. Some riders began calling the railroad the "Weary Willie." The explanation: "It went so slow and rocked all over." What a Creston journalist had proclaimed as "Iowa's brightest railway project" was hardly a showcase of modern railroading.[32]

To add to these unimpressive train operations, the CW&DM experienced a setback. On the evening of September 27, 1913, flames engulfed

During summer 1913, a company-owned steam-powered ditcher works at the West Macksburg cut to improve drainage. By railroad standards, the grade leading to this worksite was unusually steep, estimated at 5 percent. (*Author's collection.*)

the Creston depot. "The building was used as a depot and store house and several barrels of oil was [*sic*] consumed," reported the *Creston Morning American*. "The depot was of wood and burned very rapidly."[33]

If there was a grand opening for the CW&DM, it took place a few weeks after the Creston fire. That October, at the invitation of commercial interests in Macksburg, the Boosters Club and the Business Men's Club of Creston made a special trip over the road. Representatives from the Creston business and professional community and members of the Creston Concert Band packed several coaches supplied by the Burlington. The train included a car reserved for "ladies"; sponsors likely anticipated a raucous group of males. Crestonians considered the railroad as a way to attract business, and their counterparts in Macksburg wished to show that their community was full of "live wires" energized by this newly established rail link.[34]

Almost immediately the CW&DM became the transportation artery for Macksburg and the surrounding countryside. Newspapers reported that considerable livestock moved over the somewhat rickety track structure, mostly cattle and hogs destined for Swift & Company in Creston and packing plants in Omaha and elsewhere. This resembled outbound traffic throughout the sunset cluster. The little road hauled more than agricultural products such as grain and hay. Inbound carload shipments ranged from coal and lumber to cement and farm machinery. The figures for total volume are not known, but the railroad probably handled about three hundred to four hundred revenue cars during its initial year of operation.[35]

The railroad business was not easy. It took time to complete the line into Macksburg and install sidings. Eventually grain elevators appeared along with a lumber yard. Livestock pens were built in Macksburg, Zion, and several other locations en route to Creston. While the company's ditcher scoured out the big cut at West Macksburg, crews tamped the mostly dirt ballast and attended to other maintenance chores associated with a freshly installed track structure. Not only was the railroad burdened with a stiff grade east of the Grand River—reported to be a 5 percent incline, the steepest piece of trackage in Iowa[36]—it had to deal with the not-so-friendly Burlington. This sole interchange partner required (as was the custom) the CW&DM to maintain the Cumberland branch crossover near Spaulding, but much more troubling (and costly) were rate divisions on freight traffic. The Burlington moreover refused to permit reciprocal switching in Creston and often failed to supply empty freight cars. The shortline lacked any real bargaining power, and the only recourse was to file complaints with the Iowa Board of Railroad Commissioners and Interstate Commerce Commission. Residents came to blame the Burlington for the shortline's growing financial woes. "The lack of good will has been a serious handicap."[37]

Not long after the first trains chugged over the line, discussion resumed about building to Winterset. At the time of the Macksburg construction, Charles Judd had told the press that he expected to build from Macksburg to Winterset in 1913 and from there to Des Moines the following year. Any route to the Madison County capital would encounter hilly terrain and need to bridge the Middle River, making the seventeen or eighteen-mile extension expensive and time consuming. Still, backers thought that rock quarry traffic outside Winterset, which the Rock Island monopolized, justified expansion. Even though the Rock Island would likely resist competition, rate divisions with it and the Burlington were expected to become more favorable with this second outlet.[38]

Coinciding with talk of the Winterset extension, the press announced a possible albeit unlikely relationship with the Great Western. "It is reported on excellent authority that negotiations have been opened between the Creston, Winterset and Des Moines and the Chicago Great Western roads that may result in the building of the Creston road to a connection with the Great Western road at Peru and the operation of the two roads under a joint traffic arrangement or the taking over of the Creston road under an operating agreement by the Great Western." Such exchanges may have occurred, but the CW&DM never conducted a survey in that direction. A year or so later there was a rumor suggesting the company might build from Creston to the Great Western at Arispe.[39]

A FITFUL DOWNFALL

The balance sheet damped any immediate expansion plans. The income statement for the period January 21, 1913, to June 30, 1913, revealed net operating revenues of a paltry $513.11 ($13,627.89 in current dollars). While figures for the second half of 1913 are unavailable, the year 1914 led to a staggering net deficit of $16,124.79 ($428,264.67 in current dollars). "The line has been in operation under many vicissitudes practically all its life, and it is said that unless the property is placed under different management, Macksburg will be bereft of an improvement in which she took a great deal of pride," observed the contributor to the Macksburg section of the *History of Madison County and Its People*. As red ink spilled, the railroad decided that its only course of action was to seek court protection from creditors. On June 25, 1914, Clarence Wilson, Macksburg resident, farmer, and long-time supporter, became the receiver, general manager, and person who hopefully could lead the company through a successful reorganization.[40]

With additional funds raised from stockholders and the sale of several pieces of equipment including the ditcher, Receiver Wilson made essential improvements. Trackmen attended to soft spots that plagued the line during wet weather, replaced the worst ties, and installed some heavier sixty-five-pound rail. In a creative move, the company acquired a motor car for passenger, express,[41] and US mail service. Although this piece of rolling stock is a mystery, it may have been a small gasoline-powered chain-drive vehicle, a type that shortlines like the St. Joseph Valley Railway in Indiana used. Time Table No. 4, which became effective on August 18, 1914, showed that theoretically the motor car offered superior service to the mixed trains. It departed Creston Transfer at 7:15 a.m. and 3:30 p.m. and Macksburg at 8:45 a.m. and 4:55 p. m. and offered speeds about twice those of the previously scheduled runs. Yet the railroad dispatched this car only on Tuesdays, Thursdays, and Fridays, a decision based presumably on traffic needs. On Mondays, Wednesdays, and Saturdays, the slower mixed train, which handled the more lucrative shipments of carload and less-than-carload (LCL) freight, made a single round trip between Macksburg and Creston.[42]

Even though the receivership improved the CW&DM, the company in 1915 failed to generate black ink. While railroad operating revenues stood at $14,840.46 ($385,243 in current dollars), operating expenses reached a disappointing $17,683.62 ($459,048 in current dollars). The road, though, hardly squandered money. Approximately $10,500 ($272,569 in current dollars) of these expenditures involved payroll, but the yearly compensation for the thirty-one employees was low. The twenty trackmen, most of whom worked part-time, averaged $166 each ($4,309 in current dollars), and the three section foremen earned somewhat more, $220 (5,711 in current dollars). The two highest paid employees, the receiver/general manager and the locomotive engineer, annually received $1,800 ($46,726 in current dollars) and $1,200 ($31,151 in current dollars) respectively. Even though the workforce was subsequently trimmed, financial conditions the following year failed to improve. Income divided by expenses yielded a frightening operating ratio of 189. On July 1, 1916, the railroad shut down.[43]

Patrons were not about to give up on the CW&DM. Support remained strong, reinforced by the newly launched *Macksburg Independent*. Editor Charles Saiser pushed hard for a CW&DM resurrection and kept the community informed on its happenings. Although an area entrepreneur established an "Auto Passenger and Freight Service to and from Macksburg and All Neighboring Points," this alternative in the minds of backers was no substitute for an all-weather, freight-carrying railroad.[44]

The closing sparked a series of meetings. In early September 1916, at a gathering held at the home of the receiver, the approximately fifty men in attendance voted unanimously to push for solicitations to reopen the road. The feeling existed that the railroad must be extended to either Lorimor (Great Western) or Winterset (Rock Island). "It is highly desirable that more mileage be added eastward or northward to some connecting road that would give us the advantage of eastern markets and better freight rates."[45]

In order to resuscitate the CW&DM, management believed that a minimum of $18,000 ($434,257,000 in current dollars) was required, and by September 28, 1916, all but $1,600 ($38,600 in current dollars) had been raised. Prospects appeared promising for renewed service. Supporters expressed annoyance that citizens who failed to contribute. "There are men, men of ample means who ought to be interested in this project to take care all that is yet needed," observed the *Independent.* "But there are some folks who are always willing to go coasting if some one else will pull the sled to the top of the hill. Yes, they are even willing to ride up the hill."[46]

In a front-page headline on October 12, 1916, the *Independent* announced good news. "STOP—LOOK OUT FOR THE CARS!" The necessary funds had been secured and "train service will be established just as rapidly as the track and equipment will warrant." Editor Saiser continued to agitate for a connection with either the Great Western or Rock Island and within at least three years for "a line of railroad through Macksburg that will be worthy of the name and a credit to all."[47]

The *Independent* editor's words reflected what the largely farmer backers of the CW&DM believed. These men had just completed a plan that "covers a period of three years and the ultimate object is to put through connections with either the Great Western or Rock Island roads before the expiration of the time." The feeling emerged in the greater Macksburg area that "there will be no danger of another shut down on the road after it is once reopened."[48]

Restoring the CW&DM remained largely a Macksburg community affair. "Last Friday morning a hurry call was sent out for help to get the

As the Creston, Winterset & Des Moines faltered, the company sold one of its two secondhand 4-4-0 locomotives. In 1916 No. 6 likely went to a junk dealer. Its former Illinois Terminal lettering remains partially visible on the tender. This photograph, taken in the Macksburg about 1913, also shows one of the railroad's side-dump cars. (Author's collection.)

C. W. & D. M. track repaired some so that the old 7 spot [locomotive] might be taken to Creston for some repairs," reported the *Independent*. "A number of our town folks responded and by night the track was in shape so that early Saturday morning the engine was started out. Owing to dirt covered crossings and pasture fences across the track, it was not until about five o'clock that Creston was reached."[49]

On December 1, 1916, the rebirth officially occurred, although the CW&DM remained in receivership. Unlike in the past, trains handled only carload freight. Yet this second attempt at profitability turned out no better than before. Backers must have been saddened by the financials for 1917: operating revenues, $4,596.91 ($94,465.45 in current dollars); operating expenses, $10,323.10 ($210,267.31 in current dollars). Even with increased demand for railroad service because of America's entry into World War I, the future seemed bleak if not hopeless for an operation that continued to hemorrhage red ink.[50]

FINAL COLLAPSE

Underscoring the dire financial situation, the district judge who oversaw the bankruptcy expressed alarm. In June 1917, he told the receiver that "the road must not cause any more indebtedness" and that "the road had better sell to the highest bidder." The court, however, failed to follow through with its death sentence; the judge bowed to the receiver's commitment of additional funds to repair No. 7, the remaining locomotive (earlier No. 6 had been sold), and replace three thousand rotten ties. For this forthcoming track work, the company advertised: "MEN WANTED—20 MEN, white or colored; $2.00 and $2.50 per day; fare will be refunded up to $5 for 30 days' work." It was not an exaggeration that "courageous loyalty" had saved the day.[51]

The CW&DM limped along, providing service only on an as-needed basis. Operations became so intermittent that the Macksburg newspaper often reported these activities. "A joyful sound was heard here this morning," noted the March 18, 1918, issue. "It was the simple toot, toot of the old 7 spot pulling out for Creston." Less joyful were accounts of derailments. "The C. W. & D. M. experienced a delay in traffic this week due to a derailment last Wednesday, which tied up the services until Wednesday of this week," reported the *Independent*. "After working until night to get the cars back on the rails, the crew started for Creston and after a few miles travel the tender became derailed. Altogether the track repairs and putting the rolling stock on track again used up the major portion of the week." The railroad struggled, occasionally with borrowed motive power from the Burlington, to haul much-needed coal (because of wartime shortages and rationing by the US Fuel Administration), lumber, and other necessities to Macksburg. And it transported outbound grain and livestock.[52]

As the CW&DM deteriorated, rumors spread about the railroad's fate. Would the line be rehabilitated? Would the Great Western buy the road and extend it to Lorimor or East Peru? Would a junk dealer dismantle the property?[53]

In November 1918, the entangled saga of the final demise of the CW&DM began. On November 23, the receiver, with court approval, sold the railroad on the steps of the Madison County courthouse to Ralph Beaton and Sigmund Ornstein, scrap dealers from Columbus, Ohio, for $30,000 ($525,121 in current dollars). Although earlier these men had indicated that they "hoped that the road may be refinanced, rebuilt and extended," they quickly peddled the steel and rolling stock to Harris & Greenberg of Chicago, a firm also engaged in the salvage business. In early December, junkers began lifting the rails in Macksburg—because of wartime demands, scrap metal prices had soared.[54]

Response among railroad supporters was forthcoming. Richard Brown, the Creston attorney who had been active in the affairs of the company since its inception, brought suit in district court to restrain Harris & Greenberg from dismantling the line, arguing that the CW&DM had never been legally abandoned. The contention was also made that the railroad could be operated at a profit and that stockholders and taxpayers had not been fairly compensated for their investments. These arguments paralleled those made to save the Lyman–Villisca section of the Atlantic Southern. By the time the judge issued a restraining order, about six miles of track had been removed. The heavier sixty-five-pound steel rails soon went to Japan, and usable ties were sold to the public.[55]

The legal battle raged on. In May 1920, the *Des Moines Sunday Register* succinctly summarized these events. "The state of Iowa then [1919] started mandamus proceedings on complaint of various parties. Later the attorney general of the state joined the plaintiffs. Various applications to various judges were made. Some were granted; others were denied. Finally the attorney general secured a restraining order and a trial was held. The state was beaten, but on Jan. 20, 1920, it appealed the case." By summer the legal wrangling ended; the Iowa Supreme Court allowed the process of dismantling to proceed. And on June 26, 1920, the Iowa secretary of state cancelled the company's charter for failure to file the mandatory annual report for 1919.[56]

Faith in resuming rail service had amazing longevity. "We are not ready to give up," editorialized the *Independent* on December 12, 1918. "Cheer Up! Every cloud has a rainbow." Optimism for a revival continued among long-time backers of the railroad, but it was waning. Meetings continued to take place in Creston and Macksburg about how to resume operations. However, in the spring 1919 the *Independent* editor offered a rather forlorn commentary about the future of the CW&DM. "It is with mingled sorrow and gladness that we record this week that a wrecking crew started in real earnest to take up and load the rails. We are sorry to witness such a sad ending of an enterprise that has had so much put into it in the way of money, work, material, hope and ambition. And we are glad that since the end had to come the long lingering ailing is at an end and that there is yet hope for something that will far surpass anything that we have yet had." The newspaper added, "Rumors still continue to circulate."[57]

Toward the end of 1919 there remained a glimmer of hope. The salvage company expressed its willingness to sell the railroad, less the rolling stock and track materials already removed, for $50,000 ($761,708 in current dollars). "It is a fair price for the property in its present condition." But efforts to raise that amount floundered. Interestingly, other plans emerged. One called for operating a stub road from Burlington Crossing (near Spaulding) to Macksburg. More talk centered on regaining ownership and extending the line to a Great Western connection, "preferably to Peru."[58]

Then there were rumors that bordered on the absurd. A story circulated that unnamed promoters expected to build an interurban between Des Moines and Kansas City and the defunct CW&DM would be part of that route. Another speculated that a section of the old grade of the unfinished Rock Island extension between Winterset and Greenfield, which passed about four miles north of Macksburg and was never railed, might save the day. New construction and completion of the old Rock Island line would provide entry into the Madison County seat, giving the Macksburg railroad that long coveted outlet. The Creston section, however, would likely be retired.[59]

Speculation about railroad building a decade or two earlier might have had some credibility. After the war the use of motor vehicles on better roads increased dramatically. Newspapers regularly carried advertisements for new and used automobiles, frequently told of commercial trucking operations, and spotlighted road improvements. Vehicles were better mechanically and more affordable, and the viscous mud and gumbo were becoming less of a hindrance to travel. As early as 1911, Ed Smith, who edited the *Madisonian*, sensed the impending transportation revolution. "Will the motor car replace the passenger coach as a means of travel?" he asked. "If one had put this question ten years ago, his sanity might have been questioned. Today there is enough of argument in favor of the motor car to make the question a live one and there is no doubt but that the automobile has already cut deeply into the passenger receipts of the railroad companies." Smith added, "Dirt auto roads are being built and kept in good condition between the principal cities of Iowa and surrounding states. With the auto perfected and the highways further improved, the use of motor cars may soon become the ordinary mode of travel."[60]

Those individuals who sought to save the CW&DM lacked a grasp of economic realities. The railroad bled cash like a severed carotid artery; no professional analysis of its viability had ever been undertaken. The company had always been a troubled operation and neither rebuilding the line nor extending it made any sense. If there had been enough business in Macksburg and Zion, the Burlington would have acquired the miles near Spaulding to retain service. The Great Western had no reason to become involved. It focused on main stems and hardly wanted to build and buy what would never become more than a marginal branch, even if this extension siphoned some freight traffic from the Burlington in Creston and tapped two hamlets in Madison County. It was senseless for the Rock Island to acquire the remains of the CW&DM and build connecting trackage. Trunk carriers faced their own challenges, highlighted by adjustments to the end of federal wartime controls.[61]

Boosterism and sentimentality had driven proponents of a CW&DM resurrection. Many villagers and farmers expressed a genuine love of *their* railroad. "Do Your Best to Get Our Little Willie Home Again," editorialized the *Independent* in January 1920. Residents affectionately referred to the company as the "Crazy Willie & Dandy Molly," an unexplainable albeit memorable nickname. Pet names were a common occurrence during the Railway Age, with the Aunt Susie, Aunt Norie, and Ikey among other sunset carriers.[62]

Macksburg survived the loss of the CW&DM, although around the time of the railroad's dismemberment, the *Independent* folded and the lumber yard and oldest mercantile store closed. Other businesses continued, attesting to positive economic benefits the railroad had brought.

And for decades the population remained rather stable. Even in the twenty-first century, the village claims approximately one hundred residents, but in recent years it has lost virtually all commercial activities to businesses in Creston, Winterset, and Des Moines. More than a century after abandonment, there are scant physical remains. These remnants include the cement sidewalk to the site of the long-dismantled Macksburg depot, portions of grade that cross farm pastures, and the sixty-foot brick-lined well at Wilson that once provided water for locomotives. Still, there is no sprawl to disturb what little is left of "Iowa's brightest railway project."[63]

FIVE

IOWA & OMAHA
SHORT LINE RAILWAY

TREYNOR

DIFFERING FROM THE INLAND TOWNS OF COLLEGE SPRINGS, Elk Horn, Grant, and Macksburg, Treynor had a shorter history. Although settlers had arrived in Silver Creek Township in southcentral Pottawattamie County by the mid-nineteenth century, Treynor did not become incorporated until 1905, and its population by 1910 had reached a scant 122. For several decades, neighboring places remained crossroad enclaves dominated by a country store or church and supported by ethnic German (or Danish German) and Yankee farmers. Resembling country schools, churches were located near the homes of members and conveniently served families who gathered for worship and fellowship. What became Treynor had various names, including Four Corners, Eybergville, or simply Town. During the last decade of the century, this community, which included little more than a general store, blacksmith shop, two churches—German Lutheran and Free Congregational—and a few other establishments, was at times called High-Five. The name referred to a card game known also as Cinch or Double Pedro: "Its citizens would meet [in the saloon] for a game of cards called High-five." In 1893 the village obtained a post office. Its official (and permanent) name became Treynor, honoring Thomas T. Treynor, the Council Bluffs postmaster who facilitated this desired service. By 1907 the town boasted the Treynor Savings Bank, established in 1902, two general stores, two saloons, a furniture and implement store, a drugstore, a blacksmith shop, a livery barn, a school, and its churches.[1]

What the gestating Treynor needed was a railroad. Although Pot-tawattamie County claimed an impressive network of rail lines, Treynor had been missed. "The settlement of [Silver Creek] township was not as rapid as those reached by railroad," observed an early twentieth-century county history, "still there is a constant influx of inhabitants." To reach the trade and market centers of Council Bluffs (the county seat) and Omaha, it was necessary to travel more than a dozen miles in a southwesterly direction to the Wabash station at Silver City. It was about the same distance eastward to Carson, where a Chicago, Burlington & Quincy (Burlington) branch line met a Chicago, Rock Island & Pacific (Rock Island) appendage, providing connections with each road's east–west main lines at Hastings and Avoca, respectively. For farmers, who nearly always sought the Council Bluffs and Omaha grain and livestock markets, this meant transporting corn, oats, wheat, and hogs by wagon and driving cattle (rarely hogs) to Silver City. A for-hire firm supplied this transportation—Long Brothers made two weekly round trips with three-mule teams to transport livestock, grain, and other farm products to Council Bluffs and return with coal, lumber, and groceries. Because of bad roads, these movements could become nightmarish.[2]

Before Treynor residents and neighboring farmers embarked on a railroad project, there was a hint of the community's quest to improve its commercial position. It did not focus on road betterments but rather the launching in the 1890s of the Treynor Creamery Association. This short-lived enterprise produced butter and milk (perhaps hand-bottled), dominating local sales and enabling more convenient distribution to nearby markets.[3]

A SHORTLINE EVOLVES

As the new century emerged, the lure of interurban railways became widespread. Because of their not-so-splendid isolation, Treynor area residents began to discuss the possibility of building an electric road. This exciting technology inspired residents not to limit their vision to a modest trolley linking Treynor with Council Bluffs and Omaha. The goal would be a 150-mile, heavy-duty interurban between Omaha, Council Bluffs, and Des Moines capable of handling carload freight together with passengers, mail, and express. George Adams, a former express company employee and "grand promoter" from Walnut (also in Pottawattamie County), served as the principal sparkplug. Former Iowa governor Leslie Shaw, Des Moines businessman F. M. Hubbell, and an English money syndicate later became involved.

Once the economy rebounded following the Panic of 1907, a series of meetings took place in several western Iowa communities, and these discussions led to the official incorporation of the Iowa & Omaha Short Line Railway (I&OSL). This document was not filed in Iowa but instead in South Dakota, a move explained by that state's friendly corporation laws. Using the wording of contemporary documents, the railroad could "be operated by either steam, electricity, gas or gasoline," but the intent was electricity. And the projected route was indicated. Tracks would extend eastward from Council Bluffs through Treynor, Carson, Oakland, Walnut, "near Elk Horn," Exira, "via North Branch," Guthrie Center, Panora, and south of Perry, where it would connect with the Inter-Urban Railway for entrance into Des Moines. Although Adams became president, Treynorites dominated the company, serving as secretary, treasurer, and members of the board of directors. Soon the board dispatched Adams to visit major money markets, including New York, Chicago, and St. Louis, "to confer with different bond houses and large contractors that want to bid on the construction of the railroad."[4]

Backers of the I&OSL were not alone in wishing to build an interurban between Council Bluffs and Des Moines. The feeling existed among other interurban proponents that the Rock Island, whose Council Bluffs–Omaha stem was the sole direct rail connection between these cities, would be vulnerable to competition, especially for through passengers, largely because of its winding nature. Coinciding with the inception of the I&OSL was the organization of the Des Moines & Council Bluffs Railway (DM&CB), orchestrated by business interests in Des Moines and reportedly with "the financial backing of an English syndicate." Its route would run from Des Moines southeast to Knoxville and then west through Winterset, Greenfield, Lewis, Oakland, and Council Bluffs—but would miss Treynor.[5]

Resembling scores of "paper" interurbans, nothing happened in a tangible way with the DM&CB, and at first not much took place with the I&OSL. Public meetings, though, were held. Take one in Exira, an Aububon County town of about eight hundred residents. I&OSL representatives told attendees that "if the people of Exira respond to that kind of generous treatment [5 percent property tax] they can secure the local Division Terminal of the Road." It was a tantalizing incentive.[6] In late 1908, I&OLS backers adopted a much less ambitious objective: Treynor to Council Bluffs. Since a long-distance interurban appeared problematic, Treynor area residents wanted a rail link to the outside world as soon as possible. The company set its immediate sights on a connection with the Wabash Railroad at Neoga, a scheduled stop for local passenger trains about five miles from Council Bluffs Union Station. The Treynor community knew, too, that the Omaha & Council Bluffs Street Railway (O&CBStRy) was in the process of extending track from its Manawa trolley line southeast to the Iowa School for the Deaf. Discussions centered on freight moving over the Wabash and passengers taking streetcars to Council Bluffs and Omaha by connecting with the O&CBStRy near the state school.[7]

As 1909 began, newspapers reported that the I&OSL would not be operated by electricity but by steam. It would stretch the dozen miles from Treynor to a connection at Pony Creek (Neoga) with the Wabash. This trackage also would be about three miles from the O&CBStRy, "grading for which has been completed." Preliminary surveys were soon run. Rather than employing a professional locating engineer, the I&OSL hired Joel Harley Mayne, the Pottawattamie County surveyor. He engaged his office assistants to aid in this work.[8]

Activity increased during the spring and summer months. In April detailed survey work commenced. Wabash headquarters in St. Louis approved the right of future I&OSL trains to operate between Neoga and Council Bluffs. In July the shortline once more looked locally for assistance, signing W. M. Lanna, bridge contractor for Pottawattamie County, to conduct grading, build several small bridges, install culverts, and add right-of-way fencing. The company had no difficulty acquiring the hundred-foot right-of-way strip between Treynor and Neoga;

it awarded stock in exchange for land titles. In a few cases, bonds were granted. No condemnation proceedings became necessary.[9]

In fall 1909, the I&OSL had to adjust its immediate building plans. The goal of reaching a junction with the O&CBStRy collapsed when it sought to condemn land parcels owned by the Wabash between the Pony Creek area and the state school. Wabash lawyers prevented the loss of this property; construction would not occur. No explanation for the Wabash opposition was publicly stated, but it probably did not want the I&OSL to extend its service reach.[10]

Fortunately, no ongoing war occurred between the I&OSL and the Wabash. Friendly cooperation marked their relationship. Yet this did not mean that trains would soon be operating between the Neoga siding and Treynor. Construction would not start until later in 1910.

How would the "Short Line" be financed? Although details are not fully known, township property taxes may have been discussed but were never sought. This made the road unique among cluster carriers, although the ill-fated Iowa Northern Railroad was almost exclusively backed by New Vienna farmers. Prosperous agrarians from Keg Creek and Silver Creek townships became the financial engines. William Husz, William Orr, Henry Saar, Nickolous Sucksdorf, William Trede, and Bernhard Volkens supplied the bulk of the money; they bought company stock and its 6 percent short-term bonds. Their collective commitments were estimated at approximately $230,000 ($6,720,235 in current dollars). These grain, hay, and livestock producers could well open their pocketbooks, being "among the wealthiest farmers in western Iowa." Other farmers made sizable stock and bond purchases. Townspeople contributed lesser sums, although Treynor banker August Dammrow, who also owned a nearby farm, stands out as a substantial contributor.[11]

What motivated enthusiasm for the railroad and the generous response by farmers? Most of all, the richest agrarians and their neighbors longed for a rapid, dependable, and less expensive way to get cattle, hogs, and grain to market. These desires were no different from those of agrarians who donated land, invested money, and supported tax measures for the other sunset railroads. Henry Saar likely had another reason. He allegedly wanted to subdivide a portion of his farm into town lots.

Treynorites, resembling residents in other inland communities, sought convenient (and cheaper) access to coal, lumber, and consumer goods, and they desired a better way to make personal trips to Council Bluffs and Omaha. They likely were caught up in these last years of railroad fever and feared permanent isolation.[12]

Early in the construction process, I&OSL officials sought to ensure a successful outcome. In October 1909, the company hired an experienced railroader, naming M. G. Carter, former trainmaster for the Wabash at Stanberry, Missouri, as assistant general manager and general superintendent. He was described as "one of the best known and most popular railroad men of this section." (Apparently his relationship with the I&OSL was brief.) To bolster future traffic, President Adams actively (but unsuccessfully) participated in efforts to establish an independent cooperative packing plant in Council Bluffs. He joined an exploratory committee that worked with an official of Brittain & Company, a meat-processing firm in Marshalltown, Iowa.[13]

During the 1910 building season, area residents encountered more than lofty speeches and optimistic newspaper reports. They did not, however, witness modern railroad construction equipment and techniques. The small Lanna firm's workforce used mule teams to pull plows and old-fashioned metal scrapers to shape the roadbed. There was also pick, shovel, and wheelbarrow work. Technology and financial limitations explain why the building progress was painfully slow. By the close of 1910, only the three miles from the Wabash interchange toward Treynor had been readied for ties and rails. Happily, the road did not face an impending tax-payment deadline, and when needed, additional funds became available.

Completed in June 1911, the I&OSL had been an expensive undertaking. One estimate indicated that construction, rolling stock, and other essentials resulted in a final cost exceeding $400,000 ($11,270,362 in current dollars). In the 1950s, Treynor physician Dr. Robert Stephens, who had invested $800 ($22,540 in current dollars) in the railroad, recalled sarcastically: "Hell, that railroad cost more per mile than the Union Pacific main line." That, of course, was an exaggeration. Expenditures per mile stood at slightly over $23,000 ($760,540 in current dollars) compared for example to the Iowa & Southwestern (Ikey) that spent $17,720 ($481,927 in current dollars) per mile.[14]

CELEBRATION

By late June 1911, the immediate goal of Short Line backers had been realized with twelve miles of track. The road consisted of sixty-five-pound relay rail spiked to untreated ties thrown down on the grade. The track lacked ballast and tamping and had multiple soft spots. Irrespective of the delay, cost, or condition of the railroad, Treynor residents and those on nearby farms wanted to welcome the iron horse. Announced a newspaper wire story: "June 29 has been fixed as the date of celebration, and things that will not be done on that day will be those not worth noticing."[15]

The day for celebrating may have been prematurely set. By the morning of June 29, the final section of track had yet to be installed. But by noon the work gang, composed of a couple dozen Greek and Italian laborers, remained only about two hundred yards short of the newly completed depot on the north side of Treynor. The contractor employed an incentive: "A keg of beer was put in front of the depot. When the last rail was laid, they could drink the beer." Soon the keg was tapped, and the first train arrived.[16]

What took place on that hot and windy Thursday afternoon and early evening was one of the most unusual opening celebrations for any railroad, large or small. Most of the scheduled activities were predictable: speeches, a band concert, and a baseball game. A small carnival added to the festivities. When several individuals spoke before the assembled crowd, their remarks were anticipated. Perry Kearney, the local resident who presided, not only said that the occasion honored the completion of the Council Bluffs linkage but optimistically predicted that it would be the first section of an eastward line. John Hess, the Council Bluffs attorney who represented the company, eulogized the backers; O. B. Towne, member of the Commercial Club of Treynor, expressed his hope that the town would continue to grow "until it would be impossible to determine where the limits of Council Bluffs end and those of Treynor begin." And President Adams indicated that he was "not unmindful of

A newspaper artist sketched this view of Ransom Jones, a young farmer who accidently joined the performing aeronaut in a balloon ascension in Treynor during the June 29, 1911, celebration of the completion of the Iowa & Omaha Short Line Railway. Fortunately, Jones landed safely. (*Author's collection.*)

the predictions of disaster and the general impression that nothing but failure could attend the effort." The comments made by Hess, however, were interrupted by a strong gust of wind. "The guy ropes of the large tent that was erected for the accommodation of the audience gave way on the south side and created some confusion." No one was injured, and after a short delay the program resumed.[17]

The highlight of the day's festivities did not involve the hammering of a ceremonial spike or a grand dinner but rather a hot-air balloon ascension. This event had originally been announced for the morning, but because of windy conditions it was rescheduled for the afternoon. A persistent wind forced another postponement until early evening. In preparation for the ascent, a fire in an open trench superheated air to make buoyant the bulky rubber and canvas bag. The advertised program called for the "aeronaut," an unidentified itinerant balloonist, to rise above the town, perform an act from a trapeze bar, and parachute safety to the ground. That order of events never happened.

The star of the ascension would not be the balloonist but Ransom Jones, a young farmer who lived northwest of Treynor. When wind began to sway the inflated balloon, more and more spectators were asked to help contain it. Jones volunteered. "He was warned to stand back, but was too excited and too curious to keep himself clear of trouble," observed a Council Bluffs reporter. "When the word finally came to cast off, he let go with his hands, but the rope got him by the leg with a half hitch, and he was hoisted aloft with the rising balloon, willy nilly." Remembered a spectator, "He missed the bank building by 25 feet." Jones attempted to climb down from the ropes where he was clinging to reach the balloonist and his parachute. "But the parachute was not large enough to carry them both to safety on the rapidly receding ground, and the aeronaut ordered him back into the rigging." Although the aeronaut descended harmlessly, Jones remained far above the earth. Soaring to an estimated twenty-five hundred feet, he could see the lights of Omaha to the northwest. In time the hot air cooled, and the balloon gradually drifted downward. At last Jones landed in an open area four miles from the launch site. He was not hurt. "The evening stunt was pulled off therefore before a smaller crowd, and comparatively few observed the daring ride of Ransom Jones, the involuntary aeronaut."[18]

THE I&OSL COMES TO LIFE

What is known of hiring practices of these cluster railroads is sketchy, with the I&OSL being no exception. Area residents, often young men, were probably employed for maintenance and train service. It is known that the company secured the services of William Sigler, an experienced locomotive engineer. "He had been the engineer on one of the [Rock Island's] fastest trains between Des Moines and Omaha," recalled a local farmer in the 1950s. "He told me once, 'Ray, the reason I'm working for this jerkwater railroad is booze.'" The Rock Island had likely dismissed Sigler for violating "Rule G," which prohibited the consumption of alcohol. Even if he had not overcome his addiction, I&OSL officials probably believed that he would not pose serious work-related problems. After all, trains moved slowly and at times barely crept along.[19]

Once the Iowa Board of Railroad Commissioners approved the opening, the I&OSL inaugurated regular service, although operating details are limited. Early on, it apparently provided one or occasionally two daily-except-Sunday mixed trains between Treynor and Neoga, and these movements may have continued between Neoga and Council Bluffs. If they did, most passengers probably transferred to a O&CBStRy streetcar near the state school. They also could have boarded the daily northbound Wabash local that stopped at Neoga at 9:55 a.m. and arrived in Council Bluffs at 10:15 a.m. The train departed Council Bluffs for its southbound run at 5:00 p.m. and fifteen minutes later steamed into Neoga. Ample time was theoretically provided for business or shopping in the Pottawattamie capital and in neighboring Omaha.

An I&OSL train might not keep to its advertised schedule. Reminiscent of many shortlines, operations could be informal. "In the spring the engine would come chugging along a valley and all of a sudden a passenger or crew would sing out 'Mushrooms!'" recalled a Treynor resident in the 1950s, "and [the engineer] would stop the train and everyone would get off and pick mushrooms." There were likely other distractions, maybe bluebells or other wildflowers.[20]

The I&OSL lacked complexity in its physical train operations. When the company built a small yard in Treynor, it installed a hand-operated turntable. The crew members, however, did not care for the rigors of manually turning the locomotive, "so the train ran backward on one of its return trips." Running backwards was potentially dangerous, yet low speeds reduced risk of accidents. A well and water tank never appeared in Treynor. Instead, workers dug a twelve-foot square, thirty-two-foot well on a farm a mile and a half outside of town, and a gasoline pump brought water to the tender. A small engine house was also missing.[21]

The principal purpose of the railroad involved freight movements to and from Treynor, where the company had its only depot. It did employ two agents, including one housed in office space at Pearl and Broadway in Council Bluffs. The leading cattle and hog producers, who had contributed much of the capital, became the largest customers. In 1914 the state railroad board revealed that livestock constituted 30 percent of the road's freight movements. The next greatest volumes consisted of grain at 17 percent, coal at 12 percent, and lumber at 5 percent. The remainder were miscellaneous shipments, including less-than-carload (LCL) freight.[22]

Whether the I&OSL was hauling passengers or freight, operations were conducted safely—there were no recorded serious or fatal injuries. One stressful travel event, though, received considerable journalistic attention. In late January 1915, a major snowstorm and bone-chilling temperatures coupled with a minor derailment stranded the mixed train for fourteen hours. Aboard the coach were thirty-one passengers, including a dozen Treynor school teachers en route to a normal institute in Council Bluffs. During the overnight hours, the thermometer plunged and "all suffered severely from the night and the cold passenger coach." Fortunately, several male passengers secured fuel and food from nearby farmhouses. Had they failed, "some of the passengers might have perished."[23]

As with the other cluster roads, the I&OSL acquired a used 4-4-0 locomotive. This piece of motive power had once served the Milwaukee. It earned the pet name "Old Ironsides," but that was not a wholly apt moniker. It was old, but it was not reliable and remained on the property for only a short time. The Council Bluffs newspaper described it as "a very poor engine." When the company officially ended operations in 1916, its rolling stock consisted of a leased locomotive (probably from the Wabash), a passenger coach (combine), four boxcars, six flatcars, and two coal cars. Its equipment roster resembled that of most modest shortlines, including other cluster carriers.[24]

Early on, directors must have sensed that earnings posed a threat to the long-term health of their railroad. They surely realized it would take time to improve trackage, equipment, and the traffic base. For the year 1912, a time when the national economy thrived, operating revenues totaled $9,871.49 ($268,459 in current dollars), but expenses amounted to a staggering $18,548.43 ($504,446 in current dollars). There were other financial obligations, including overdue interest payments on outstanding debt. This produced a yearly net loss of $26,238.05 ($713,590 in current dollars).[25]

Everyone involved with the I&OSL understood that it faced a challenging future. Although the railroad failed to make operating expenses, it provided Treynor with much appreciated freight and passenger service. And as with the Iowa & Southwestern (Ikey), Wells Fargo held the express franchise. The arrival of this steel outlet stimulated new and existing businesses. The Fullerton Lumber Company, an area chain operator, became a notable arrival. In 1911 this building materials firm established its Treynor yard. Soon Charles Hammer constructed a grain elevator, and F. H. Schultz relocated his hog oiler manufacturing plant to a siding so "he could have daily shipping facilities." Public demand and significantly reduced coal costs led the town to open a municipal light and power plant, and builders responded to a shortage of private dwellings. A boom was on.[26]

What should be the proper course of action for the struggling I&OSL? Although several well-healed farmers took out mortgages on their land to provide operating funds, the railroad in early summer 1913 suspended operations because of a cash shortage. The directors, backed by the ten largest bondholders, concluded that their best response would be a receivership. These investors held most of the $150,000 ($3,983,909 in current dollars) of short-term construction bonds that had matured on June 10, 1911. That legal strategy was immediately pursued. On July 10, 1913, a Pottawattamie County district court judge granted the application. Hopefully, the various claims against the railroad, including a substantial one made by contractor W. M. Lanna, could be resolved and service resumed. August Dammrow, Treynor Savings Bank cashier and I&OSL director and bondholder, assumed the role of receiver. Once again trains rolled.[27]

The income statement for 1914 hardly looked encouraging. Revenues for operations totaled $10,625.90 ($278,572 in current dollars), but railroad expenses reached $12,752.77 ($334,339 in current dollars). The overall operating losses stood at $3,297.01 ($86,442 in current dollars), showing a sizeable reduction from the red ink generated the previous year. An extensively reported lawsuit was brought in early 1915 against Receiver Dammrow. It was filed by Enid Shaw, the former governor's daughter and investor in the ill-fated attempt by the Shaw syndicate to gain control of the Atlantic Northern & Southern Railroad (AN&S) and I&OSL. In March she won a settlement for $3,000 plus interest and costs for a note given to her by her father. "The jury gave all that Miss Shaw asked, the verdict being for $3,510.00 ($91,116 in current dollars)." It is uncertain whether she ever received that amount. By then it was doubtful that anyone honestly believed the plans of Adams, Shaw, and their associates to consolidate the I&OSL with the AN&S would materialize. It was sheer fantasy to think these properties would be extended to Des Moines or anywhere else.[28]

Even though the operating ratio had shown an improvement, first mortgage bondholders expressed concern about their multithousand-dollar investments. Receiver Dammrow filed papers with the district court to sell the railroad, and on September 12, 1915, the judge ordered it sold. Although various parties sought to have their claims honored, the court decreed that the first in line would not be the first mortgage bondholders but the county taxing authority and the Lanna Construction Company. The consensus among the knowledgeable was that a sale would never generate enough money to satisfy every claimant.[29]

COLLAPSE AND DEMISE

After lengthy legal delays, the court-ordered sale finally took place in February 1916, and W. M. Lanna won the bidding. He agreed to pay $24,000 ($579,010 in current dollars) for the I&OSL, far below the cost of construction. Yet finalization of that commitment became a drawn-out process. Lanna received seven extensions from the court while he negotiated for the disposal of the railroad to other parties, but he could not raise the necessary funds. Said the court: "It appearing that W. M.

Lanna has failed to carry out his bid for the property in conformity with the bid approved by the count on March 1, 1916, the sale is annulled and the order set aside." On October 11, 1916, the judge commanded Receiver Dammrow to advertise for a second bidding in the *Council Bluffs Nonpareil*, *Omaha Daily Bee*, and *St. Louis Post-Dispatch*. This event was scheduled for October 30, 1916, at the Pottawattamie County Courthouse main entrance.[30]

Before its second and final sale, the I&OSL limped along with frequent service disruptions, the track structure continuing to require extensive and expensive repairs. The railroad drifted rapidly into decrepitude, and by spring of 1916 "transportation slum" aptly described the property. During this time, rumors circulated about its fate. The most common supposition was that the O&CBStRy would take control of the property, electrify it, and maybe extend it to other parts of Pottawattamie County or beyond. A more plausible one suggested that the Wabash would acquire ownership; after all, the I&OSL in 1915 still generated several hundred carloads of freight. Would this be another Ikey rumored possibility? One farfetched notion involved intervention by William B. McKinley, Champaign, Illinois, banker and US congressman. This wealthy entrepreneur controlled one of the nation's largest interurbans, the Illinois Traction Company or "McKinley System." It recently had bridged the Mississippi River to provide entry into St. Louis and seemed destined to reach Chicago. The McKinley organization also had invested in electric power plants in southwestern Iowa, suggesting an interest in this part of the state.[31]

Since no outside party sought to acquire the I&OSL and none of the previous local interests, including well-to-do farmers, had the will to make additional investments, the prudent alternative seemed to be abandonment. Already the railroad had suspended operations, reportedly on June 30, 1916.[32]

If and when the I&OLS disappeared, residents might not have viewed the event as a transportation disaster, seriously damaging the local economy. Motorized vehicles had already made their presence in the county, and public roads were improving. Recent happenings offered livestock producers an alternative method of shipping their hogs to the South Omaha market. The "auto truck" provided that hauling recourse.

"The first few shipments will be just experimental," explained hog-collar manufacturer F. H. Shultz in July 1916, soon after the railroad shutdown. "The transfer company which is handling the hogs is making us a rate of 35 cents per hundred for the first few batches and then when they have something to go on they will draw up a regular schedule." Added Shultz: "By truck it takes only two hours and a half to get hogs from home to Omaha yards, and the shrunk [shrinkage in body weight] is not as heavy as when shipping on the railroad." The truck delivery service worked and continued. When the I&OSL quit permanently, rack and ruin did not follow for livestock shippers.[33]

The closing chapter of the Treynor Short Line developed into a legal muddle. The announced winner of the public auction was Herman Sonker, "witnessed by a big crowd of men about the court house." Sonker, who represented a Kansas City "syndicate," bid $21,250 ($512,665 in current dollars) for the property. August Dammrow and George Adams also participated, bidding $20,000 ($482,508 in current dollars) and $19,500 ($470,445 in current dollars) respectively. "This is taken to mean that the purchasers [syndicate] will demand either further support from the community or will endeavor to secure concessions of some sort in consideration of the road being opened for traffic," observed the *Nonpareil*. "There was an air of much secrecy about the future of the line and the purpose of the bidder."[34]

In a strange twist, Sonker, who apparently had developed a relationship with Adams, did not walk away with ownership of the I&OSL. On November 8, 1916, Receiver Dammrow sold the railroad at an undisclosed price to Edward Wickham, a Council Bluffs financier and building contractor, and awarded him a deed of ownership. Although the amount of this cash transaction was not publicly announced, it probably exceeded what Sonker had agreed to pay. When Sonker learned of this deal, he took legal action, but his efforts failed to defeat the new owner. The court awarded control to Wickham. Sonker did score a success in the state, pouncing on the much larger and abandoned Chicago, Anamosa & Northern Railroad. In December 1916, he won ownership of this property, dismantling it for its junk value the following year.[35]

What did loser Sonker and winner Wickham expect to do with the I&OSL? The former, in conjunction with Adams, supposedly planned to operate the defunct railroad and extend it eastward, perhaps through Walnut to Oakland.[36] The latter made it clear that he would not junk the shortline. "Wickham definitely declared that his intention is to rehabilitate the road and put it into operation. He had no dreams at present of extending the line, but said that if it proved feasible or desirable, he has the money to make the extension without putting it up to the people of Treynor." These positive dispositions toward the I&OSL surely pleased its supporters, though they never happened and were only wishful thinking.[37]

Accounts of Wickham's intentions became contradictory. One indicated that he had sold the property to the Joe Joseph Brothers Company, a Cincinnati, Ohio, junk dealer. Somewhat later Wickham was identified as being behind the formation of the Iowa & Omaha Interurban Railway Company, designed to operate the line in conjunction with the O&CBStRy. By this time, interurban building had virtually ended in the country, and streetcar extensions were mostly shelved because of the war.[38]

At last, the I&OSL had an ending. The *Nonpareil* reported that Wickham and his attorneys had been unsuccessful in their efforts to entice the Wabash to take over the I&OSL, and so Wickham sold the metal to the Cincinnati company—likely for a tidy profit. "The consideration will probably run somewhere between $40,000 [$821,990 in current dollars] and $50,000 [$1,027,488 in current dollars], depending upon the value of the material, laid down upon the cars when ready for shipment." The removal work was scheduled to begin on July 1, 1917, and the rails were thought destined for rerolling in Moline, Illinois. That may not have happened; as with other cluster railroads abandoned during World War I, those who possessed scrap steel cashed in on its soaring price. It seems likely that a St. Louis firm acquired the metal from that Cincinnati concern in October 1917 and quickly removed the rails. By late fall, the defunct I&OSL had become a stripped roadbed with hundreds of broken and rotten ties strewn about. The single-story Treynor depot was sold, cut in half, and moved. Much later, some residents wrongly believed that the railroad did have a final value: "The steel was shot at the Germans."[39]

The lifting of I&OSL rails coincided with the first time any significant mileage of the national railroad network had been junked. "In 1917 there was 451 miles of railroad actually taken up," reported *Railway Age*. It added, "The abandonment of railroads in the past year marks a very important state in the economic development of the country." The I&OSL joined the *Railway Age* listing of defunct shortlines.[40]

The life and death of the I&OSL involved only a small population and a single community. Nevertheless, the road's fate was long remembered by area residents—and probably not fondly. The failure of the railroad had its greatest negative impact on its principal backers. "Henry Saar put in a total of 98 thousand dollars [$2,364,292 in current dollars] in cash or land," observed a feature writer for the *Omaha World-Herald* in 1956. "His son Arthur Saar lost a 160-acre farm estimated to be worth two hundred dollars [$4,825 in current dollars] an acre at the time. Nick Suckstorff [*sic*], another cattle feeder and investor, lost 75 thousand dollars [$1,809,407 in current dollars] in the deal." Financial setbacks, though exceptional, affected most individuals who had invested directly or indirectly in these cluster shortlines. When backers had opened their pocketbooks, their support for railroad projects had not been irrational acts. What they experienced was a sea-change in transportation. The rapidly developing Motor Age doomed the vast majority of these newly opened, agriculturally dependent shortlines. This was true in Iowa and throughout America.[41]

SIX

DES MOINES & RED OAK RAILWAY

GESTATION OF AN INTERURBAN

RAILROAD HISTORIANS, BOTH PROFESSIONAL AND AMATEUR, have chronicled extensively the electric interurban industry. There exists the classic work by George Hilton and John Due, *The Electric Interurban Railways in America*, a carefully crafted study published more than sixty years ago. There are scores of focused semischolarly studies, some of which the Central Electric Railfans' Association has produced for more than eighty years. Moreover, a variety of pieces that have appeared in academic journals and enthusiast publications add to this literature. Articles discuss unbuilt or "paper" traction projects. A cursory glance suggests that *all* aspects of the interurban experience have been covered. A few obscure electrics have yet to be examined, and some warrant greater attention, including the enduring and profitable Piedmont & Northern Railway of the Carolinas.[1]

A void still remains. It involves interurbans that fall in a category between paper entities and wholly or partially operational lines. The number of such firms is unknown but might total less than a dozen. Specifically, these interurbans (or at least, lines projected as such) were chartered and *partially* built. Maybe a significant amount of grading, bridging, and culvert work took place, but they never turned a wheel. These companies, in Iowa or elsewhere, may have been reconstituted (in the minds of their promoters) as carriers that would employ internal combustion, for example McKeen motor cars, or become conventional steam roads.

An illustration of a stillborn interurban—yet one that started to take shape physically—is the Des Moines & Red Oak Railway (DM&RO). This line, which was planned to link the Iowa capital with the Montgomery County seat, emerged during the heyday of intercity traction excitement. The DM&RO is a textbook example of this neglected dimension of interurban and early twentieth-century shortline history.

Although multiple steam shortlines emerged in western Iowa during the sunset era, rumors flourished that they might become longer, connected, and ideally electrified. Talks ensued about linking the Iowa & Southwestern (Ikey) with the Atlantic Northern & Southern (AN&S) and somehow tying the Iowa & Omaha Short Line (I&OSL) to the AN&S. There was speculation that the Ikey would extend into northwestern Missouri; the Creston, Winterset & Des Moines (CW&DM), née Creston, Winterset & Des Moines Electric Railway, would enter Des Moines or at least Winterset or possibly East Peru or Lorimor, where a connection would be forged with the Chicago Great Western Railroad; the I&OSL would build east from Treynor to the Iowa capital; and the AN&S would seek Sioux City. If the AN&S did not arrive in the state's third largest city, the line would "definitely" be built to Manning, where it would interchange with three trunk lines. The AN&S, CW&DM, and I&OSL were proposed as interurbans, and the Ikey during its gestation and near the end of its life might conceivably have become one. Not to be overlooked was the Minneapolis, Kansas City & Gulf Electric Railway, a highly publicized lunatic-fringe proposal. In 1907 promoters sought to construct an interurban that would connect the Twin Cities and Galveston, Texas, and serve Des Moines, Kansas City, Wichita, Oklahoma City, Dallas, and Houston together with scores of intermediate places (roughly the route of today's Interstate 35). The company planned to build in sections, installing the first between Minneapolis and Des Moines. "As each section is completed it will be immediately placed in operation, thus producing revenues." The Panic of 1907 ended all discussion about constructing this "wrong way transcontinental" interurban. In this rarified atmosphere, the Red Oak & North Eastern Interurban Promotion Company (RO&NEIPCo), precursor of the DM&RO, appeared.[2]

By the turn of the twentieth century, Red Oak, a lively county seat of 4,355, benefited from a mixed economic base. In addition to serving as a thriving agricultural trading center, it sported various manufacturing concerns. These included an iron foundry, cannery, and the Thomas D. Murphy Company, a nationally recognized publisher of calendars. Adding to the community's vitality were three financial institutions: Farmers National Bank, Red Oak National Bank, and Red Oak Trust & Savings Bank. The town also enjoyed good railroad connections. In 1869 the westward-advancing Burlington & Missouri River Railroad, a Chicago, Burlington & Quincy Railroad affiliate (Burlington), arrived from the East and soon reached Council Bluffs, where it linked up with the Union Pacific–Central Pacific transcontinental route. A few years later, the Burlington installed a thirty-seven-mile branch from Red Oak southwestward to its Council Bluffs–Kansas City line in Hamburg, Iowa. Then, as part of a branch line–building blitz in southern Iowa and northern Missouri in the late 1870s and early 1880s, it constructed twenty miles north from Red Oak to Griswold. These additions were designed to generate feeder traffic and to stymie incursions by the Jay Gould system into "Burlington territory." The Chicago, Rock Island & Pacific (Rock Island), probably to protect its domain, built a fifteen-mile extension south from Atlantic to Griswold, effectively blocking movement northward by the Burlington. Gould posed the greater threat, but after the mid-1880s the likelihood of penetration lessened and by 1890 had disappeared. The prosperous Burlington continually improved operations along its main stem, which by 1882 had reached Denver, Colorado. At the turn of the century, the company double-tracked and reduced grades and curvatures along sections of its primary route across Iowa, and before World War I it erected brick passenger depots in most Hawkeye State county seats. The state-of-the-art Red Oak depot opened in 1903. It featured a restaurant ("lunchroom"), being the only depot between Creston and Omaha to have one.[3]

Except for Council Bluffs and Sioux City, Red Oak was unusual in western Iowa in that it once had a street railway. This two-mile animal-car line, which opened in the early 1880s, connected hotels in the commercial core with the Burlington station. The company's mule cars operated on a day-long schedule, but later they met only the principal passenger trains. In the early twentieth century, this hometown firm, which never was much of a moneymaker, faced an assessment for a street-paving project. Rather than pay, it shut down. Its history supported a contemporary observer who opined that "it seems to be a well known fact that a street railway or an opera house in a town or city of less than 25,000 will not pay." Apparently, there were never plans to electrify the Red Oak operation or to make it the core for a rural trolley or a longer interurban.[4]

The idea of an electric railroad nevertheless materialized in Red Oak. Following the wave of interurban building that followed the brief Panic of 1903, Red Oak and Montgomery County residents discussed the possibility of obtaining this much ballyhooed transportation form. In a front-page editorial, "Needs for New Year," the *Red Oak Express* on December 29, 1905, listed as a top priority "an electric road connecting Shenanhoah and Atlantic." This wish-list also included a hospital, normal school, and "park within easy distance of the square to serve as a resort for our townspeople and also for a Chautauqua ground." Red Oak boosters sought to make their community "The City of Progress and Enterprise" and "The Hub and Metropolis of S.-W. Iowa."[5]

Enthusiasm for an electric railroad is understandable. If a community lacked adequate steam railroad service or faced a monopoly, an interurban could be a godsend. Traction companies allowed farmers, villagers, and others convenient access to socioeconomic opportunities offered by urban places, and merchants and professionals could tap an expanded trading and service area. Interurbans fostered goodwill between urban and rural localities. Traveling salesmen could make their calls with greater ease and efficiency. When in operation, electric lines maintained frequent passenger service; cars typically ran on hourly schedules during much of the day while steam roads often provided at best only double-daily service. Such scheduling meant trains might arrive and depart at inconvenient times. Electric cars stopped at most public road crossings to accommodate riders. Some interurbans, including most of those operating in Iowa, handled steam road equipment. In the public mind, a multipurpose electric road would have a positive impact on competing steam carriers, improving service and reducing rates. It was widely assumed that with an interurban, real-estate values, both urban and rural, would increase, even soar. "They universally pay their owners well and do wonders in developing the cities they touch and in increasing the value of contiguous farm land," argued an Iowa editor in 1907. If the interurban company generated its own electricity, the excess could be sold along its route. For farmers this could be meaningful for needs ranging from powering electric lights to grinding feed and pumping water. Everyone realized that electric traction offered a practical alternative to the poor-quality Hawkeye State roads. Furthermore, interurban cars were clean, quiet, and potentially fast. As final clinchers, their stock would appreciate and pay cash dividends, and their bonds would yield regular payments.[6]

As the new century began, a series of public meetings in western Iowa discussed building electric interurbans, including at least two proposals that would serve Red Oak. The first promising one came in summer 1906 when Clarence Ross and Charles Judd of the Engineering, Construction & Securities Company announced their plan to acquire electric light plants in Atlantic and Red Oak. Facilities would supply power for a connecting twenty-five-mile interurban. This Atlantic and Red Oak line would parallel the Griswold branches of the Rock Island and Burlington, but it failed to advance much beyond the planning stage.[7]

A false start hardly dampened interurban enthusiasm. "There is scarcely any doubt that a new railroad of some kind, probably an electric interurban, will be built from this county in a northeasterly direction in the near future," predicted a Red Oak editor in April 1907. "A notable vacancy consisting of a broad and rich territory without railroads is to be found between Montgomery County and the capital city." Not only did the Red Oak press reveal a keen interest in such a project, but newspapers in Des Moines began to support an interurban to the southwest. Boosters wanted Des Moines (1910 population of 86,368) to become a traction hub, envying the electric railway network that had catapulted another state capital, Indianapolis, Indiana, into a "first-class city." With the presence of the Inter-Urban Railway and the evolving Fort Dodge, Des Moines & Southern Railroad, could the Indianapolis model be emulated? Perhaps. A Missouri newspaper sensed acute interurban fever in the Iowa capital. "Interurban lines out of Des Moines have been so successful that the people of that place look favorably upon any projects of this kind." Electric railways meant urban growth and prosperity, or so traction proponents argued. "The modern interurban road is the latest achievement of the railroader's art," asserted the *Red Oak Express*. Intercity electric roads oozed modernity.[8]

Even though the Panic of 1907 disrupted the American economy, financial conditions by the following year had improved markedly. On April 25, 1908, interurban advocates, led by Red Oak Canning Company executive B. B. Clark and Red Oak attorney and Iowa Supreme Court justice Horace Deemer, organized what was called the Red Oak & North Eastern Interurban Promotion Company, designed to build the approximately one hundred miles to Des Moines. (This awkward name commonly became shortened to the Red Oak & Northeastern.) Quickly the firm, with an authorized capital stock of $10,000 ($292,181 in current dollars) and operating from an office on the south side of the Red Oak public square, began to raise both awareness and funds for preliminary work. A typical (and predictable) pitch went as follows: "Red Oak need waste no effort in trying to get factories. Get a new road first and the factories will come of their own accord." The company invited area residents to visit the office and learn more. "Come in without knocking. The latch string is always out."[9]

Even though the RO&NEIPCo made Des Moines its announced objective, backers did not rule out other destinations. In April 1908, an official of the Thomas D. Murphy Company attended a meeting of interurban zealots held at Amity College in College Springs. "Red Oak was more than anxious to build a road that would give them a Southern outlet," reported the local newspaper. The most likely route would be "Red Oak, through Nyman, Yorktown, Page Center, College Springs, Elmo, Mo., Burlington Junction and Maryville, Mo. at which point there is a corporation now existing for the purpose of building [an interurban] road from that place to St. Joseph, Mo." Wishful thinking, of course.[10]

"ON TO DES MOINES!"

The route between Red Oak and Des Moines was never set in stone. Initially the RO&NEIPCo found encouragement in several (mostly small) communities between these two endpoints. Civic-minded citizens of Grant, Greenfield, Stuart, Redfield, Adel, and Waukee expressed interest. Greenfield and Adair County citizens seemed especially anxious to gain access to an interurban. "The line would mean especially much to Adair county, which now has a smaller railroad mileage, considering its area, than any other county in Iowa." After word spread of the proposed project, individuals in Dexter, located between Stuart and Redfield, indicated that they wanted to be included. "To reach Dexter would not be difficult and would add very little to the mileage of the road and would probably help some in getting around engineering difficulties," opined a RO&NEIPCo spokesman.[11]

With what officers considered ample enthusiasm and money, efforts began to turn the interurban dream into reality. In June 1908, a contract was signed with the Roberts & Abbott Company of Cleveland, Ohio, "as good an engineering firm as there is in the country," with instructions to determine construction costs and potential earnings for "an electric passenger railway and also as an electric freight railway." Line locators started their preliminary survey. "The road from Red Oak to Des Moines is going through and it is going just as fast as money and energy can push it," proclaimed the *Express*. "If you are in the way, jump one side quickly and turn in and help push. On to Des Moines!"[12]

Week after week the Red Oak press updated readers with its "Some Interurban News" column. In July the likelihood of the road passing through Grant seemed remote. Railroad backers there favored the proposed steam-operated Villisca line of the AN&S. The RO&NEIPCo, however, took comfort in the support of residents of Mount Etna, an unincorporated inland village in Adams County about fifteen miles east of Grant: "They are willing to put up all the money necessary for a preliminary survey and would gladly give all the money asked for the promotion of the road itself." By September 1908, the Roberts & Abbott firm had completed its work between Des Moines and Mount Etna and turned to the remaining Mount Etna and Red Oak section.[13]

After survey work ended, newspaper coverage dwindled. "So little has been heard or said about the business of the interurban electric line from Red Oak to Des Moines that many may have gotten the idea that the business was a dead issue," commented the *Express* in May 1909.

"Such is not the case, however, and there are some people in the deal who will not let go as long as there is a fighting chance." Added the newspaper: "The time is ripe for Red Oak boosters to get busy." Somewhat later the RO&NEIPCo reported a cash balance of $1,318.50 ($38,524.48 in current dollars), based on nearly $7,000 ($204,500 in current dollars) in funds generated from town and country supporters. The largest expenditure had been for the preliminary survey; it cost $3,520.27 ($102,856.71 in current dollars). The till was not empty, but it hardly overflowed.[14]

Those who wanted the interurban felt better after a widely reported meeting took place in Des Moines on July 19, 1909. The city's *Register and Leader* told of a crowd of area businessmen at the Savory Hotel who applauded the presentations made by representatives of the RO&NEIPCo. The audience, most of whom belonged to the Greater Des Moines Committee, sensed that the Capital City could penetrate profitably a region that had inferior linkages to its businesses and services. Their reasoning was sound. "The result is that merchants in Red Oak and other towns are either compelled to buy their goods in Omaha or to depend on getting them from Chicago, despite the long distance rather than trust to the uncertainties of connections from Des Moines." Attendees expected that "the entire volume of grain and cattle shipments would be directed toward Des Moines instead of to markets outside the state, [as] is necessary under present conditions. In return Des Moines manufacturers and wholesalers would have a new country opened to them in which to dispose of their wares and products." The thought of consumers—hungry passengers pouring into Des Moines—pleased them as well. A representative of the Agar Packing Company of Des Moines made this point: "The field south of this city is virgin, and vast fortunes await the men who invest their money in interurban railroads. Winterset, Indianola, Greenfield, and other cities of that class are now accessible only by almost useless steam railway branches."[15]

Sentiments expressed in Des Moines elevated expectations. Red Oak and Montgomery County residents were reminded that proponents of the RO&NEIPCo remained wide awake. "In the vernacular of the street, they have been 'saying nothing but sawing wood.' They have sawed a lot of it and it seems to fit, too, and it is now announced that the

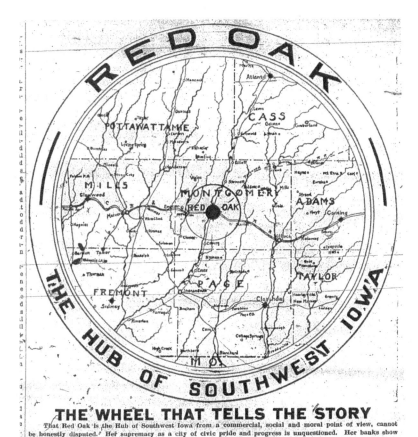

THE WHEEL THAT TELLS THE STORY

That Red Oak is the Hub of Southwest Iowa from a commercial, social and moral point of view, cannot be honestly disputed. Her supremacy as a city of civic pride and progress is unquestioned. Her banks show the greatest volume of business, and her postoffice receipts are unequalled. She is the richest city in the richest section of one of the richest states in the union. She already has more public improvements than any other city of twice her size in the state, and is still going ahead with paving and other progressive works. She is already one of the most important shipping points along the main line of the greatest railroad in Iowa, and is the nucleus for north and south branch lines which bring what would otherwise be remote sections into the reach of first-class railroad facilities. She contemplates the early construction of an interurban railroad which will be the incentive for the building of still more roads until Red Oak will be the converging point of several distinct lines and becomes a prominent railroad center. As evidence that Red Oak is also the geographical center—the Hub, as it were—of Southwest Iowa, it is only necessary to glance at the above map, which is a true reproduction of an official map of the territory covered. Stand up for Red Oak, and watch her grow!

Red Oak boosters sought to "put the icing on the cake" with the Des Moines & Red Oak interurban. Its construction would prove (and guarantee) that the Montgomery County capital was "The Hub of Southwest Iowa." (*Author's collection.*)

long-projected interurban is no longer a dream, as some have considered it, or a mere hope, as others have felt, but a practical project which is so far and so thoroughly shaped up in all its details that it is now but a question of 'building the road.'"[16]

By this time the route had been altered significantly. Rather than passing through the several communities strung along the Rock Island west of Des Moines, the interurban would veer northeast from Mount Etna and pass through Greenfield (1910 population of 1,379) and Winterset (1910 population of 2,818) on its way to the Capital City. More funds could likely be raised from citizens of these Adair and Madison County seats than from communities along the Rock Island, although advocates of the gestating Creston, Winterset & Des Moines Railroad also expected financial backing from Winterset. This county seat, monopolized by the Rock Island, could theoretically win both the Red Oak and Creston projects and enjoy the benefits of multiple outlets. Another consideration for the RO&NEIPCo might have been the partially graded right-of-way that stretched between Greenfield and Winterset, built by the Rock Island but never railed. On June 23, 1910, officers of the RO&NEIPCo officially altered their charter. "The incorporation was amended by striking the out the words 'Grant, Stuart, Redfield, and Adel.'" The replacement clause indicated that the road would run "between Red Oak and Des Moines, Greenfield, Winterset or such other points as the board of the directors may determine." A new line survey followed.[17]

Interurban fever spread. The excitement of the hoped-for railroad prompted the *Express* editor to place several large banners immediately above the front-page masthead. One read: Toot! Toot! All Aboard for Up the Line to Des Moines Via the R. O. & N. E. R. R. And another: The Interurban Has Passed the Doubtful State—Better Get in Game Early.[18]

Other towns sought action and seemed energized about prospects. "Everyone along the route wants a railroad," observed the *Greenfield Transcript*. "This is altogether a different proposition from anything ever offered our people before and it is earnestly desired by the Transcript that the people have a thorough understanding of the matter. When it is seen in the proper light the men in charge will have no trouble in disposing of the stock at home." The Greenfield sentiment was that the

Burlington failed to provide the town, twenty-one miles north of Creston, with adequate service on its forty-seven-mile Cumberland branch.[19]

Red Oak journalists kept readers aware of the advantages of the
anticipated electric railway. In a November 1909 piece, readers were
told that "no other interurban in the state has better prospects as a paying proposition to the stockholders. Look at the railroad map of Iowa.
You will find that the people in all other parts of the state are building
interurbans and wherever built they are prospering." Much was made
of the expected economic impact on the community. "The new road is
to be operated from Red Oak. From 50 to 125 men will then make their
headquarters here. We will say 50 families, which is a very conservative
estimate." These questions were raised, "Will Red Oak be a loser when
the new road is built? Say, can you name one city of any importance that
would have ever become so with but ONE railroad? Can you give one
single way in which Red Oak is to grow much larger than it now is unless
we build a NEW railroad—the Red Oak & Northeastern? You cannot do
it." These arguments were interchangeable with ones made by apostles
of boosterism in Clarinda, Creston, and elsewhere.[20]

While the RO&NEIPCo was dedicated to improved rail outlets
for the projected service territory, a dramatic change took place. Likely
because of cost considerations, the company directors backed off from
their initial commitment of building a *true* interurban that would require a power source, electrical substations, and a network of poles and
overhead wire. The front page of the November 19, 1909, issue of the
Express featured a photograph and story about "The New Interurban
Cars." Instead of conventional traction equipment, promoters opted for
McKeen cars, built by the McKeen Motor Car Company of Omaha.
These pieces of sleek, self-propelled rolling stock with their knife-edge
front, rounded rear section, porthole windows, leather and mahogany
interior, and seventy-foot-long body were starting to appear largely in the
trans-Chicago West. This creation of William R. McKeen Jr., superintendent of motive power for the Union Pacific, was a mechanical-chain drive
railcar designed to be cheaper to operate than a steam-powered train. A
contemporary source estimated the cost at only fifteen cents per mile.
In 1905 McKeen introduced his first gasoline units, and by 1911 more

than seventy were in service on multiple roads, particularly on branch lines and shortlines but also for local operations on main and secondary routes. They became an emblem of modernity. "Passengers on the R. O. & N. E. railway will ride in the latest and most approved gasoline motor cars such as are already in use on the following roads: Union Pacific road in Nebraska, Kansas and Colorado, Illinois Central in Illinois [and] Chicago & Northwestern in Wisconsin." The newspaper suggested that McKeen cars were just as good if not better than standard interurban equipment and that they would have the same impact on service. "The cars of this kind are most comfortable at any time of year or in any kind of weather. No cinders or smoke to bother. Easy-riding and speedy." The copy continued: "Farmers living along the Red Oak & Northeastern will have no need of automobiles. There will be cars every hour on the new road. When a farmer wants to come to town what will he do? Simply go to the nearest place where the interurban crosses a road, hail a car and get on." Potentially the best features of both an electric and steam road would be realized. Did RO&NEIPCo backers realize that McKeen cars had the habit of inconveniently breaking down between stations? Probably not.[21]

The rejection of a traditional interurban was supported by a subsequent piece in the *Express* on "Handling Interurban Freight." Although the described schedule reflected what some electric roads provided their freight customers, the announced activities for this revenue sector indicated a steam shortline. "There will be two regular freight trains a day, one each way. A freight will run from Greenfield to Red Oak and

Facing top, Officials of the Des Moines & Red Oak decided not to string overhead wire, believing that McKeen cars could adequately serve their needs. Interestingly, one Iowa interurban, Charles City Western Railway (CCW), which in 1911 opened its Charles City–Marble Rock line, used both a McKeen car and steam power similar to what the DM&RO planned. *(Don L. Hofsommer collection)*

Facing middle, Four years later, the CCW built between Charles City and Colwell and electrified to become a twenty-one-mile interurban, yet it briefly retained its McKeen car. *(Author's collection.)*

Facing bottom, Several major steam roads, including Union Pacific, acquired McKeen units. *(Don L. Hofsommer collection.)*

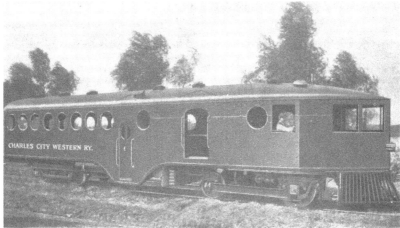

from Red Oak to Greenfield. [This] will constitute one division of the road. The other division will be from Greenfield to Des Moines." The article announced that the company, typical of freight-hauling electric interurbans, planned to install multiple sidings, allowing farmers the convenience of receiving and shipping carload freight, particularly livestock. With McKeen cars moving frequently up and down the line, the writer reminded readers that "with a passenger car with capacity for light freight, milk cans, etc., passing every hour, and a regular freight twice a day, could the farmers wish or ask for anything better in the way of shipping facilities?" It is possible that a McKeen car would pull one or two standard freight cars. Interestingly, speculation continued that if adequate funding were raised, the Red Oak company would embrace electric traction, becoming more than a "wireless" interurban. Yet by late 1911, the *Electric Railway Journal* stated flatly that "this company will be operated by steam and not by electricity."[22]

Irrespective of the type of railroad the RO&NEIPCo sought to become, proponents relentlessly pushed their construction plans. On Christmas Eve 1909, the *Express* reminded everyone that an "Interurban [Is] an Improvement." It was a hard-sell approach, especially directed toward farmers. "You CANNOT lose by investing in the Red Oak & Northeastern. It WILL increase the value of your land, and besides that it WILL make you good interest on your investment." These were hardly novel arguments.[23]

As the new year began, the RO&NEIPCo concentrated on having farmers donate land along the resurveyed route. Individuals would not be signing over large pieces of property but rather the standard hundred-foot-wide right-of-way strip. "Sixty-five per cent of the right of way of Interurban roads of the State of Indiana was DONATED by farmers along the line," noted the *Express*. "Iowa beats that for at least some of Iowa's Interurbans were put through with ALL or practically ALL right of way DONATED." The Red Oak road should not be an exception.[24]

A good response followed. The *Express* began to publish "THE ROLL OF HONOR," a weekly listing of farmers who donated land for the right-of-way. In one instance, the newspaper used the headline "Lifters vs. Leaners," again employing moral suasion to convince farmers to contribute. By March 1910, the honor roll included fifty-three donors. This listing made those not backing the project conspicuous by their absence. Still, Herschel Clovis, right-of-way agent, also took options to purchase land, and by July an estimated one-third of the projected 104-mile route had been acquired. In September more encouraging news came when he reported that he had secured 90 percent of the right-of-way for the seventy miles between Red Oak and Winterset. "Much of the right-of-way is being donated or paid by shares of stock." Clovis did not expect that much land would need to be taken through legal condemnation.[25]

The RO&NEIPCo promoters did more than solicit right-of-way donations and make option-purchase agreements; they simultaneously sought aggressively to raise stock subscriptions. A list published in spring 1910 revealed ninety-four individual contributors and thirty-four business sponsors in Red Oak. The goal of $75,000 ($2,113,192 in current dollars) for the community's share in the project seemed certain, promoting the belief that the "Red Oak & Northeastern Railroad is practically assured, and it will be but a question of a short few months when construction will be well under way on this great project which will give to the city an additional connecting link with the outside world." By September pledges in Red Oak neared $100,000 ($2,817,590 in current dollars).[26]

At the other end of the proposed road, Des Moines, support grew. In June 1910, the *Register and Leader* reported that three commercial organizations, Des Moines Commercial Club, East Des Moines Commercial League, and the Greater Des Moines Committee, planned to solicit stock subscriptions and agreed to raise $200,000 ($5,635,181 in current dollars). As with subscriptions made by residents of Red Oak and other online communities, "no subscriber should be required to pay any amount upon said subscription until the road is built and in operation." At this point an investor would hardly be making a risky commitment.[27]

Reports remained upbeat. On October 4, 1910, the *Des Moines Daily Capital* announced that city backers would soon begin a ten-day "whirlwind campaign" to raise stock subscriptions. That same day the *Register and Leader* revealed that 95 percent of the right-of-way had been obtained, given outright or acquired through the granting of stock. Elsewhere it was also reported that trackage rights over local electric roads could be arranged for access into the heart of the Capital City, reducing construction costs. Apparently, the only place along the intended route where money posed a challenge was in the vicinity of Winterset, "where it is thought other roads are endeavoring to embarrass the road." (The Rock Island was likely the culprit.) The *Daily Capital* disclosed that the company had secured a townsite, located on the W. I. Hully farm about two miles north of Grant, where the line would cross the soon-to-open AN&S. Herschel Clovis closed the deal, and he continued to secure the right-of-way for the interurban. This was not what businessmen in Grant wanted to hear; competitive stores might blossom forth in their midst. These merchants might pay a price for backing the AN&S rather than the RO&NEIPCo.[28]

Notwithstanding the stream of encouraging news, the Red Oak–Des Moines project would not be cheap. Construction standards would be that of a quality branch line, meaning heavy rail (perhaps seventy pounds to the yard), rock ballast, and white oak ties. One contractor estimated the costs to be $2,228,000 ($62,775,918 in current dollars), or $22,000 ($619,869 in current dollars) per mile, including labor and materials.[29]

While reports circulated that the potential gross earnings for the interurban would be substantial, amounting annually to nearly $700,000 ($19,723,134 in current dollars)—a farfetched figure—the subscription drive in Des Moines generated less than $100,000 ($2,817,590 in current dollars). The amount fell short by half of the announced goal. This lack of pledged capital did not auger well for the project and dampened enthusiasm in Des Moines and elsewhere.[30]

IMOGENE EXTENSION

As 1911 dawned, optimism faded sharply. The RO&NEIPCo directors decided that it would be prudent to consider an additional route "to establish beyond any further doubt the fact that the R. O. & N. E. is at last to be realized." Although backers did not abandon plans for building through Greenfield and Winterset to Des Moines, they believed that a 13.5-mile line southwest of Red Oak would be a smart interim move. The concept was to forge a connection with the friendly Wabash about a mile

and a half north of Imogene, a community of 341 residents in northeast-
ern Fremont County. Before reaching Red Oak, track would pass near
Coburg, a Montgomery County village of 177 residents situated on the
Red Oak–Hamburg branch of the Burlington.[31]

Additional reasons existed for building the "Southern Extension."
If the core route never materialized, this outlet would allow businesses
in Red Oak to break the Burlington stronghold. "In a broader sense [the
Imogene connection] will benefit Red Oak materially by opening direct
channels to markets not now reached except by circuitous routes. It will
give us not only competitive service to and from the large cities of the
east, but more direct means of reaching St. Louis and other points to the
south via the Wabash, and to Kansas City, Omaha, and points beyond
as well as intermediate points," editorialized the *Express*. "Very satisfactory traffic arrangements have been made with the Wabash, and excellent freight and passenger connections." An accommodating Wabash
also aided both the Ikey and I&OSL. If plans developed as anticipated,
construction materials for the core Des Moines line could move over
this trackage.[32]

By June 1911, dirt had begun to fly on the Imogene project. The company had purchased the needed equipment, namely an elevator grader,
plows, scrapers, and dump wagons, and had engaged an experienced
local contractor who owned a powerful steam traction engine. Initially,
construction gangs attacked the easy grades and two minor cuts. A
stream of visitors, including company officers and supporters from Red
Oak and elsewhere, flocked to inspect the major work site: Jenks Hill
near the Mills-Montgomery County line. Although the previous work
had not been unusually difficult, this cut measured about eighteen feet
in depth and required removal of about twenty thousand cubic yards of
dirt. Observers probably examined the construction camp that served
approximately thirty locally recruited laborers. "Here we found down in
a glen a very pleasant eating house, a good [water] pump, and everything
to make the life of the railroaders as comfortable as possible."[33]

Progress continued, and expectations soared. "The prospects of
building are good," opined a Wabash official, "but no track has been
laid as yet." Although the harsh winter of 1911–1912 delayed construction, grading, except for two small sections, was completed between the

Wabash interchange and the Burlington crossover on the outskirts of Red Oak by summer 1912. The missing links resulted from the inability to acquire title to several right-of-way parcels, forcing condemnation proceedings.[34]

In March 1912, the legal name of the RO&NEIPCo changed. At the insistence of Des Moines backers, the road received a less cumbersome name, and the firm became the Des Moines & Red Oak Railway Company (DM&RO). No one objected; after all, supporters believed that the railroad had moved beyond the promotion stage. By having Des Moines appear first in the corporate title, this moniker was expected to make it easier to gain more financial support.[35]

Although excitement for the interurban had outwardly lessened in Des Moines, established arguments for the Red Oak to Capital City line remained. "It is the biggest open territory outside of Des Moines," reported the *Register and Leader* in the spring of 1912. "The entire traffic zone of the Des Moines & Red Oak is 900 square miles. Des Moines has splendid train service in all other directions except into this territory." These points were added: "At present it is almost as easy to go to Chicago from the territory between Winterset and Red Oak as it is to come to Des Moines. It takes six hours to come to Des Moines now from Red Oak. The new interurban will bring Des Moines within a three hours' ride from Red Oak. The territory is probably the most fertile and productive in the state. The country is well developed already."[36]

Notwithstanding rebranding, the financial picture by 1912 revealed serious challenges for the DM&RO, pointing to why Red Oak failed to gain a second railroad and why Des Moines, Winterset, Greenfield, and intermediate points also never got the road. Work on the Southern Extension had been pricey and imprudent. The costs of survey, machinery, labor, and construction materials had already amounted to about $29,000 ($788,707 in current dollars) per mile. Heavy expenditures, it was believed, would be amortized as building advanced from Red Oak to Des Moines. Still additional expenses awaited the company before it could open the Imogene connection. The pesky Nishnabotna River, most of all, required either a steel span or less expensive wooden trestle. Although crossties, bridge timbers, and culvert pipes had been purchased, there remained the price of rails, ties, and other track materials, rolling stock, and the Red Oak depot and support facilities. Labor, too, would have to be factored into the final cost. Financing came from paid-in subscriptions and the pocketbooks of company officials. An audit of the books in August 1912 revealed that cash subscriptions had generated $34,651 ($942,397 in current dollars), and another $8,910 ($242,323 in current dollars) came from loans made by directors. There had been discussion of issuing construction bonds for the 13.5-mile line, but management decided to seek tax aid from two local sources, Red Oak City and West Township of Montgomery County.[37]

During this period, startup steam and electric railroads regularly relied on taxpayer dollars. Of the sunset carriers, the I&OSL was the sole exception. Usually the tax was modest, a short-term millage assessment on property. In return, taxpayers received stock in the project. There was the standard stipulation that the railroad had to be completed by a definite date before public funds would be paid. Since the line sliced through West Township, backers of the Wabash connection sought assistance from these taxpayers. (For some unexplained reason, no tax election was contemplated for Monroe Township in Fremont County, where the line would interchange with the Wabash.) In the special West Township balloting, held on July 2, 1912, the proposal went down to a resounding defeat, 45 yes and 142 no. Voters may have questioned the prospects for a successful project, or they were mostly satisfied with existing rail service, being within a reasonable driving distance to stations in Essex and Imogene. As always, there was the possibility that they objected to a tax increase. "The result in West township may not rightly be considered a real blow to the project," commented the *Express*. Yet work ground to a halt. "So far as the Imogene end of the railroad is concerned the proposition will be temporarily abandoned."[38]

Hope persisted. Backers of the DM&RO believed that a special tax issue in Des Moines and several other locales would generate the funds needed to allow the railroad to be built. With tax victories, especially in Des Moines, bonding companies would willing accept the debt, but the first goal was to gain the approval of Red Oak taxpayers.[39]

In August 1912, much excitement developed in Red Oak about the special election scheduled for the last day of the month. The proposition called for property owners to decide whether to approve a 2.5 percent property tax for two years. When passed, about $40,000 ($1,087,872 in current dollars) of public funds would be invested in the DM&RO if it was completed by the close of 1914. Once again, taxpayers would receive stock proportionate to their assessments.[40]

Although most of the business community endorsed the tax proposition and there was strong newspaper backing, not everyone favored financing the stalled DM&RO. Opponents, whom the *Express* called members of the "Knockers League," allegedly engaged an outsider to drum up opposition. "His slimy literature is sent broadcast over the city. He is doing this disreputable work for hire; he has no interest in the matter except the money he receives for his dirty ink." But there were strong counterresponses. Merchants and others placed placards in their windows: WE ARE FOR THE RAILROAD AND RED OAK. Readers of the *Express* were again told of the advantages of a line to Greenfield, Winterset, and Des Moines, and published testimonials from prominent citizens of Clarinda explained how valuable the recently opened Ikey had become.[41]

Then came election day—a Saturday—and voters turned out in droves throughout the Red Oak wards. Electioneering had varied. "During the past two weeks, those for and against the tax have waged a bitter warfare," reported the *Nonpareil*. "Each side adopted the plan of sending daily bulletins by mail and every form of political cunning has been resorted to for influencing voters at the election today." Added the Council Bluffs newspaper: "Prominent officials in the Murphy Calendar Company are also interested in the proposed railroad, and late this afternoon dozens of automobiles were employed in conveying the several hundred women employed by the calendar company to the polls." Later the *Express* denied any coercive or untoward acts, but whether there had been any was moot. Voters overwhelmingly favored the tax subsidy; the male vote was 745 yes and 277 no, and the female balloting went 453 yes and only 40 no. "The way women turned out was enough to convert most of us to become suffragists," opined the *Express*. When results were announced that evening, spirited celebrations followed. "The serenaders or 'shot gun' parade was some noisy and were indiscriminate in their favors and their performance was looked upon will all due forbearance.

Some of the younger boosters became almost overenthusiastic, but no harm was done."[42]

COLLAPSE

For the moment all seemed to bode well for the DM&RO project, yet it was not to be. Efforts to hold tax elections in Des Moines and elsewhere fizzled. The failure of Red Oak interests to rail the nearly completed road-bed to Imogene hardly helped. A last-ditch effort in spring 1913 to call a special election in Des Moines to vote a tax subsidy went nowhere. Still, an optimistic management purchased seven lots on Coolbraugh Street in Red Oak for its station grounds. "The new depot will be a block nearer the square than the Burlington freight depot and two or three blocks nearer than the passenger station." But not one section of track or even a single tie was ever laid for the DM&RO. The Red Oak press became largely silent about the railroad, noting a few small public expenditures. The largest involved payment of $596.16 ($15,833.65 in current dollars) during 1913, presumably for the station real estate.[43]

Another inkling of why the Des Moines & Red Oak Railway col-lapsed came in late 1915. "There is a belt of territory generally described as lying between the 'Q' [Burlington] and the Rock Island, at one end of which is Des Moines and at the other Red Oak, that ought to accom-modate another steam railroad," observed a Des Moines writer, "and that undoubtedly would have accommodated a steam railroad before this if it were not for the difficulties experienced in financing a new railroad in between two old ones." The Burlington and Rock Island may have played a role in stymying the DM&RO. Earlier the Burlington had done its best to prevent bonding firms from taking debt of both the Ikey and CW&DM. Neither the Burlington nor the Rock Island wanted the Shaw syndicate to take control of the bankrupt AN&S and to see a connecting Des Moines to Council Bluffs road.[44]

The difficulty of successfully placing public debt apparently plagued Red Oak and Montgomery County. Not long after the victory of the railroad tax levy, Harris Trust and Savings Bank, a powerful Chicago financial institution, refused, without explanation, to accept any county road and bridge bonds. When the economic vitality of Red Oak is considered, this action is surprising. Was this the doing of the Burlington? Moreover, bonding agents knew of the repeated struggles and failures of the several sunset roads in western Iowa. Since these other upstart sunset carriers, with the exception of the Atlantic Northern (née AN&S), failed to generate sufficient revenues to cover fixed costs, DM&RO securities would be chancy.[45]

Strangely, there remained rumors that the Des Moines to Red Oak interurban might still take shape. In December 1915, the Greater Des Moines Committee backed the project and argued that it remained a thoroughly practical undertaking. Alas, nothing tangible occurred.[46]

Red Oak boosters soldiered on. At the annual banquet of the local commercial club held at the Johnson Hotel in May 1916, a feeling of optimism prevailed. The talk, however, was not about railroads electric or otherwise but about improved roads. Montgomery County Engineer C. D. Forsbeck made much of the evolving Good Roads Movement. "A radical change in conditions in our county during the past few years has brought a demand for good roads," explained Forsbeck. "The farmers want good roads, and the owners of automobiles are demanding them." In 1916 the federal government pledged itself to a network of highways, which in part subsidized the developing automobile industry. The future of intercity transportation in America would be with better roads and not independent shortline railroads, no matter their form of motive power.[47]

For some time, the nearly thirteen miles of naked grade of the stillborn Des Moines & Red Oak interurban reminded observers that a monumental shift had occurred in preferred modes of transportation. It would also awaken memories that backers of the DM&RO had made a gallant effort to build an electric road or possibly a conventional steam shortline. Surely if the Motor Age had been slower to evolve, the raw roadbed might have been finished, and trains operated. If the interurban had succeeded, it might have been an electric road of note. It never would have been a major carrier of passengers, but there existed the potential for profitable carload freight, agricultural products and likely rock from limestone quarries near Winterset. The road could have lasted into the era of the Great Depression or maybe longer.

In some ways the histories of two twilight Midwestern roads, Missouri & Kansas Interurban Railway (M&KIRy) and Woodstock & Sycamore Traction Company (W&STCo), might have been replicated. In 1907 the M&KIRy, known as the Strang Line after its promoter W. B. Strang, opened twenty miles of track between Kansas City and Olathe, Kansas. In a reversal of the initially announced plans of the DM&RO, the Strang Line began with gasoline motor cars but electrified in 1909 due to the inadequacies of its initial motive power. A substantial freight business kept that company functioning until its abandonment on the eve of World War II. The saga of the W&STCo might also have been repeated. In 1910 this twenty-six-mile railroad began service between the Illinois communities of Sycamore and Marengo (Woodstock was never reached). The company opted for a McKeen gas-electric car, never electrified, and became junk in 1918.[48]

Irrespective of the possibilities for freight revenue, the combination of all-weather roads, more dependable motor vehicles, and reasonably priced fuel would have ultimately killed the Des Moines & Red Oak Railway. In the decade from 1928 to 1937, the national interurban industry crumbled. Motorized America sealed the fate of most electrics, except those with substantial carload freight revenues that the cost-saving diesel locomotive revolution helped sustain after World War II. Even dieselized steam roads started to stumble because of modal competition. By the early 1950s, observers concluded that the Railway Age had ended.

SEVEN

EPILOGUE

THE FIVE IOWA SUNSET CLUSTER RAILROADS MIGHT APPEAR
to deserve eternal obscurity, being at best minor footnotes to American
railroad history. After all, their *total* length barely exceeded one hundred
miles. Their average life span, moreover, covered about five years, and
the Des Moines & Red Oak Railway (DM&RO) never turned a wheel.
There is one exception: the initial component of the Atlantic Northern
& Southern Railroad (AN&S), the reorganized Atlantic Northern Railroad, operated until 1936. But after twenty-nine years, automobile, bus,
and truck competition and the Great Depression finally killed it off. Few
physical traces of these roads remain; the former Iowa & Southwestern Railway (Ikey) depot in College Springs rests on the grounds of
the Nodaway Valley Historical Museum in Clarinda, and the one-time
Sciota AN&S depot has become a public park fixture in Elk Horn. Even
small artifacts are scarce. Collectors of railroadiana occasionally find annual passes and real-photo postcards for the four built carriers, but there
are few if any company-issued public timetables and no known marked
switch keys, locks, and hand lanterns. It is doubtful model railroaders

Facing, Physical remains of the Iowa & Southwestern (Ikey) consist of traces of the
long-abandoned right-of-way and its former College Springs depot. After the railroad
closed, this structure was moved to a lot in College Springs to serve as a private
residence. Ultimately, it was transported to Clarinda to become part of the Nodaway
Valley Historical Museum complex. (*Author's photographs.*)

have immortalized any of these shortlines in their O- or HO-gauge layouts.[1]

The five sunset railroads illustrate the value of local history studies. The adage "all history is local" is deceptively simple, but it contains a degree of truth. Uncovering what occurred with these shortlines reveals dimensions of economic and social life and changes that occurred in multiple communities, illuminating past events and reflecting larger currents. "A good understanding of the past," argue historians David Kyvig and Myron Marty, "whether designated as memory or history, needs to take into account nearby as well as national and international developments."[2]

These obscure western Iowa shortlines hold importance—and not merely for chronicling nearby history. For one thing, they reflect the national eagerness, perhaps impatience, for interurban railways during the formative years of the twentieth century. Although the Hawkeye State never became a preeminent leader in electric mileage, many of its citizens, especially farmers and villagers, expressed keen interest in what was a technological revolution in transportation. Supporters of these five roads experienced interurban fever, but their electric dreams went unfilled. Furthermore, most interurbans built during the second wave of construction, from after the Panic of 1907 to the outbreak of the European war in 1914, lacked profitability. During this time, scores of proposed interurbans remained just paper entities, and in hindsight that was fortuitous. The money-conscious backers of the DM&RO, the most notable of these cluster traction projects, may have realized the principal flaw in interurban building, namely high initial costs. That surely explains why backers came to express enthusiasm for self-contained gasoline motor cars even though they were highly unreliable. Nevertheless, these "wireless" cars offered the promise of reducing the expense of electric railway construction but retaining interurban-like operating qualities. Would-be interurban promoters also had the option of selecting traditional steam power. Affordable and serviceable pieces were readily available from railroads and used equipment dealers. Indeed, the four sunset carriers acquired American Standard locomotives. These 4-4-0s were the backbone of motive power rosters everywhere in

In 1932 photographer Clyde Fulton caught a somewhat battered, one-of-a-kind motor car in the Atlantic yards of the Atlantic Northern Railway. Economical to operate, this unit handled US mail, express, and passengers, commonly youngsters going to and from school. *(Courtesy of Railway & Locomotive Historical Society.)*

the nineteenth century and remained so on shortlines for decades to
come. At times the best bottom-line option, however, was to lease motive power. The Ikey and Iowa & Omaha Short Line (I&OSL) embraced
that strategy. The Creston, Winterset & Des Moines (CW&DM) and the
Atlantic Northern each reduced operating expenses by augmenting their
steam locomotives with gasoline-powered rail motor cars. Employees
of the latter company showed creativity, installing a Model T engine in
a homemade wooden box-like contraption mounted on flanged wheels.
For years it transported mail, express, and a small number of passengers
(often schoolchildren). Locals called this bizarre vehicle the "Toonerville trolley" or simply the "trolley."[3]

Whether projected as an interurban or built as a steam shortline,
trunk railroads showed mixed feeling about these upstarts. The Chicago,
Burlington & Quincy Railroad (Burlington) repeatedly revealed enmity
toward these companies, especially the Ikey. The Chicago, Rock Island
& Pacific Railroad (Rock Island), probably because of its distressed finances, displayed a greater willingness to cooperate with the AN&S
and later with the Atlantic Northern. The Wabash Railroad revealed a
friendliness toward the Ikey, I&OSL, and the graded Imogene section
of the DM&RO. It sought to capture business from the Burlington in
Clarinda and Red Oak and to gain traffic from the former inland towns
of College Springs and Treynor.

Part of value of exploring these unheralded cluster roads is that
they attracted small, unstudied development firms. In three of these
case studies, the Engineering, Construction & Securities Company
(EC&SCo), listed as Chicago based and led by Clarence A. Ross, president, and Charles B. Judd, chief engineer, became involved. The firm
viewed Iowa, specifically its southern and western sections, as an attractive place for doing business. The EC&SCo was a partnership with
probably few employees, either permanent or temporary. Both Ross and
Judd had considerable professional experience when they arrived in the
Hawkeye State. For nearly a decade, Ross had been associated with the
Westinghouse Electric & Manufacturing Company, having supervised
the building of the Ardmore (Indian Territory) Electric Company and
the Eldorado Springs (Missouri) Electric Company. He also had financial interests in that Eldorado Springs facility and a power company in

Holton, Kansas. Early on, Judd had become involved with interurbans. In the late 1890s, he served as president of the unbuilt Grand Rapids & Belding Traction Company, and later he became associated with other Midwestern interurban projects. These included electrification shortly before World War I of the twenty-five-mile Centerville, Albia & Southern Railway, trackage previously operated under steam by the Iowa Central Railway. Their work was financially risky and not easy. Ross had to deal with boosters and bankers, and both men encountered problems with projects that had limited financial resources.

The EC&SCo entered Iowa about 1906 with a grand plan. The booming and closely spaced bituminous coal-mining communities in the southern section attracted its attention. Ross and Judd believed that traction lines from larger towns to mining camps could be easier to promote than agriculturally based shortlines; after all, "miners spent, farmers saved." At this time the region lacked an operating interurban. The firm first constructed the three-mile Oskaloosa–Buxton Electric Railway, which opened in 1907, and almost immediately turned its attention to building the Albia Interurban Railway. "The promoters state it is their ultimate aim to include Ottumwa [the dominant metropolis] in the network of electric lines and to give this city direct communication with all the mining camps in the vicinity of Oskaloosa and Albia." The Ross company failed to extend Oskaloosa trackage the ten miles beyond the coal-mining village of Beacon to the booming and predominately African American coal town of Buxton. Its residents suffered from poor service offered by the Chicago & North Western, being situated at the end of a long branch line that missed any place of importance. Success, however, came in Albia. Not only did Ross and Judd, "the interurban hustlers," and their partner Ottumwa attorney and entrepreneur Calvin Manning buy out the local power plant, but in late 1907 they constructed the community-funded Albia Interurban Railway three miles south to the coal camps of Rizerville and Hocking. Late the following year, electrified trackage reached the much larger mining town of Hiteman, eight miles northwest of Albia. Plans to build the dozen miles from Albia north to Buxton and four miles west to the Ward mines fizzled. Later the EC&SCo built artificial ice and steam heating plants in this Monroe County seat.[4]

In 1908 two promoters of the Albia Interurban Railway stand alongside Car No. 1 on the northwest corner of the public square in this Monroe County seat. Charles Ross is standing third from the left, and Calvin Manning is to his right. Locally financed, Ross and Manning worked out an imaginative arrangement where young men assisted in construction work, being paid half in cash and the balance in common stock. (*Author's collection.*)

Although the full activities of Ross and Judd and their EC&SCo remain somewhat obscure, they embraced the age of electricity. Yet they also supported construction of steam railroads, including the AN&S, Ikey, and CW&DM. Even though these roads were projected as electrics, there was only a remote possibility that once opened they might come under wire. Considering their backgrounds and successes in the southern Iowa coalfields, Ross and Judd preferred the interurban option. Nonetheless, paying clients were paying clients.

The EC&SCo filled a void. Trunk roads employed large and powerful entities, namely, major banks, investment houses, and well-known construction companies. They showed little or no interest in small, late-day agriculturally dependent shortlines, most of which appeared

problematic. It is unlikely that Clarence Ross resembled Colonel Be-
riah Sellers, the slippery promoter in the 1873 satirical novel *The Gilded
Age: Tale of Today* by Mark Twain and Charles Dudley. If he had shared
any of the Colonel's unscrupulous traits, local railroad advocates might
have embraced them. When Brookfield, Missouri, sought an interurban
during that second wave of construction, the editor of the *Brookfield Gazette* believed a promoter of that ilk could be useful in getting a project
off the ground.[5]

These sunset carriers demonstrate the critical role played by govern-
mental units, the activities of which were hardly uniform. Municipal and
township entities were generally receptive to railroad projects, reflecting
community enthusiasm for a first or second railroad. Passage of generous
tax subsidies became commonplace. Yet there were cases when election
outcomes disappointed backers. Red Oak overwhelmingly voted aid
for the DM&RO, but West Township in the same county did not. State
regulatory bodies consistently supported the interests of their citizenry.
In the 1870s, Iowa helped to spearhead modern railroad regulation with
its Granger laws. Later, its Board of Railroad Commissioners backed
freight customers in Clarinda when they complained about the refusal
of the Burlington to cooperate with the Ikey on matters of reciprocal
switching and freight rates and divisions. Compared to the Interstate
Commerce Commission's (ICC) handling of similar concerns, the Iowa
board acted with certainty and dispatch. The initial decision by the ICC
in the Ikey case had been poorly conceived and was "so ambiguous in its
terms as to make a second application to the Interstate Commerce Commission necessary." It failed to render a final verdict before the railroad
slipped into fatal free fall. An ICC case might drag on for years. What it
did—or in this situation, didn't do—indicates how its overall policies
support the contention of historian Albro Martin that federal government actions led to "enterprise denied" for the industry. In this instance,
only a small road was affected. It might be a stretch, but the ICC delay,
which contributed to the death of the Ikey, is reminiscent of *Jarndyce v.
Jarndyce*, a legal case described in the Charles Dickens novel *Bleak House*
that went on forever.[6]

While a government agency might negatively impact an upstart
shortline, these railroads could also face serious internal shortcomings.

The majority of early twentieth-century Midwestern roads were usually run by local merchants, bankers, and farmers who lacked railroad experience. Although well-intentioned, they commonly made poor decisions, likely due to the absence of consultations with railroad professionals about business practices and train operations. Interestingly, a carefully researched report existed for the Ikey but was probably never shared with its management. When the Wabash took a serious look at the property in 1915, it hired J. W. Kendrick, an experienced railroad consultant, to scrutinize the Ikey's strengths and weaknesses. He found much less of the former and more of the latter. Kendrick described various shortcomings, including this one: "It is a mistake for engine and train crews to be paid by the month, irrespective of the number of trips that they make." He explained: "At the present time two trains are run in each direction between Clarinda and Blanchard daily except Sunday. This movement is more than would be necessary to handle the business if it were not for the fact that the engines owned by the Company (both of those owned being out of commission) and the one leased at present from the Wabash are not suited to use upon this line with its heavy grades." Paying these crews on an adjusted mileage basis would have been the wiser course of action. Nonprofessionals, too, saw weaknesses in grassroots management. In 1911 the *Des Moines Register and Leader* editorialized about the problems that faced the AN&S: "Farming is one thing, building and operating railroads is another. Railroading is not a profitable game for the amateur." Two years later, the editor of the *Villisca Review* echoed these thoughts. He did not mince words about why the company had failed: "The history of the AN&S road from its inception down to the present time has been more or less a nightmare. It was operated by men who knew little of actual railroading." Moreover, there are no known formal meetings held between managers of two or more of these sunset cluster carriers, although there may have been exchanges of correspondence or other contacts.[7]

From a company perspective, the four operating cluster roads benefited from not having to negotiate with the railroad brotherhoods. Work stoppages occurred, but they were spontaneous and not union orchestrated. When a former member of the Brotherhood of Locomotive Engineers took a comparable position on the I&OSL, he surely allowed his union membership to lapse. By avoiding a unionized labor force, these shortlines saved on wages, paying considerably less than trunk and terminal roads. Furthermore, there often existed a family feeling among rank-and-file employees and between them and their patrons. These relationships were no different in the vast majority of shortlines, past and present.

Service reflected a similar affability. The freight needs of cluster customers were handled in as rapid and personalized a manner as possible, and passengers customarily were treated with the same consideration. They could request stops most anywhere, and they might board where they pleased as well. Trunk roads usually didn't show the same thoughtfulness on their branch lines, although interurbans did.

There was little diversity among these sunset cluster railroads—simplicity dominated their operations. There were usually no or limited Sunday train movements, excluding special excursions, and just one or two trains during the remainder of the week. None of the roads adopted the telegraph, and only the Atlantic Southern of the reconstituted AN&S installed a telephone line. Carriers lacked dispatchers and may not have used train orders, relying on oral instructions and written switch-lists. Signals were nonexistent except where the shortline crossed another railroad. When the AN&S and CW&DM met branches of the Rock Island and Burlington at grade, wooden crossing gates were installed. This was probably how main-line Rock Island trains in Atlantic were protected. When shortlines appeared, public telephone service was commonly available in villages and towns, and this means of communication was probably used by customers to contact depot agents. Farmers, however, usually needed to make in-person contacts with railroad personnel due to the slowness of extending telephone access into the countryside.[8]

What is striking but hardly shocking about these cluster railroads is the extent to which they reveal the American optimism and boosterism that enveloped much of the nation. The pervasive feeling was that the present was superior to the past, and the future held greater promise. The twentieth century would hopefully yield unstoppable prosperity; railroads contributed to that worldview. Farmers, who expected land values to rise, frequently expanded their acreages. They acquired labor-saving equipment and adopted better farming practices, perhaps inspired by progressive neighbors or grant college specialists and later by US Department of Agriculture extension agents. Community residents generally saw progress in growth. The anticipated or achieved results were rising population and accompanying wealth, displayed best in increased real-estate values. Booth Tarkington put it well in *The Magnificent Ambersons* when he described boosters in mythical Oakland City, Indiana: "They were optimists—optimists to the point of belligerence—their motto being 'Boost! Don't knock!' And they were hustlers, believing in hustling and in honesty because both paid." Tarkington made this point: "The more prosperous my beloved city, the more prosperous Beloved I!" The editor of the *Red Oak Express* consistently promoted the DM&RO using language similar to that of other journalists associated with the cluster. He made this claim: "Now then, help make Red Oak a second Omaha and all real estate will go up proportionately. Every thinking man knows that this would be sure to occur." BOOST! DON'T KNOCK became an oft-repeated battle cry for civic uplifters. Newspapers, especially in smaller communities, did much to advance progressive endeavors.[9]

Optimism and boosterism, no matter their intensity, produced constructive results with the advent of these four functioning shortlines. There would be livestock auctions, town-lot sales, new and remodeled houses, business openings and expansions, and other betterments. The din and clatter of saws and hammers became familiar and welcomed sounds. One outcome was the appearance of hometown newspapers. Grant and Macksburg residents saw the debut of the *Grant Chief* and the *Macksburg Independent*. When the Atlantic Southern and CW&DM shut down, both weeklies struggled and by 1921 had suspended publication. And there was enhancement of the quality of community life. Communities large and small launched or enlarged their summertime Chautauquas, religious gatherings, old settlers reunions, and other local events.

The timing of the cluster railroads was unfortunate. If they had appeared a generation or two earlier, most surely would not have experienced early deaths. Their overall impact would undoubtedly have been greater; these roads could have been ongoing engines of development and prosperity. Still, their future would have been limited because they were principally short-haul grain and livestock carriers, lacking

sustainable mineral deposits, major industries, or other durable rail customers. Not to be overlooked is the depression that ravaged the nation
during 1920–1921, and the continued decline of farm income throughout
the Roaring Twenties. In Iowa, the Midwest, and elsewhere, too, the
last railroads built were often among the first to shut down. With modal
competition and all-weather roads, these carriers had largely outlived
their usefulness—their trains were on the fast track to Extinctionville.
Sunset-era promoters, of course, were not clairvoyant; it remained the
Railway Age. "When the iron rail network was built to completion in the
half-century before World War I, the nation needed nearly every railroad
that was constructed," concludes historian John Stover. "In a day when
the farm wagon was the main mode of transport, closely spaced lines
with depots located every few miles made real sense." Simply stated,
trade centers were dependent on railroads and horse-drawn conveyances. Rail construction rarely surpassed contemporary needs.[10]

There were hints of drastic change in transportation technologies.
Immediately prior to World War I, newspapers reported the growing
use of automobiles for intercity travel. Take this 1916 personal column
entry: "Miss Agnes Bedford, a former teacher and principal of College
Springs public schools, drove in from Idana, Kans., last week in her Ford.
She never asks the rail roads any questions now when she wants to go
anywhere, just jumps into her car, pulls the lever and goes." The distance
covered was approximately two hundred miles. The automobile Bedford
owned was that ultrapopular Ford Model T, which became less expensive. By 1916 a Model T cost about 50 percent of its original list price.
(Ford built more than fifteen million Model Ts between 1908 and 1927.)
The Model T and other automobile makes represented a new American
freedom by putting the nation on wheels. Town residents acquired the
earliest horseless carriages, and rural families followed suit only after
they became less expensive and more dependable and country roads
improved. Even before World War I, the attitude toward automobiles
evolved in that they were no longer playthings of the rich. Still, there
were those in the immediate postwar years who naively believed that
they would not cause the death or serious decline of short- or long-haul
railroad passenger service. "When people will get over their joy riding

spree when their bellies are empty and the credit exhausted, passenger demand will recover." Notwithstanding naysayers, "automania" swept America.[11]

On the eve of World War I, commercial truck usage began to emerge. Shortly after the I&OSL suspended operations, Treynor area farmers learned the value of employing trucks to haul hogs to market. It did not take long before cattle moved in this manner to area slaughterhouses. By the 1920s, this form of transport had become widespread in the Hawkeye State. In 1925 *Railway Age* pointed out that 40 percent of livestock received by the Iowa Packing Company in Des Moines arrived by "motor truck." The distance traveled was mostly from a twenty-five to thirty-mile radius, but "will be extended to 100 miles or more with completion of all-weather roads." This estimation supported what US secretary of agriculture William Marion Jardine announced that same year; he did not expect railroads would encounter truck competition for distances exceeding thirty miles. But that was all to change dramatically. Mud was becoming less likely to mire the most powerful vehicles or even cake their wheels. This decade also saw expansion of interstate trucking operations, which negatively impacted the railroad industry, large and small carriers alike.[12]

These sunset cluster shortlines, except for the northern section of the AN&S, never had a fair trial to demonstrate their commercial value. Most midwestern railroads could not be expected to show profitability during their first years of operation. Maintenance expenses were high until the roadbed became seasoned. Betterments ranging from depots to sidings were ongoing. Moreover, it took time for managers to determine what degree of service traffic demanded, and customers, accustomed to going elsewhere, needed to readjust. As new business developed with the improving quality of operations, a railroad became more appreciated and financially stronger.

When abandonment occurred, communities served exclusively by these sunset carriers felt the loss, yet departure of the iron horse usually did not prove immediately fatal. Morton Mills is representative. In "Town Grows Without Railroad," a newspaper reporter in 1923 wrote that "the lumber yards, stores and other business places that the town boasted of when the railroad ceased to exist are still doing a good business. The town steadfastly refuses to die." Notable exceptions were those hamlets that had sprung up at trackside; they declined or vanished much sooner. In time, however, broken communities dotted the landscape. These places could not handle the impact of motorized vehicles, good roads, business centralization, and farm mechanization and consolidation. Convenient access to a railroad often made little difference.[13]

As with all business closures, there were the human repercussions, which could be long lasting. They involved more than lost investments, though some of these were sizeable for backers and taxpayers. The enormous dollar losses sustained by the handful of farmers who bankrolled the I&OSL stand out. Those associated with these struggling shortlines surely encountered sleepless nights and recurrent anxieties. Hans Rattenborg is an example: the constant strain of managing the affairs of the AN&S ruined his health. "It was while engaged in this project that Mr. Rattenborg's health was broken," noted his obituary, "and he never fully regained his former health." Moreover, unpleasant memories linger. Observed Elaine Artlip, who coproduced a sesquicentennial video on Grant: "The very mention of the road is guaranteed to raise the blood pressure of descendants of those who invested heavily in the project." A woman who grew up on a farm near Grant agreed. She recalled decades after the Atlantic Southern suspended operations that her father, who made a substantial investment in the building of the AN&S, fretted for years about its failure. In fact, she did not care to talk about "that railroad."[14]

NOTES

1. SUNSET YEARS

1. *American Railroad Journal*, November 9, 1850.

2. William D. Middleton, George M. Smerk, and Robert L. Diehl, eds., *Encyclopedia of North American Railroads* (Bloomington: Indiana University Press, 2007), 1132; "Railway Lines Abandoned During the Year 1920," *Railway Age* 70 (January 7, 1921): 151.

3. George W. Hilton and John F. Due, *The Electric Interurban Railways in America* (Stanford, CA: Stanford University Press, 1960), 186, 331, 346, 398; William F. Gephart, *Transportation and Industrial Development in the Middle West* (New York: Columbia University Press, 1909), 231–241.

4. It can be argued that the San Diego & Arizona Railway was the last transcontinental railroad. Construction began in 1911 and was completed eight years later, resulting in a 156-mile line that linked the Southern Pacific at El Central, CA, with San Diego.

5. John F. Stover, *The Life and Decline of the American Railroad* (New York: Oxford University Press, 1970), 107–109; *Railway Statistics of the United States of America for the Year Ending June 30, 1910* (Chicago: Gunthorp-Warren, 1911), 80, 85.

6. Hilton and Due, *The Electric Interurban Railways in America*, 44.

7. *Railroad Gazette* 44 (January 24, 1908): 130.

8. Herbert S. Schell, "The Dakota Southern, A Frontier Railway Venture of Dakota Territory," *South Dakota Historical Review* 2 (October 1936): 99; *Clarinda* (IA) *Herald*, December 16, 1909; *Des Moines* (IA) *Register and Leader*, April 4, 1912.

9. See H. Roger Grant, "The Railroad Right-of-Way," *Railroad History* 221 (Fall-Winter 2019): 4–5. Canals usually required a wider swath of land. The first long distance ditch in the United States, the Santee Canal in South Carolina, used a corridor width of 210 feet.

10. "J. A. Harris and Wife to Atlantic Northern & Southern Ry. Co." July 11, 1907, Filled for Record the 23rd of September AD 1907 at 11 A.M., A. K. Coomes [Cass County, IA] Recorder B-212, P 482, document in possession of author.

11. Edward Lewis, *American Shortline Railway Guide* (Milwaukee, WI: Kalmbach, 1986), 54.

12. James Patrick Morgans, *John Todd and the Underground Railroad: Biography of an Iowa Abolitionist* (Jefferson, NC: McFarland, 2006), 47–59, 154–155; Otha

D. Wearin, "The Tabor and Northern Railroad," *Annals of Iowa* 38 (Fall 1966): 427–430; W. W. Merritt Sr., *A History of the County of Montgomery from the Earliest Days to 1906* (Red Oak, IA: Express, 1906), 79; Catharine Grace Barbour Farquhar, "Tabor and Tabor College," *Iowa Journal of History and Politics* 41 (October 1943): 387–388.

13. Frank B. Tracy, "The Farmer's Railroad," *McClure's Magazine* (May 1899): 35–42. See also H. Roger Grant, *Self-Help in the 1890s Depression* (Ames: Iowa State University Press, 1983), 74–100.

14. H. Roger Grant, "Captive Corporation: The Farmers' Grain & Shipping Company, 1896–1945," *North Dakota History* 49 (Winter 1982): 4–10.

15. James W. Whitaker, *Feedlot Empire: Beef Cattle Feeding in Illinois and Iowa, 1840–1900* (Ames: Iowa State University Press, 1975), 126; Earle D. Ross, *Iowa Agriculture: An Historical Survey* (Iowa City: State Historical Society of Iowa, 1951), 118–120. See Allan G. Bogue, *From Prairie to Cornbelt: Farming on the Illinois and Iowa Prairie in the Nineteenth Century* (Chicago: University of Chicago Press, 1963) for an examination of the rapid evolution of Iowa agriculture.

16. *Cedar Rapids Gazette* quoted in the *Current-Press* (College Springs, IA), August 26, 1909; Edwin Percy Chase, "Forty Years of Main Street," *Iowa Journal of History and Politics* 34 (July 1936): 253; *Evening Nonpareil* (Council Bluffs, IA), July 27, 1917.

17. *Historical Statistics of the United States, Colonial Times to 1957* (Washington, DC: US Bureau of the Census, 1960), 12–13; Leland L. Sage, *A History of Iowa* (Ames: Iowa State University Press, 1974), 216–217; *Page County Democrat* (Clarinda, IA), December 12, 1910. As early as the mid-1890s one writer noted the decline of small towns in Iowa but concentrated on eastern sections of the state. See Henry J.

Fletcher, "The Doom of the Small Town," *Forum* 19 (April 1895): 214–223.

18. *Evening Nonpareil* (Council Bluffs, IA), February 1, 1908.

19. George Rogers Taylor, *The Transportation Revolution, 1815–1860* (New York: Holt, Rinehart and Winston, 1951), 29–31; William H. Thompson, *Transportation in Iowa: A Historical Summary* (Ames: Iowa Department of Transportation, 1989), 5; Ben Hur Wilson, "Planked from Burlington," *Palimpsest* 16 (October 1935): 309–328.

20. John King, "John Plumbe: Origins of the Pacific Railroad," *Annals of Iowa* 6 (January 1904): 288–296; Ora Williams, "When Railroads Were Sought," *Annals of Iowa* 31 (Winter 1952): 166; *Reports of the President and Engineer of the Fort Wayne, Lacon and Platte Valley Air Line Railroad Company* (Cincinnati, OH, 1854), 1–2; Don L. Hofsommer, *Steel Trails of Hawkeyeland: Iowa's Railroad Experience* (Bloomington: Indiana University Press, 2005), 8.

21. Hofsommer, *Steel Trails of Hawkeyeland*, 23.

22. Donovan L. Hofsommer, "A Chronology of Iowa Railroads," *Railroad History* 132 (Spring 1975): 71–80; *A Chronology of American Railroads: Including Mileage by States and by Years* (Washington, DC: Association of American Railroads, 1955): 7; Ben Hur Wilson, "Abandoned Railroads of Iowa," *Iowa Journal of History and Politics* 26 (January 1928): 6; *Fiftieth Annual Report of the Board of Railroad Commissioners for the Year Ending December 1, 1927* (Des Moines: State Printer, 1928), 8.

23. Technically, the second line abandonment in Iowa occurred in 1879, and it involved the narrow-gauge St. Louis, Keosauqua & St. Paul Railroad. This short-lived road operated for less than four years. A year later, the Rock Island Railroad acquired the right-of-way and installed a 4.5-mile branch from Mt. Zion

into Keosauqua. This trackage lasted until 1976.

24. Wilson, "Abandoned Railroads of Iowa," 41; George W. Hilton, *American Narrow Gauge Railroads* (Stanford, CA: Stanford University Press, 1990), 397; Hofsommer, *Steel Trails of Hawkeyeland*, 35; *Poor's Manual of the Railroads of the United States* (New York: Poor's Railroad Manual, 1916), 283; S. B. Evans, ed., *History of Wapello County, Iowa, and Representative Citizens* (Chicago: Biographical, 1901), 148; Harrison L. Waterman, ed., *History of Wapello County Iowa* (Chicago: S. J. Clarke, 1914), 1:321, 2:23; A. P. Butts, *Walter Wilson and His Crooked Creek Railroad* (Webster City, IA: Fred Hahne, 1976) 73–74.

25. *Moody's Manual of Railroads and Corporation Securities* (New York: Moody Manual, 1911), 686; *Poor's Manual of the Railroads of the United States* (New York: Poor's Railroad Manual, 1906), 601, 603; Gary L. Holzinger, *The Wapsie Valley Route: Chicago, Anamosa & Northern Railway* (Quasqueton, IA: Quasqueton Area Historical Society, 2022), 10–11, 39–40, 47, 56; Wilson, "Abandoned Railroads of Iowa," 29–30, 45–46, 56; *Adams County Free Press* (Corning, IA), October 4, 1916.

26. H. Roger Grant, ed., *Iowa Railroads: The Essays of Frank P. Donovan, Jr.* (Iowa City: University of Iowa Press, 2000), 218.

27. The three Iowa interurbans with a steam railroad heritage are the Charles City Western Railway; Fort Dodge, Des Moines & Southern Railway; and Iowa Southern Utilities.

28. Hilton and Due, *The Electric Interurban Railways in America*, 357–365; *Fiftieth Annual Report of the Board of Railroad Commissioners*, 10.

29. Western Iowa experienced several proposed interurbans. An insert map in the January 1911 issue of *Electric Railway Journal*, for example, shows an interurban projected between Sioux City and Council Bluffs.

30. Wearin, "The Tabor and Northern Railroad," 427–430; Wilson, "Abandoned Railroads of Iowa," 61–62.

31. Major railroads commonly used separately organized companies for their branch line projects for one principal reason: if the line failed financially, it would not adversely affect the parent firm.

32. Mildred Throne, "The Repeal of the Iowa Granger Laws, 1878," *Iowa Journal of History* 47 (October 1949): 289–324 and 51 (April 1953): 97–130; Richard C. Overton, *Burlington Route: A History of the Burlington Lines* (New York: Alfred A. Knopf, 1965), 111, 164, 520–521; W. W. Baldwin, comp., *Chicago, Burlington & Quincy Documentary History: Volume Two Lines in Iowa and Missouri* (Chicago: Chicago, Burlington & Quincy Railroad, 1929), 232, 245, 348, 365, 382, 462, 1021, 1030.

33. H. Roger Grant, *A Mighty Fine Road: A History of the Chicago, Rock Island & Pacific Railroad Company* (Bloomington: Indiana University Press, 2020), 50; Overton, *Burlington Route*, 165.

34. Sage, *A History of Iowa*, 311.

35. Thompson, *Transportation in Iowa*, 69, 93; George S. May, "Getting Out of the Mud," *Palimpsest* 46 (February 1965): 96–115.

36. *Red Oak* (IA) *Express*, December 10, 1909.

37. *Clarinda Herald*, February 25, 1915.

38. Karl Detzer, *Culture Under Canvas: The Story of Tent Chautauqua: The Story of Tent Chautauqua* (New York: Hastings House, 1958), 69.

39. Burlington Route Time Tables, November 1910; *Page County Democrat*, April 14, 1908; Frank P. Donovan Jr., "The Manchester & Oneida Railway," *Palimpsest* 38 (September 1957): 345.

40. H. Roger Grant, "Hard Luck Town: College Springs, Iowa," *Iowa Heritage Illustrated* 92 (Spring 2011): 2–9; "The Story of Grant: In Honor of the 150th Birthday Celebration, June 21, 2008,"

video produced by Elaine Artlip and Janet Taylor.

2. ATLANTIC NORTHERN & SOUTHERN RAILWAY

1. The north–south directional designation in a railroad corporate name also occurred elsewhere: Louisiana North & South Railroad, Muscatine North & South Railroad (Iowa), North & South Railroad (Wyoming), North & South Carolina Railroad, North & South Railroad of Georgia, and North & South Texas Railroad. East–west names were fewer: East & West Railroad Company of Alabama and East & West Louisiana Railroad.

2. *Evening Nonpareil* (Council Bluffs, IA), January 3, 1908; *Thirty-Eighth Annual Report of the Board of Railroad Commissioners for the Year Ending December 6, 1915* (Des Moines: State of Iowa, 1917), 63, hereafter cited as *Thirty-Eighth Annual Report*.

3. Lila Hoogeveen and Shiona Putnam, *Images of America: Atlantic* (Charleston, SC: Arcadia, 2010), 40–41, 48–49.

4. H. Roger Grant, *A Mighty Fine Road: A History of the Chicago, Rock Island & Pacific Railroad Company* (Bloomington: Indiana University Press, 2020), 21, 34, 36, 38; Tom Savage, *A Dictionary of Iowa Place-Names* (Iowa City: University of Iowa Press, 2007), 30; *One Hundred Years of Pioneering and Progress: Atlantic, Iowa* (Atlantic, IA, 1968), 33; *Red Oak* (IA) *Express*, January 4, 1910.

5. *Atlantic* (IA) *Telegraph*, January 3, 1908.

6. Arthur Herman, *The Viking Heart: How Scandinavians Conquered the World* (Boston: Houghton Mifflin Harcourt, 2021), 264–265; *Des Moines* (IA) *Register and Leader*, February 9, 1913; Jette Mackintosh, "'Little Denmark' on the Prairie: A Study of the Towns Elk Horn and Kimballton in Iowa," *Journal of American Ethnic History* (Spring 1988): 46; Thomas Peter Christensen, *A History of Danes in Iowa*

(New York: Arno Press, 1979), 13; Ronald D. Bro, *Out of Denmark: An Immigrant Story* (Decorah, IA: Anundsen, 2009), 7.

7. Edward S. White, *Past and Present of Shelby County Iowa* (Chicago: B. F. Brown, 1915), 1:274, 427; Thorvald Hansen, "Danish Immigrant Materials: The Archives of Grand View College," *Annals of Iowa* 45 (Spring 1980): 315; Leah D. Rogers, "Architectural and Historical Survey of the Danish Community of Kimballton Audubon County, Iowa" (Final Report Prepared for Kimballton Historic Preservation Commission and the State Historical Society of Iowa Historic Preservation Bureau, June 30, 1993), hereafter cited as Rogers Report, 15; Herman, *The Viking Heart*, 285.

8. Rogers Report, 16, 19.

9. Savage, *A Dictionary of Iowa Place-Names*, 122; *Evening Nonpareil*, January 30, 1908; Mackintosh, "'Little Denmark' on the Prairie," 58–59; Rogers Report, 7–8.

10. *Villisca* (IA) *Review*, March 12, 1902, June 18, 1902, August 27, 1902; *Red Oak Express*, April 18, 1902.

11. *Red Oak Express*, August 31, 1906; *Elk Horn Community History* (Elk Horn, IA: privately printed, 2000), 117; *Des Moines* (IA) *Sunday Register*, December 2, 1928; *Atlantic* (IA) *News-Telegraph*, February 16, 1932; Rogers Report, 21; *Villisca Review*, January 5, 1911; *Sunday Nonpareil*, May 26, 1907; *Atlantic News*, January 8, 1908, *Atlantic News-Telegraph*, February 16, 1991.

12. *Audubon County Journal* (Exira, IA), February 6, 1908; *Poor's Manual of Railroads of the United States* (New York: H. V. & H. W. Poor, 1910), 1200; *Evening Nonpareil*, February 4, 1907.

13. *Villisca Review*, January 5, 1911; M. W. Savage to Charles F. Wells, May 2, 1911, in possession of author.

14. *Elk Horn Community History*, 118; *Atlantic* (IA) *Messenger* quoted in *Red Oak Express*, January 4, 1907.

15. *Audubon County Journal*, April 4, 1907; *Evening Nonpareil*, June 24, 1907; *Elk Horn Community History*, 118.

16. *Elk Horn Community History*, 118.

17. *Elk Horn Community History*, 118.

18. *Elk Horn Community History*, 119; *Audubon County Journal*, February 8, 1908.

19. *One Hundred Years of Pioneering and Progress*, 34; *Atlantic News*, January 3, 1908. Special dinners to honor workers and guests went well when provided on sunset cluster railroads. But there was at least one exception in Iowa at such a celebration. When the Burlington & Missouri River Railroad (Burlington) arrived in Ottumwa during the late summer of 1859, the community dinner for workers did not go as planned. "The citizens of Ottumwa had provided a free dinner on long tables beneath the shade of the trees; when the food was placed on the tables, the throng did not wait for dinner to be announced, but made a rush and grab, and swept everything off the tables. The dinner was a failure, not because there was not enough provided, but through the waste and selfishness of those who wanted more than a fair share of the victuals." S. B. Evans, ed., *History of Wapello County, Iowa, and Representative Citizens* (Chicago: Biographical, 1901), 73.

20. *Elk Horn Community History*, 119.

21. The American Standard locomotive with a 4-4-0 wheel arrangement was introduced in 1836 and immediately became immensely popular. By the 1870s more than 80 percent of the country's steam engines featured this design. For decades thousands of these 4-4-0s became available on the used market. F. H. Whyte, an official with the New York Central Lines, created this classification scheme by noting the number of pilot wheels, drivers, and trailing wheels to identify steam locomotives. Thus the "American" or "Eight Wheeler" features a four-wheel pilot, two pairs of coupled drivers, and no trailing wheels.

22. *Poor's Manual of the Railroads* (1910), 1200; *Evening Nonpareil*, January 3, 1908, January 10, 1908, January 26, 1908; *Audubon County Journal*, January 9, 1908; Barbara Lund-Jones and John W. Nielsen, eds., *Embracing Two Worlds: The Thorval Muller Family of Kimballton* (Blair, NE: Lur Publications, 1998), 106.

23. *Evening Nonpareil*, January 6, 1908.

24. *Poor's Manual of Railroads of the United States* (1910), 1200; *Official Guide of the Railways* (New York: National Railway, January 1911), 1165; Lila Hoogeveen and Shiona Putnam, *Images of America: Cass County* (Charleston, SC: Arcadia, 2011), 106.

25. Rogers Report, 21; *Des Moines Sunday Register*, December 2, 1928.

26. Rogers Report, 21; *Poor's Manual of Railroads of the United States* (1910), 1200; *Current-Press* (College Springs, IA), August 12, 1909; *Evening Nonpareil*, April 16, 1908, August 4, 1908; *Thirty-Third Annual Report of the Board of Railroad Commissioners for the Year Ending December 5, 1910* (Des Moines: State Printer, 1910), 392.

27. Mackintosh, "'Little Denmark' on the Prairie," 53; Lund-Jones and Nielsen, eds., *Embracing Two Worlds*, 93–105; *Audubon County Journal*, July 8, 1909, July 30, 1909.

28. *Villisca Review*, January 5, 1911.

29. *Villisca Review*, January 5, 1911.

30. *Villisca Review*, June 18, 1908.

31. *Villisca Review*, January 5, 1911; *Evening Nonpareil*, December 19, 1910.

32. *Villisca Review*, January 5, 1911; *Evening Nonpareil*, December 19, 1910.

33. *Villisca Review*, January 5, 1911.

34. *Villisca Review*, January 5, 1911.

35. *Villisca Review*, January 5, 1911.

36. Frederick A. Talbot, *Railway Wonders of the World* (London: Cassell, 1924), 78–79.

37. *Villisca Review,* January 5, 1911; *Current-Press,* December 12, 1910; *Evening Nonpareil,* December 27, 1910; *Red Oak* (IA) *Sun,* December 16, 1910.

38. *Villisca Review,* January 5, 1911.

39. *Villisca Review,* January 5, 1911; *Clarinda* (IA) *Herald,* January 5, 1911; *Red Oak Express,* December 30, 1910.

40. *Evening Nonpareil,* December 17, 1910, January 7, 1911, January 11, 1911, January 13, 1911; *Villisca Review,* January 26, 1911; *Adams County Free Press* (Corning, IA), January 21, 1911; *Atlantic Daily Telegraph* (Atlantic, IA), January 6, 1911. Hans Rattenborg, whose railroad experiences contributed to declining health, died on February 15, 1932, at age fifty-nine. *Atlantic News-Telegraph,* February 16, 1932.

41. *Evening Nonpareil,* December 29, 1911.

42. *Evening Nonpareil,* January 15, 1911, January 29, 1911.

43. *Evening Nonpareil,* February 4, 1911, February 8, 1911, February 17, 1911.

44. *Red Oak Express,* March 3, 1911; *Evening Nonpareil,* March 3, 1911, March 4, 1911, March 8, 1911.

45. *Evening Nonpareil,* April 28, 1911; *Red Oak Express,* April 28, 1911.

46. *Thirty-Eighth Annual Report,* 63.

47. *Denison* (IA) *Review,* November 11, 1914; *Red Oak Express,* May 10, 1912.

48. *Thirty-Eighth Annual Report,* 64; Elaine Artlip and Janet Taylor, "The Story of Grant, 1858–2008," 2008 video in possession of author; *Red Oak Sun,* October 25, 1912; *Red Oak Express,* October 16, 1911; *Villisca Review,* July 23, 1914; *Des Moines Register and Leader,* October 19, 1913.

49. *Villisca Review,* January 20, 1911, September 21, 1911, October 26, 1911, October 31, 1912, November 14, 1912, July 3, 1913, February 12, 1914; *Red Oak Sun,* February 16, 1912, November 1, 1912, January 24, 1913; *Thirty-Eighth Annual Report,* 64. For commentary on tent Chautauqua, see Frank Luther Mott, *Time Enough: Essays in Autobiography* (Chapel Hill: University of North Carolina Press, 1962), 88–103, Karl Detzer, *Culture Under Canvas: The Story of Tent Chautauqua* (New York: Hastings House, 1958), and Roger E. Barrows, *The Traveling Chautauqua: Caravans of Culture in Early 20th Century America* (Jefferson, NC: McFarland, 2019).

50. *Villisca Review,* December 1, 1910.

51. *Villisca Review,* March 27, 1913, August 14, 1913, September 18, 1913.

52. *Villisca Review,* January 22, 1914, February 5, 1914, February 26, 1914, July 23, 1914.

53. *Villisca Review,* November 4, 1914.

54. *Daily Nonpareil,* May 7, 1936.

55. Hoogeveen and Putnam, *Images of America: Cass County,* 103, 106; *Des Moines Register,* June 15, 1961; *Evening Nonpareil,* March 10, 1921, January 23, 1922.

56. *Red Oak Sun,* September 5, 1913.

57. *Villisca Review,* July 3, 1913.

58. *Des Moines Register and Leader,* March 22, 1913; David Hudson, Marvin Bergman, and Loren Horton, eds., *The Biographical Dictionary of Iowa* (Iowa City: University of Iowa Press, 2008), 456–457; *Denison Review,* March 30, 1932.

59. *Evening Nonpareil,* April 12, 1912, November 5, 1911, December 29, 1911, January 16, 1912; *Daily Times* (Davenport, IA), November 30, 1911; *Des Moines Register and Leader,* May 26, 1912.

60. *Evening Nonpareil,* September 28, 1911, October 29, 1911, December 3, 1911; William B. Friedricks, *Investing in Iowa: The Life and Times of F. M. Hubbell* (Des Moines: Iowan Books, 2007), 45–53, 83–88; *Page County Democrat* (Clarinda, IA), January 25, 1912.

61. Frank P. Donovan Jr., "Edwin Hawley," *Trains & Travel* 12 (September 1952): 52.

62. *Evening Nonpareil,* November 10, 1911; Don L. Hofsommer, *The Tootin' Louie: A History of the Minneapolis & St. Louis Railway* (Minneapolis: University

of Minnesota Press, 2005), 120; interview with Don L. Hofsommer, July 16, 2021.

63. *Evening Nonpareil*, November 7, 1911.

64. *Evening Nonpareil*, March 18, 1912.

65. *Evening Nonpareil*, April 8, 1912, June 25, 1912, June 26, 1912, July 17, 1912; *Nebraska State Journal* (Lincoln), May 26, 1912; *Sunday Nonpareil*, May 19, 1912, June 23, 1912.

66. *Evening Nonpareil*, July 18, 1912.

67. *Evening Times-Republican* (Marshalltown, IA), July 20, 1912; *Sunday Nonpareil*, July 21, 1912.

68. *Evening Nonpareil*, July 29, 1912, August 3, 1912, August 5, 1912, August 30, 1912, October 25, 1912, November 1, 1912; *Denison Review*, August 7, 1912.

69. *Evening Nonpareil*, December 10, 1912, December 12, 1912.

70. *Evening Nonpareil*, February 24, 1913, March 2, 1913, April 9, 1913; *Des Moines Register and Leader*, March 4, 1913; *Clarinda Journal*, May 29, 1913.

71. *Evening Nonpareil*, May 19, 1913, June 16, 1913, July 28, 1913, August 10, 1913, February 5, 1914; *Thirty-Eighth Annual Report*, 63.

72. *Sioux City* (IA) *Journal*, November 17, 1914; *Des Moines Register and Leader*, November 12, 1916; *New York Times*, February 1, 1912.

73. *Thirty-Eighth Annual Report*, 63; *Adams County Free Press* (Corning, IA), January 6, 1915.

74. *Thirty-Eighth Annual Report*, 63–64; *Des Moines Register and Leader*, September 29, 1915; *Davenport* (IA) *Weekly Democrat and Leader*, August 14, 1913.

75. *Thirty-Eighth Annual Report*, 66.

76. *Villisca Review*, September 18, 1913; *Thirty-Eighth Annual Report*, 77; *Des Moines Register and Leader*, August 10, 1913, November 11, 1914.

77. *Thirty-Eighth Annual Report*, 77–78.

78. *Poor's Manual of Railroads of the United States* (New York: Poor's Railroad Manual, 1915), 1132; *Red Oak Express*, July 23, 1915.

79. *Thirty-Eighth Annual Report*, 77–79; *Evening Nonpareil*, January 14, 1915; *Des Moines Register and Leader*, October 1, 1915.

80. *Villisca Review* quoted in *Adams County Free Press*, January 6, 1915.

81. *Evening Nonpareil*, March 19, 1915.

82. *Red Oak Express*, November 12, 1915; *Des Moines Register and Leader*, September 30, 1915; *Evening Nonpareil*, January 24, 1916.

83. *The Railway Library, 1915* (Chicago: Stromberg, Allen, 1916), 69–70.

84. *Evening Nonpareil*, January 26, 1916, January 27, 1916; *Red Oak Express*, February 4, 1916.

85. *Red Oak Express*, May 19, 1916.

86. *Evening Nonpareil*, July 4, 1916, July 5, 1916; *Clarinda Herald*, January 4, 1917.

87. *Grant Chief* (Grant, IA), February 22, 1917.

88. *Adams County Free Press*, May 30, 1917.

89. *Grant Chief*, November 5, 1914; "More Railway Lines Abandoned Than Built," *Railway Age* 66 (January 3, 1919): 57; *Evening Nonpareil*, November 16, 1914, February 28, 1917; *Villisca Review*, December 30, 1914; *Thirty-Ninth Annual Report of the Board of Railroad Commissioners for the Year Ending December 4, 1916* (Des Moines: State of Iowa, 1917), 201–202.

90. Miscellaneous Record, Book 248, page 112, Cass County Office of the Recorder; *Elk Horn Community History*, 116; *Evening Nonpareil*, August 6, 1913.

91. *Evening Nonpareil*, October 28, 1913, March 12, 1915, September 12, 1915, November 1, 1915; *Register and Leader*, September 1, 1915.

92. *Poor's Manual of Railroads of the United States* (1915), 1132; Interstate Commerce Commission, Valuation Docket No. 448, Tentative Valuation Report of the Property of Atlantic Northern Railway Company, as of June 30, 1918, 3.

93. *Evening Nonpareil*, October 27, 1919; *Des Moines Sunday Register*, November 2, 1919; Miscellaneous Record, Book 269, page 564, Cass County Office of the Recorder.

94. James Grant, *The Forgotten Depression: 1921: The Crash That Cured Itself* (New York: Simon & Schuster, 2014); Dorothy Schwieder, "Rural Iowa in the 1920s," *Annals of Iowa* 47 (1983): 104–115.

95. *Poor's Manual of Railroads* (New York: Poor's, 1922), 1277; *Moody's Manual of Investments* (New York: Moody's Investors Service, 1926), 833; *Fiftieth Annual Report of the Board of Railroad Commissioners* (Des Moines: State of Iowa, 1927), 197–198.

96. *Elk Horn* (IA) *Review*, 1928, clipping in possession of author.

97. This second Atlantic Northern steam locomotive, built by the Rhode Island Locomotive Works in 1886, came from the Burlington. In 1916 it had been rebuilt in the Burlington's Galesburg, IL, shops. At the time of liquidation, this classic 4-4-0 was sold to the Manchester & Oneida Railway, where it remained in active service until that shortline closed in 1951. Frank P. Donovan Jr., "The Manchester & Oneida Railway," *The Palimpsest* 38 (September 1957): 387.

98. *Moody's Steam Railroads* (New York: Moody's Investors Service, 1934), 436; H. H. Fulton, "A Small Line That's Still Going Strong," *Railroad Stories* 12 (September 1933): 86; *Des Moines Register*, July 23, 1933.

99. *Fifty-Eighth Annual Report of the Board of Railroad Commissioners for the Year Ending December 2, 1935* (Des Moines: State of Iowa, 1936), 316–317; *Elk Horn Review*, June 2, 1983; *Omaha* (NE) *Evening Bee-News*, September 11, 1935; *Evening Nonpareil*, December 8, 1935, December 11, 1935, January 5, 1936; "To the Stockholders of Atlantic Northern Railway Company," n.d., copy in possession of author.

100. *Evening Nonpareil*, July 28, 1936, October 30, 1936, November 2, 1936; *Elk Horn Community History*, 116.

101. *Evening Nonpareil*, January 3, 1936, February 4, 1936.

102. *Evening Nonpareil*, December 29, 1936; *Elk Horn Community History*, 121.

103. *Elk Horn Community History*, 121.

3. IOWA & SOUTHWESTERN RAILWAY

1. The origin of the Ikey nickname is unclear. Larry Polsley, a Blanchard, Iowa, native, surmises that it had a negative connotation. "Ikey was name put on [the railroad] by folks who weren't so fond of the plan and it stuck." Larry Polsley to author, April 29, 2021. John Ayto and John Simpson, editors of the *Oxford Dictionary of Modern Slang* (New York: Oxford University Press, 2010), 108, suggest that it might be a pejorative antisemitic slur. There are other possible meanings, including having a good opinion of oneself and being crafty. Whatever the explanation, Ikey became used by the public throughout the greater Page County area to identify the Iowa & Southwestern Railway/Railroad, rather than I&S, I&SW, or Southwestern. There was another unusual local nickname—the College Springs *Current-Press* newspaper was affectionately known as "The Gooseberry."

2. Prior to 1904, Le Claire in Scott County would have challenged the claim by College Springs that it was the largest town in Iowa without a railroad. The federal census listed its 1900 population as 997, although a decade later it had dropped to 690. In November 1904 the Iowa & Illinois Railway (later Clinton, Davenport & Muscatine Railway) opened between Davenport and Clinton with Le Claire being an important station. Although an electric interurban, its builders constructed their line to relatively high standards, allowing it to interchange steam railroad rolling

stock. In 1940 the Davenport, Rock Island & Northwestern Railroad, a subsidiary of the Burlington and Milwaukee Railroads, took over the fourteen miles between Davenport and Le Claire when the CD&M shut down its Clinton operations.

3. Larry Polsley to author, April 27, 2021; Tom Savage, *A Dictionary of Iowa Place-Names* (Iowa City: University of Iowa Press, 2007), 39; *Current-Press* (College Springs, IA), September 3, 1908, December 16, 1909; *Tingley* (IA) *Vindicator* quoted in *Clarinda* (IA) *Herald*, April 14, 1908, April 18, 1908; H. Roger Grant, "Hard-Luck Town: College Springs, Iowa," *Iowa Heritage Illustrated* 91 (Spring 2011): 5; *Page County Democrat* (Clarinda, IA), September 1, 1910.

4. *Current-Press*, April 5, 1906, June 21, 1906.

5. *Current-Press*, September 3, 1908, August 12, 1909; *Clarinda Herald*, July 23, 1909.

6. *Current-Press*, April 4, 1908, April 16, 1908, August 12, 1909; *Evening Nonpareil* (Council Bluffs, IA), August 21, 1908.

7. *Railroad Gazette* 44 (January 24, 1908): 130.

8. *Current-Press*, April 23, 1908.

9. *Clarinda Herald*, January 21, 1909; *Current-Press*, January 28, 1909.

10. *Clarinda Herald*, July 22, 1909; *Winterset* (IA) *Madisonian*, November 28, 1907.

11. *Clarinda Herald*, February 11, 1909; *Current-Press*, July 22, 1909; undated clipping, "William Smith Farquhar," Nodaway Valley Historical Museum, Clarinda, IA; W. L. Kershaw, *History of Page County Iowa* (Chicago: Clarke, 1909), II, 58–60; Larry Polsley to author, April 28, 2021; J. W. Kendrick, *Report of Valuation, Iowa & Southwestern Railway, April 15, 1915*, Box 1–91 in John W. Barriger III papers, John W. Barriger III National Railroad Library, St. Louis, MO, hereafter cited as Kendrick Report.

12. *Current-Press*, August 12, 1909.

13. *Clarinda Herald*, July 22, 1909.

14. *Current-Press*, July 22, 1909.

15. *Clarinda Herald*, September 30, 1909.

16. *Clarinda Herald*, July 22, 1909, August 19, 1909, January 27, 1910; *Page County Democrat*, September 2, 1909, August 11, 1910.

17. Leland L. Sage, *A History of Iowa* (Ames: Iowa State University Press, 1974), 255; *Clarinda Herald*, December 16, 1909, December 23, 1909; *Page County Democrat*, December 23, 1909.

18. *Clarinda Herald*, February 2, 1910; *Page County Democrat*, February 3, 1910.

19. *Clarinda Herald*, July 21, 1910; *Page County Democrat*, August 11, 1910.

20. *Current-Press*, September 1, 1910, November 10, 1910; *Page County Democrat*, September 9, 1910.

21. *Page County Democrat*, December 1, 1910.

22. *Clarinda Herald*, October 13, 1910, October 27, 1910.

23. *Clarinda Herald*, December 12, 1910; *Evening Nonpareil*, January 2, 1911; *Sunday Nonpareil*, January 8, 1911.

24. *Page County Democrat*, April 4, 1911.

25. *Clarinda* (IA) *Journal*, October 19, 1911; *Current-Press*, October 19, 1911; *Evening Nonpareil*, October 18, 1911; *Page County Democrat*, November 11, 1911.

26. *Current-Press*, November, n.d., 1911.

27. *Clarinda Journal*, November 23, 1911, November 30, 1911; *Clarinda Herald*, November 30, 1911; Kendrick Report.

28. *Current-Press*, January 4, 1912. The Ikey had yet to receive its first locomotive, described as a "good engine from the New York Central." It expected delivery in early January. *Clarinda Herald*, January 4, 1912. The Ikey would acquire more power and rolling stock. From the Lake Shore & Michigan Southern (NYC), it received a 4-4-0 and 4-6-0; an elderly combine from the Wabash; an "ancient" coach from the Pennsylvania; and three freight cars, namely a boxcar, flatcar, and

"cinder car" from unknown sources. All this equipment was well past its prime and affordable.

29. *Evening Nonpareil*, January 2, 1912; *Des Moines* (IA) *Register and Leader*, January 14, 1912; *Clarinda Journal*, January 4, 1912.

30. *Clarinda Journal*, January 4, 1912; *Des Moines Register and Leader*, January 14, 1912; *Page County Democrat*, January 4, 1912.

31. *Clarinda Journal*, January 4, 1912.

32. Kendrick Report.

33. *Clarinda Journal*, February 1, 1912; *Page County Democrat*, February 15, 1912.

34. *Page County Democrat*, May 30, 1912; *Current-Press*, May 23, 1912.

35. *Clarinda Herald*, July 18, 1912.

36. *Clarinda Herald*, August 1, 1912, November 21, 1912; *Thirty-Seventh Annual Report of the Board of Railroad Commissioners for the Year Ending December 7, 1914* (Des Moines: State Printer, 1915), 424.

37. *Red Oak* (IA) *Express*, August 30, 1912.

38. *Clarinda Herald*, November 28, 1912, October 9, 1913; *Russell's Railway Guide and Hotel Directory* (Cedar Rapids, IA: Russell's Railway Guide, November 1913), 59; *Des Moines Register and Leader*, February 8, 1913.

39. *Clarinda Journal*, May 2, 1912; *Clarinda Herald*, August 15, 1912.

40. *A History of Amity College, College Springs, Iowa* (Bedford, IA: Waubonsie Chapter DAR, 1977), 16.

41. *Clarinda Journal*, July 3, 1913; *Clarinda Herald*, July 3, 1913. The widow of John George sued the Ikey for negligence and asked for a $30,000 ($786,557 in current dollars) settlement. The judge dismissed the case for lack of evidence. *Current-Press*, December 3, 1914.

42. *Clarinda Herald*, April 17, 1913, April 24, 1913.

43. *Current-Press*, January 23, 1913; *Clarinda Herald*, January 30, 1913.

44. *Clarinda Herald*, January 30, 1913, April 3, 1913; *Thirty-Eighth Annual Report of the Board of Railroad Commissioners for the Year Ending December 6, 1915* (Des Moines: State Printer, 1916), 232; *Clarinda Journal*, September 9, 1915, April 27, 1916.

45. *Clarinda Herald*, January 22, 1914, March 12, 1914; Kendrick Report; *Page County Democrat*, June 11, 1914.

46. *Page County Democrat*, February 4, 1915.

47. *Thirty-Seventh Annual Report of the Board of Railroad Commissioners for the Year Ending December 7, 1914*, 338; *Clarinda Herald*, April 29, 1915; *Current-Press*, April 22, 1915; *Clarinda Journal*, April 29, 1915.

48. *Clarinda Journal*, April 29, 1915.

49. *Clarinda Journal*, July 22, 1915; *Current-Press*, August 26, 1915; *Clarinda Herald*, September 9, 1915.

50. *Clarinda Herald*, August 12, 1915.

51. *Clarinda Journal*, April 27, 1916; *Current-Press*, May 4, 1916.

52. *Clarinda Journal*, April 27, 1916; *Clarinda Herald*, April 27, 1916.

53. *Thirty-Ninth Annual Report of the Board of Railroad Commissioners for the Year Ending December 4, 1916* (Des Moines: State of Iowa, 1917), 314–316; *Clarinda Herald*, June 29, 1916, November 2, 1916; *Page County Democrat*, May 16, 1916.

54. *Page County Democrat*, July 16, 1916, October 5, 1916.

55. H. Roger Grant, *"Follow the Flag": A History of the Wabash Railroad Company* (DeKalb: Northern Illinois University Press, 2004), 133; Kendrick Report.

56. *Page County Democrat*, November 9, 1916.

57. *Page County Democrat*, January 11, 1917.

58. *Clarinda Herald*, February 28, 1918.

59. *Clarinda Herald*, April 26, 1917; *Page County Democrat*, June 13, 1918.

60. *Mineral Resources of the United States, 1917, Part I Metals* (Washington,

DC: US Department of the Interior, 1921), 302.

61. *Clarinda Herald*, November 7, 1918.

62. *Current-Press*, April 10, 1919.

63. Larry Polsley to author, January 17, 2022; *Clarinda Herald*, August 8, 1912, April 24, 1913.

4. CRESTON, WINTERSET & DES MOINES RAILROAD

1. *Atlas of Madison County, Iowa* (Philadelphia: Harrison & Warner, 1875); *A. T. Andreas Illustrated Historical Atlas of the State of Iowa* (Chicago: Lakeside Press, 1875); *History of Madison County, Iowa* (Des Moines: Union Historical Society, 1879), 388–89; *Macksburg and Neighbors* (n.p., n.d.), Book 1, 175.

2. Creston proclaimed itself as the blue grass capital of Iowa. The Blue Grass League of Southwestern Iowa sponsored the building of the short-lived Blue Grass Palace. This structure, opened in 1889, celebrated the hay fields and pastures of the region. See *Creston* (IA) *News-Advertiser*, June 21, 2021.

3. W. W. Baldwin, comp., *Chicago, Burlington & Quincy Railroad Company Documentary History: Volume 2 Lines in Iowa and Missouri* (Chicago: Chicago, Burlington & Quincy Railroad, 1929), 1057–1058; Des Moines & Kansas City Railway public timetable, n.d. (ca. 1891); George W. Hilton, *American Narrow Gauge Railroads* (Stanford, CA: Stanford University Press, 1990), 397.

4. George W. Hilton and John F. Due, *The Electric Interurban Railways in America* (Stanford, CA: Stanford University Press, 1960), 3–44; H. Roger Grant, "Electric Traction Promotion in the South Iowa Coalfields," *Palimpsest* 58 (January-February 1977): 18–29; *Current-Press* (College Springs, IA), May 5, 1904.

5. *Courier* (Waterloo, IA), February 7, 1901, February 19, 1901; *Ottumwa* (IA) *Tri-Weekly Courier*, March 26, 1901; *Evening*

Times-Republican (Marshalltown, IA), June 30, 1902.

6. *Evening Times-Republican*, June 30, 1902, October 15, 1902, December 22, 1902.

7. *Evening Times-Republican*, October 15, 1902. While not proposed as an interurban, there was another failed effort to provide Creston a second railroad. When the Burlington relocated and double-tracked its main line through Union County, it left an abandoned roadbed between Talmage and Creston. Promoters saw this as an opportunity to link the Great Western interchange at Talmage to Creston. Commented a circulated report, "It would seem that Creston is now in fair way to secure another line of railroad and that line will be the Chicago Great Western." Backers of this scheme would either sell the fifteen-mile line to the Great Western or operate it as an independent shortline. *Sioux City* (IA) *Journal*, August 10, 1905.

8. Hilton and Due, *The Electric Interurban Railways in America*, 363–365; *Des Moines* (IA) *Register and Leader*, August 12, 1906.

9. Hilton and Due, *The Electric Interurban Railways in America*, 363–365; *The Official Guide of the Railways* (New York: National Railroad, June 1904), 683, 712, 732; *Des Moines Register and Leader*, June 23, 1907.

10. George A. Ide, *History of Union County, Iowa* (Chicago: Clarke, 1908), 51; *Des Moines Register and Leader*, March 4, 1908.

11. Tom Savage, *A Dictionary of Iowa Place-Names* (Iowa City: University of Iowa Press, 2007), 139–40; *Winterset* (IA) *Madisonian*, January 23, 1908; *Macksburg* (IA) *Independent*, May 8, 1919.

12. *Winterset Madisonian*, February 27, 1908, March 5, 1908; *Des Moines Register and Leader*, March 14, 1908.

13. *Des Moines Register and Leader*, March 5, 1908, March 9, 1908, September 27, 1908.

14. *Creston* (IA) *Semi-Weekly Advertiser,* January 19, 1909.

15. *Creston Semi-Weekly Advertiser,* January 19, 1909.

16. *Des Moines* (IA) *Capital,* March 23, 1909.

17. *Winterset Madisonian,* April 8, 1909, July 1, 1909; *Electric Railway Journal* 34 (July 3, 1909): 57; *Current-Press,* April 23, 1908.

18. *Winterset Madisonian,* July 8, 1909; *Creston Semi-Weekly Advertiser,* July 13, 1909; *Electric Railway Journal* 34 (September 18, 1909): 450, 34, (October 23, 1909): 925, 37 (March 18,1911): 483, 37 (June 3, 1911): 997, 37, (November 4, 1911): 1013; *Railway World* 55 (October 13, 1911): 867; *Creston City and Union County Directory* (Des Moines: R. L. Polk, 1913), 65. In 1910 leadership faced a setback when lightning struck and killed Jerry Wilson (1842–1910), who farmed 1,300 acres west of Macksburg. Yet the Wilson family continued to back the road, and according to one source "is largely responsible for the fact that a railroad has been extended into Macksburg." *History of Madison County, Iowa, and Its People* (Chicago: Clarke, 1915) 3, 138–143.

19. *Winterset Madisonian,* October 7, 1909; Ben Hur Wilson, "Abandoned Railroads of Iowa," *Iowa Journal of History and Politics* 26 (January 1928): 23–25; *Thirty-Eighth Annual Report of the Board of Railroad Commissioners for the Year Ending December 6, 1915* (Des Moines: State Printer, 1915), 62–63; *Creston Semi-Weekly Advertiser,* December 29, 1910; H. Roger Grant, *"Follow the Flag": A History of the Wabash Railroad Company* (DeKalb: Northern Illinois University Press, 2004), 91; *Clarinda* (IA) *Journal,* September 5, 1912; *Ottumwa Tri-Weekly Courier,* July 15, 1909.

20. *Clarinda* (IA) *Herald,* November 18, 1909.

21. See Donald L. McMurry, *Great Burlington Strike of 1888: Case Study in Labor Relations* (Cambridge, MA: Harvard University Press, 1956).

22. *Winterset Madisonian,* January 27, 1910, September 29, 1910.

23. Diane Burdette, Office of Iowa Secretary of State, to author, February 6, 2008, hereafter cited as Burdette letter; *Articles of Incorporation of the Creston, Winterset and Des Moines Railroad Company,* Book C-5, 241; *Annual Report of the Creston, Winterset & Des Moines R. R. Co. to the Interstate Commerce Commission of the United States for the Year Ended June 30, 1915,* 1, Interstate Commerce Commission Records, Record Group 134, National Archives and Records Administration, College Park, MD, hereafter cited as *1915 ICC Annual Report; Creston Weekly Advertiser,* July 20, 1911, September 21, 1911; *Winterset Madisonian,* October 5, 1911.

24. *Winterset Madisonian,* January 31, 1912.

25. *Winterset Madisonian,* June 12, 1912, August 7, 1912.

26. *Winterset Madisonian,* August 7, 1912; *Page County Democrat* (Clarinda, IA), August 22, 1912; *1915 ICC Annual Report.*

27. *Creston* (IA) *Plain Dealer,* October 12, 1912; *Des Moines Register and Leader,* November 23, 1912; *[Map] Board of [Iowa] Railroad Commissioners* (Chicago, 1915).

28. *Creston Plain Dealer,* October 12, 1912; *Poor's Manual of Railroads, 1915* (New York: Poor's Railroad Manual, 1915), 1990; *Official Railway Equipment Register* 30 (January 1915): 719.

29. *Winterset Madisonian,* November 6, 1912, November 20, 1912; *Des Moines Register and Leader,* November 10, 1912.

30. *Winterset Madisonian,* December 25, 1912, January 1, 1913, January 8, 1913; *Evening Nonpareil* (Council Bluffs, IA), January 2, 1913; *Omaha* (NE) *Daily Bee,* January 3, 1913; *Des Moines Register and Leader,* January 1, 1913.

31. *Evening Nonpareil,* January 8, 1913, January 22, 1913; *1915 ICC Annual Report.*

32. *Creston Daily Advertiser,* July 7, 1913; *Winterset Madisonian,* February 26, 1913; *Russell's Railway Guide* (Cedar Rapids, IA: Russell's Railway Guide, November 1913), 47; *Union County Iowa History* (Creston, IA: Union County Historical Society, 1970), 12.

33. *Creston* (IA) *Morning American,* September 28, 1913.

34. *Creston* (IA) *Advertiser-Gazette,* October 8, 1913, October 10, 1913.

35. *Creston Morning American,* September 2, 1913, November 21, 1913, November 30, 1913; *Thirty-Sixth Annual Report of the Board of Railroad Commissioners for the Year Ending December 1, 1913* (Des Moines: State Printer, 1913), 426–429.

36. No railroad in Iowa challenged the CW&DM with such a steep grade. The nearest competitor was the Crooked Creek Railroad with a 4 percent grade. Both the Colfax Northern Railway and the Tabor & Northern Railroad had 3 percent grades. "These are small railroads, and do not handle heavy trains," remarked the Iowa Board of Railroad Commissioners, "but the testimony in this case would indicate that light trains are and can be handled on this road [CW&DM]." *Thirty-Eighth Annual Report of the Board of Railroad Commissioners for the Year Ending December 4, 1916* (Des Moines: State of Iowa), 32.

37. Interview with Ralph Breakenridge, Macksburg, IA, August 24, 2007, hereafter cited as Ralph Breakenridge interview; H. Roger Grant, ed., *Iowa Railroads: The Essays of Frank P. Donovan, Jr.* (Iowa City: University of Iowa Press, 2000), 222; *Decisions of the Interstate Commerce Commission of the United States, No. 8936* (Washington, DC, 1918), 377–778; *Macksburg Independent,* October 26, 1916.

38. *Winterset Madisonian,* April 16, 1913; *Grand Island* (NE) *Daily Independent,* July 16, 1912.

39. *Courier* (Waterloo, IA), April 6, 1914; *Ottumwa Tri-Weekly Courier,* April 20, 1915.

40. *Thirty-Sixth Annual Report of the Board of Railroad Commissioners,* 340–441; *1915 ICC Annual Report; History of Madison County Iowa and Its People,* 1, 355.

41. The Adams Express Company, which served the Burlington, operated over the CW&DM. It was the logical firm for the job.

42. *Creston Advertiser-Gazette,* January 2, 1915.

43. *Thirty-Eighth Annual Report of the Board of Railroad Commissioners for the Year Ending December 6, 1915,* 256; *1915 ICC Annual Report; Poor's Manual of Railroads, 1918* (New York: Poor's Railroad Manual, 1918), 1331; *Thirty-Ninth Annual Report of the Board of Railroad Commissions for the Year Ending December 4, 1916,* 196, 272. The financial difficulties that the CW&DM encountered did not deter a group of Creston businessmen from launching the Creston Connecting Railway in early 1915. The CW&DM model would be followed: "The railroad will be run by steam, electricity, gas, gasoline or any other motive power." This projected dozen-mile road would provide Creston with another outlet, a connection to the southeast with the Great Western at Arispe. The Creston Connecting Railway, though, was stillborn. *Red Oak* (IA) *Express,* May 28, 1915.

44. *Macksburg Independent,* August 24, 1916, August 31, 1916.

45. *Macksburg Independent,* September 9, 1916.

46. *Macksburg Independent,* October 5, 1916.

47. *Macksburg Independent,* October 12, 1916.

48. *Sunday Nonpareil* (Council Bluffs, IA), October 22, 1916.

49. *Macksburg Independent,* November 9, 1916.

50. *Annual Report of the Creston, Winterset & Des Moines Railroad Co. to the Interstate Commerce Commission for the Year Ended 31, 1917*, Interstate Commerce Commission Records, Record Group 134, National Archives and Records Administration, College Park, MD; *Fortieth Annual Report of the Board of Railroad Commissioners for the Year Ending December 3, 1917* (Des Moines: State Printer, 1917), 405.

51. *Macksburg Independent*, May 17, 1917, June 26, 1917; *Des Moines Tribune*, July 14, 1917.

52. *Macksburg Independent*, June 7, 1917, March 18, 1918, August 22, 1918.

53. *Macksburg Independent*, September 5, 1918, October 31, 1918. Because of high wartime scrap prices and patriotism, metal dealers sought out liquidating steam shortlines, including the thirty-five-mile Chicago, Anamosa & Northern Railway in eastern Iowa. Dan Kelliher and Frances Davis, "Buys Whole Railroads to Junk'em," *Railroad Man's Magazine* 35 (April 1918): 547–556.

54. *Macksburg Independent*, November 14, 1918, December 12, 1918; *Adams County Free Press* (Corning, IA), November 30, 1918.

55. *Macksburg Independent*, December 19, 1918, October 9, 1919, November 6, 1919, November 27, 1919, April 8, 1920.

56. Burdette letter; *Macksburg Independent*, May 20, 1920, June 17, 1920.

57. *Macksburg Independent*, December 12, 1918, March 24, 1919.

58. *Macksburg Independent*, December 18, 1919.

59. *Macksburg Independent*, November 7, 1918, May 15, 1919.

60. *Creston Morning American*, October 21, 1913; *Macksburg Independent*, August 3, 1916, October 9, 1919; *Winterset Madisonian*, June 15, 1911.

61. Richard C. Overton, *Burlington Route: A History of the Burlington Lines* (New York: Knopf, 1965), 310–318; H.

Roger Grant, *The Corn Belt Route: A History of the Chicago Great Western Railroad Company* (DeKalb: Northern Illinois University Press, 1984), 89–92; William Edward Hayes, *Iron Road to Empire: The History of 100 Years of Progress of the Rock Island Lines* (New York: Simmons-Boardman, 1953), 200–205.

62. *Macksburg Independent*, January 8, 1920; interview with Georgena Breakenridge, Macksburg, IA, August 24, 2007.

63. Ralph Breakenridge interview.

5. IOWA & OMAHA SHORT LINE RAILWAY

1. *History of the Community of Treynor* (Treynor, IA: Treynor Town & Country Club, 1961), 19–20; *Omaha* (NE) *Daily Bee*, August 30, 1910; Tom Savage, *A Dictionary of Iowa Place-Names* (Iowa City: University of Iowa Press, 2007), 221; Homer H. Field and Joseph R. Reed, *History of Pottawattamie County, Iowa From the Earliest Historic Times to 1907* (Chicago: Clarke, 1907), 1:236.

2. Field and Reed, *History of Pottawattamie County*, 1:236; *Omaha* (NE) *World-Herald Magazine*, March 18, 1956.

3. *History of the Community of Treynor*, 20.

4. *Pierre* (SD) *Weekly Press*, October 20, 1908; *Audubon County Journal* (Exira, IA), October 22, 1908, December 3, 1908.

5. *Audubon County Journal*, December 7, 1908; *Omaha Daily Bee*, August 14, 1908.

6. *Audubon County Journal*, October 22, 1908.

7. Richard Orr, *O&CB: Streetcars of Omaha and Council Bluffs* (privately printed, 1996), 204.

8. *Evening Times-Republican* (Marshalltown, IA), January 26, 1909; *Omaha Daily Bee*, April 11, 1909.

9. *Omaha Daily Bee*, April 11, 1909, July 27, 1909.

10. *Omaha Daily Bee*, October 27, 1909.

11. *Omaha Daily Bee*, September 26, 1912.

12. *Omaha World-Herald Magazine*, March 18, 1956.

13. *Omaha Daily Bee*, October 27, 1909; *Evening Times-Republican*, March 3, 1910; *Ottumwa* (IA) *Tri-Weekly Courier*, March 10, 1910.

14. *Omaha World-Herald Magazine*, March 18, 1956; *Thirty-Sixth Annual Report of the Board of Railroad Commissioners for the Year 1913* (Des Moines: State Printer, 1914), 339.

15. *Ottumwa Tri-Weekly Courier*, June 22, 1911.

16. *Omaha World-Herald Magazine*, March 18, 1956.

17. *Evening Nonpareil* (Council Bluffs, IA), June 30, 1911.

18. *Evening Nonpareil*, June 30, 1911; *Omaha World-Herald Magazine*, March 18, 1956; *St. Joseph* (MO) *News-Press*, July 1, 1911. Another Iowa railroad-related hot-air balloon mishap, albeit less dramatic than the one in Treynor, occurred the following year. The event was a community celebration held in Quasqueton on September 17, 1912, to welcome the thirty-five-mile Chicago, Anamosa & Northern Railway. Due to a miscommunication, the female balloonist and parachutist fell out of the basket shortly after liftoff but was uninjured. The balloon continued its flight and later floated harmlessly to the ground. Gary L. Holzinger, *The Waspsie Route: Chicago, Anamosa & Northern Railway* (Quasqueton, IA: Quasqueton Area Historical Society, 2022), 55, 63.

19. *Omaha World-Herald Magazine*, March 18, 1956.

20. *Omaha World-Herald Magazine*, March 18, 1956.

21. *Omaha World-Herald Magazine*, March 18, 1956.

22. *Thirty-Seventh Annual Report of the Board of Railroad Commissioners for the*

Year Ending December 7, 1914 (Des Moines: State Printer, 1915), 424–429.

23. *Webster City* (IA) *Freeman*, February 2, 1915.

24. *Evening Nonpareil*, October 11, 1916; *Omaha Daily Bee*, October 17, 1916.

25. *Thirty-Fifth Annual Report of the Board of Railroad Commissioners for the Year Ending December 2, 1912* (Des Moines: State Printer, 1913), 296, 300–301.

26. *History of the Community of Treynor*, 20.

27. *Evening Times-Republican*, July 11, 1913; *Evening Nonpareil*, July 10, 1913, July 12, 1913; *Register and Leader* (Des Moines, IA), July 15, 1913.

28. *Fifty-Seventh Annual Report of the Board of Railroad Commissioners* (1914), 338–339; *Denison* (IA) *Review*, March 31, 1915.

29. *Sunday Nonpareil*, September 20, 1914.

30. *Ottumwa Tri-Weekly Courier*, February 23, 1916; *Evening Nonpareil*, October 11, 1916; *Omaha Daily Bee*, October 19, 1916.

31. *Sunday Nonpareil*, September 20, 1914; *Evening Nonpareil*, October 11, 1916.

32. Ben Hur Wilson, "Abandoned Railroads of Iowa," *Iowa Journal of History and Politics* 26 (January 1928): 46.

33. *Evening Times-Republican*, July 24, 1916.

34. *Evening Nonpareil*, October 30, 1916.

35. *Evening Nonpareil*, November 10, 1916; *Beatrice* (NE) *Daily Sun*, March 13, 1926; Wilson, "Abandoned Railroads of Iowa," 30.

36. George Adams continued his efforts at railroad promotion. As the I&OSL faltered, he reportedly sought to build a rail line from Atlantic, IA, toward Minneapolis–St. Paul. As of fall 1914, Adams claimed his route had been located as far north as North Branch, a village in Guthrie County, IA. Apparently this scheme quickly failed. There was an additional project: constructing a railroad between

O'Neill, NE, and Mitchell, SD. Adams's financial fate subsequently took a sharp nosedive. The 1920 federal manuscript census listed Adams as a custodian in Lewis, IA. He was then fifty-seven years old. *Evening Nonpareil*, October 15, 1914, October 16, 1916.

37. *Evening Nonpareil*, November 10, 1916.

38. *Evening Times-Republican*, May 24, 1917, July 9, 1917.

39. *Evening Nonpareil*, May 21, 1917; *Adams County Union-Republican* (Corning, IA), May 30, 1917; Wilson, "Abandoned Railroads of Iowa," 46; *Omaha World-Herald Magazine*, March 18, 1956. During World War I, Edward Wickham made a fortune as head of the National Construction Company of Omaha building cantonments for the federal government. In March 1925, at age fifty-eight, he committed suicide, attributed to the recent accidental death of his wife and his own poor health. *Iowa City* (IA) *Press-Citizen*, March 12, 1925.

40. "1,300 miles of Railroad Abandoned," *Railway Age* 64 (January 4, 1918): 49–50.

41. *Omaha World-Herald Magazine*, March 18, 1956.

6. DES MOINES & ROAD OAK RAILWAY

1. George W. Hilton and John F. Due, *The Electric Interurban Railways in America* (Stanford, CA: Stanford University Press, 1960). Two representative CERA book publications are Norman Carlson, ed., *Iowa Trolleys* (Chicago, 1975) and Johnnie J. Myers, *Texas Electric Railway* (Chicago, 1982). See also H. Roger Grant, "'Interurbans Are the Wave of the Future': Electric Railway Promotion in Texas," *Southwestern Historical Quarterly* 23 (Fall 1980): 148–156.

2. *Minneapolis Journal*, June 23, 1907.

3. W. W. Bildwin, comp., *Chicago Burlington & Quincy Railroad Company Documentary History*, vol. 2, *Lines in Iowa and Missouri* (Chicago: Chicago, Burlington & Quincy Railroad, 1929); Richard C. Overton, *Burlington Route: A History of the Burlington Lines* (New York: Alfred A. Knopf, 1965), 237–238.

4. Carlson, ed., *Iowa Trolleys*, 185; Theodore M. Stuart, *Past and Present of Lucas and Wayne Counties Iowa* (Chicago: Clarke, 1913) 1:85.

5. *Red Oak* (IA) *Express*, December 29, 1905, August 9, 1912.

6. Samuel E. Moffett, "The War on the Locomotive: The Marvelous Development of the Trolley Car System," *McClure's Magazine* 20 (March 1903): 451–462; James Glen, "The Interurban Trolley Flyers," *World's Work* (January 1907): 8406–8407; H. Roger Grant, "Electric Traction Promotion in the South Iowa Coalfields," *Palimpsest* 58 (January/February 1977): 18–29; *Fort Dodge* (IA) *Messenger*, November 4, 1907; William H. Thompson, *Transportation in Iowa: A Historical Summary* (Ames: Iowa Department of Transportation, 1989): 93.

7. *Red Oak Express*, August 31, 1906.

8. *Red Oak Express*, August 31, 1906; Hilton and Due, *The Electric Interurban Railways in America*, 363–365; *Andrew County Republican* (Savannah, MO), quoted in the *Current-Press* (College Springs, IA), June 21, 1906; *Red Oak* (IA) *Sun* quoted in the *Clarinda* (IA) *Herald*, December 16, 1909.

9. Office of Recorder, Montgomery County, Iowa, Miscellaneous Record No. 25, 317–319; *Red Oak Express*, April 12, 1907, May 29, 1908, December 3, 1909.

10. *Current-Press*, April 23, 1908.

11. *Des Moines* (IA) *Register and Leader*, April 27, 1908; *Red Oak Express*, May 29, 1908.

12. *Red Oak Express*, June 12, 1908.

13. *Red Oak Express,* July 3, 1908, September 15, 1908.

14. *Red Oak Express,* May 14, 1909, May 28, 1909.

15. *Des Moines Register and Leader,* July 20, 1909; *Red Oak Express,* January 14, 1910. Although dominated by Red Oak businessmen, the RO&NEIPCo consisted of individuals who lived along the proposed route, including in Des Moines, Greenfield, and Winterset. A concerted effort was made not to make this ambitious undertaking a wholly Red Oak venture.

16. *Red Oak Express,* August 13, 1909.

17. *Mackburg* (IA) *Independent,* May 15, 1919; Office of Recorder, Montgomery County, Iowa, Miscellaneous Record No. 29, 44–45. In 1903 the Rock Island acquired the stock of the Des Moines & Southern Railroad, a company launched by local interests. Some grading occurred between Winterset and Greenfield before the project quickly collapsed. H. Roger Grant, *A Mighty Fine Road: A History of the Chicago, Rock Island & Pacific Railroad Company* (Bloomington: Indiana University Press, 2020), 44.

18. *Red Oak Express,* September 17, 1909, January 21, 1910.

19. *Red Oak Express,* October 16, 1909.

20. *Red Oak Express,* November 12, 1909, November 26, 1909, December 3, 1909, December 10, 1909, December 24, 1909, January 7, 1910.

21. *Red Oak Express,* November 19, 1909; Maury Klein, *Union Pacific: The Rebirth, 1894–1969* (New York: Doubleday, 1989), 296–298; *Akron* (OH) *Beacon Journal,* September 30, 1908.

22. *Red Oak Express,* November 26, 1909; *Electric Railway Journal* 38 (November 4, 1911): 1013.

23. *Red Oak Express,* December 24, 1909.

24. *Red Oak Express,* December 31, 1909, January 21, 1910.

25. *Red Oak Express,* January 14, 1910, January 28, 1910, March 18, 1910, September 2, 1910.

26. *Red Oak Express,* March 25, 1910, April 8, 1910, September 16, 1910.

27. *Des Moines* (IA) *Sunday Register and Leader,* June 5, 1910.

28. *Des Moines* (IA) *Daily Capital,* October 4, 1910; *Atlantic* (IA) *Evening News,* September 22, 1910; *Adams County Free Press* (Corning, IA), October 12, 1910; *Des Moines Register and Leader,* October 4, 1910.

29. *Red Oak Express,* September 16, 1910.

30. *Red Oak Express,* November 4, 1910.

31. *Red Oak Express,* June 23, 1911.

32. *Red Oak Express,* June 23, 1911; *Railway Age Gazette* 51 (July 14, 1911): 105.

33. *Red Oak Express,* July 14, 1911, September 15, 1911; *Cedar Rapids* (IA) *Evening Gazette,* October 19, 1911.

34. *Railway Age Gazette,* 51 (August 4, 1911): 269; *Red Oak Express,* August 30, 1912.

35. *Red Oak Express,* April 5, 1912; *Page County Democrat* (Clarinda, IA), March 28, 1912.

36. *Des Moines Register and Leader,* March 24, 1912.

37. J. W. Kendrick, *A Report upon the Wabash Railroad* (Chicago, 1912), 24–25, copy in the John W. Barriger III National Railroad Library, St. Louis, MO; *Red Oak Express,* August 26, 1912.

38. *Red Oak Express,* July 5, 1912.

39. *Red Oak Express,* August 30, 1912.

40. *Red Oak Express,* August 16, 1912.

41. *Red Oak Express,* August 30, 1912.

42. *Sunday Nonpareil* (Council Bluffs, IA), September 1, 1912; *Red Oak Express,* September 6, 1912.

43. *Red Oak Express,* April 25, 1913, May 2, 1913, April 24, 1914.

44. *Red Oak Express,* December 17, 1915; *Clarinda Herald,* July 21, 1910; *Madisonian* (Winterset, IA), June 12, 1912.

45. *Red Oak Express,* December 31, 1915.

46. *Des Moines Register and Leader,* December 12, 1915. As the final rumor of a possible interurban between Des Moines and Red Oak circulated, there involved the remote possibility that the profitable Waterloo, Cedar Rapids & Northern electric might take control of the out-of-service steam Chicago, Anamosa & Northern Railway, which connected the Iowa communities of Anamosa and Quasqueton, and acquire the mostly graded ten miles of roadbed built by the never-railed Iowa & Northwestern Railway near Quasqueton (Wapsipinicon River) to Rowley. These properties would then be linked with the WCF&N at Brandon and become electrified. See Gary L. Holzinger, *The Wapsie Valley Route: Chicago, Anamosa & Northern Railway* (Quasqueton, IA: Quasqueton Area Historical Society, 2022), 38, 75, 86.

47. *Red Oak Express,* May 26, 1916.

48. Hilton and Due, *The Electric Interurban Railways in America,* 367; William E. Robertson, *The Woodstock and Sycamore Traction Company* (Delavan, WI: National Bus Trader, 1985).

EPILOGUE

1. "College Spring Depot Arrives," *Nodaway Valley Historical Society News,* October 2006, 1; *Clarinda* (IA) *Herald-Journal,* April 9, 2008.

2. David E. Kyvig and Myron A. Marty, *Nearby History: Exploring the Past Around You,* 3rd ed. (Lanham, MD: AltaMira Press, 2010), 8.

3. H. H. Fulton, "A Small Line That's Still Going Strong," *Railroad Stories* 12 (September 1933): 86; *Elk Horn Community History* (Elk Horn, IA: privately printed, 2000), 120; Warren Watson to author, February 8, 2022. The "Toonerville trolley" name came from "Toonerville Folk," the popular contemporary syndicated cartoon strip drawn by Fontaine Fox.

4. H. Roger Grant, "Electric Traction Promotion in the South Iowa Coalfieds,"

Palimpsest 58 (January/February 1977): 18–29; *Ottumwa* (IA) *Tri-Weekly Courier,* February 7, 1907, February 9, 1907, October 15, 1910; *Des Moines* (IA) *Register and Leader,* December 15, 1907; *Des Moines* (IA) *Tribune,* January 31, 1910.

5. Lewis Atherton, *Main Street on the Middle Border* (Bloomington: Indiana University Press, 1954), 235.

6. J. W. Kendrick, *Report of Valuation, Iowa & Southwestern Railway,* April 15, 1915, Box 1–91 in John W. Barriger III National Railroad Library, St. Louis, MO, hereafter cited as Kendrick Report.

7. Kendrick Report; *Des Moines Register and Leader,* February 4, 1911; *Villisca* (IA) *Review,* October 16, 1913.

8. *Thirty-Eighth Annual Report of the Board of Railroad Commissioners for the Year Ending December 6, 1915* (Des Moines: State Printer, 1917), 77.

9. Booth Tarkington, *The Magnificent Ambersons* (New York: Doubleday, Page, 1918), 388–389; *Red Oak* (IA) *Express,* April 22, 1910.

10. John F. Stover, *The Life and Decline of the American Railroad* (New York: Oxford University Press, 1970), 239–240.

11. *Clarinda* (IA) *Herald,* August 10, 1916; *Sidetrack* (Fourth Quarter, 2019): 7.

12. *Railway Age* 87 (July 27, 1925): 325.

13. *Evening Nonpareil* (Council Bluffs, IA), December 4, 1923. As abandonments increased after World War I, the loss of railroad service could have an immediate negative impact on communities served by a single carrier. In 1924 *Railway Age* published an analysis of the effect the impending shutdown of the Chicago, Peoria & St. Louis Railroad would have on its service territory: "[Shippers] cannot carry on their businesses without dependable and adequate transportation and the condition of roads in Illinois is such that daily truck operation is impossible for most of the towns which would be affected by the abandonment of the railroad." The study

also noted that "merchants are dependent almost entirely on shipments from outside points to maintain their stock. Without the railroad these shipments will have to be brought in my truck and, as been shown, this will be extremely difficult if not impossible, during a considerable part of the year." "What About the Patrons of an Abandoned Road?" *Railway Age* 76 (May 3, 1924): 1077–1079.

14. *Atlantic News-Telegraph*, February 16, 1932; Interview with Mrs. Charles "Gerrie" Slemmons, March 1, 1981.

INDEX

Index pages in *italics* indicate illustrations

H. ROGER GRANT is author of numerous books, including *Visionary Railroader, John W. Barriger III, Railroaders without Borders, Railroads and the American People,* and *A Mighty Fine Road.* He is Kathryn and Calhoun Lemon Professor of History at Clemson University.

FOR INDIANA UNIVERSITY PRESS

TONY BREWER Graphic Designer

DAN CRISSMAN Trade and Regional Acquisitions Editor

SAMANTHA HEFFNER Trade Acquisitions Assistant

BRENNA HOSMAN Production Coordinator

KATHRYN HUGGINS Production Manager

DAVID MILLER Lead Project Manager/Editor

STEPHEN WILLIAMS Marketing and Publicity Manager

JENNIFER WITZKE Graphic Designer